The Troubled Origins of
the Italian Catholic Labor Movement,
1878–1914

The Troubled Origins of the Italian Catholic Labor Movement, 1878–1914

Sándor Agócs

Wayne State University Press · Detroit 1988

Library of Congress Cataloging-in-Publication Data

Agócs, Sándor, 1932–
   The troubled origins of the Italian Catholic labor movement,
1878–1914 / Sándor Agócs.
      p.   cm.
   Bibliography: p.
   Includes index.
   ISBN 0–8143–1938–6 (alk. paper)
      1. Trade-unions, Catholic—Italy—History.   2. Church and social
problems—Italy—Catholic Church—History.   3. Church and labor—
Italy—History.   4. Catholic Church—Doctrines—History.
I.   Title.
HD6481.2.I8A38   1988
331.88′0945—dc19   87–31961
                                                           CIP

Contents

Acknowledgments

For building up the source base of this study, I am indebted to several Italian research libraries. They complied with my requests for years, and located, copied, and sent information in what must have seemed to them an unending stream. My heartfelt thanks go to the directors and staffs of the Biblioteca Apostolica Vaticana, the Biblioteca Nazionale in Rome and Florence, the Biblioteca Universitaria Alessandrina and the Biblioteca di Storia Moderna in Rome, and the Biblioteca Marucelliana in Florence, as well as the Interlibrary Loan Department of Wayne State University Libraries in Detroit.

I would also like to thank my good friend Professor Melvin Small, who read and critiqued a draft of this essay, and to express an old indebtedness to A. William Salomone, who years ago did his best to turn me into a good historian, directing my first research efforts with unfailing patience, pointed suggestions, and always valid criticisms. I hope that, after he reads this study, Professor Salomone will still allow me to call him *maestro,* my teacher, as was my habit when as a graduate student I conversed with him in Italian.

I also wish to acknowledge the help I received from my wife in both conceptualizing and styling this study. This was so substantial that I am tempted to suggest she is responsible for some of the errors and omissions that I am sure remain in this volume. But I assume responsibility for all of them, knowing that those who are familiar with the scholarship of Professor Carol Agócs would not believe me otherwise. My two children, Kati and Peter, also deserve an acknowledgment for their patience in putting up with the preoccupations and work involved in producing this volume that severely limited my availability to them for quite a long time.

My thanks are also due to Ms. Joanne Lemon, who typed the manuscript. Because of her uncanny ability to decipher my utterly illegible handwriting, she saved me barrels of time. Ms. Yvonne Reineke and Ms. Judy Wedeles read parts of the manuscript and suggested stylistic improvements. Surrounded by such a talented and workaholic matriarchate, it was all so easy!

Introduction

In a series of articles published during the 1970s,[1] I pointed to the Neo-Thomistic intellectual current as the source of some of the most important ideas and paradigms of Italian Catholic social philosophy at the turn of the nineteenth century. In applying this thesis to the history of the Italian Catholic labor movement during its formative years, I have expanded the methodological scope of my previous works. Whereas those were essentially exercises in the history of ideas, in this study I have attempted to produce a hybrid of intellectual and social history by anchoring ideas in reality, by relating social ideas to social institutions, notably, the particular organizational forms and activities of the Catholic labor movement.

Monographic studies that have dealt, often marginally, with the early history of the Italian Catholic labor movement are now obsolete, having been published during the 1960s. Thus a book-length treatment integrating the research evidence that has emerged during the last two decades is overdue. A synthesis, which this volume represents, is also timely because it will help orient research on this subject as the relevant materials in the Vatican Archives are about to become available.

The evidence that forms the basis of this study comes mostly from those who occupied positions of leadership: the Vatican hierarchy, the episcopate, and the laymen who headed the central organizations of Italian Catholic Action. Intellectual history presenting the motivations and intentions of leaders is an indispensable part of historiography, for it is the first step toward the discovery of ever-present tensions between ideas and reality, between the custodians of ideals motivating social movements and the activists charged with putting these ideals into practice. A study of the intentions and directives of leaders is especially relevant in connection with religious hierarchies such as the leadership of the Catholic church, for in such institutions directives from above have an unusual salience. In such cases the tensions between leaders and followers also become especially dramatic because of the particular form of legitimacy with which the leadership is endowed, an authority derived from God.

I approach history from a perspective that places social ideas and action, rather than political developments, at the center of the stage. Italian historiography, until recently, had a one-sided political orientation and tended to focus on political ideas, trends, and events as central in the historical process. Because of this political emphasis, the tools, the basic concepts found in the works that cover my historical period, were of limited use, if not misleading, for the study of social ideas—especially if one's aim was to examine these concepts as they related to social action.

Italian historians describe Catholic political attitudes, for instance, as ranging between the extreme positions of "conservative" and "moderate." Conservativism implies an uncompromising, rigidly intransigent adherence to the Vatican's position in connection with the Roman Question, a confrontation between the church and the Italian state that resulted from the incorporation of the Papal States into united Italy. To put it bluntly, Italian Catholic conservatives were caught in an impasse to which there appeared to be no solution given the unwillingness of the political ruling classes to undo the Risorgimento. Moderates, on the other hand, favored an end to the deadlock through a compromise between the church and the state, and wanted to lift the Non Expedit, the ban placed by the Vatican on the participation of Italian Catholics in national elections as long as the Roman Question remained unsolved.

If Unification set the political alignment of Italian Catholics, their social attitudes developed in response to the Social Question, which centered on the living conditions of the working classes. In confronting the *questione sociale,* the church attempted to come to terms with modern industrial society. This effort brought Catholics face to face with the developing labor movement and class conflict. The activists' inclination to accept the inevitability of class antagonism gave rise to a struggle within Italian Catholic Action that became especially bitter during the papacy of Pius X (1903–14). He considered class conflict and strikes contrary to the spirit of Christianity and, to prevent them from occurring, imposed on Italian Catholic Action severe organizational restrictions, which he justified by reference to Neo-Thomistic ideas.

The pope's insistence upon the mixed organization of labor, for instance, was connected with Thomistic social philosophy. The mixed union, which was to include both capitalists and workers, was conceived by Neo-Thomistic conservatives like Pius X as indispensable for the proper practice of *caritas* (charity), the all-important theological principle aimed at uniting society by establishing a symbiotic relationship between various social strata. The Thomistic principle of charity implied a "tutelage" by the "superior classes" of the interests of the workers, the "inferior classes," as conservatives preferred to call them. But the insistence upon the mixed union became the source of a conflict between aged conservative leaders, often high-ranking churchmen, and young activists, who, daily facing reality, knew that the Italian workers had no inclination to submit to permanent social inferiority. Thus, if only because they wanted to be successful in their organizational efforts, activists such as Giulio Rusconi and Giorgio Gusmini pressed for the acceptance of the simple union that included only the workers. The social autonomy of the simple union expressed the rising class-consciousness of the Italian workers.

Some members of the church hierarchy, like Cardinal Alfonso Capecelatro and Bishop Geremia Bonomelli, not only sympathized with the activists but shared many of their ideas. By the same token, some of the young activists were perfectly orthodox in outlook and behavior. Nevertheless, the conflict between paternalistic ideals and social reality reflected a veritable generation gap between leaders and activists in Italian Catholic Action. This generation gap was even more obvious in politics, with the activists usually taking supermoderate positions and thereby incurring the wrath of conservative church leaders. Activists such as Filippo Meda and Luigi Sturzo represented a new generation that matured after Unification. For them the loss of papal temporal power was not a personal experience but an historical event; it was an accomplished fact. The Non Expedit, which deprived Catholic citizens of Italy of their political rights and reduced them to pawns in a chess game between the Vatican and the Italian ruling classes, appeared to the activists as a wasted sacrifice, since it had been in effect for more than thirty years without producing any apparent results. The political inaction enforced by the Non Expedit, which appeared perfectly justified to aged leaders like Pius X, came to be seen by many of the young activists as senseless and self-defeating, since it prevented Catholics from putting into practice through political action the principles their social philosophy held dear. Thus, from the very beginning of his papacy, Pius X faced intense and constant pressure from the activists for the lifting of the Non Expedit, a pressure that he resisted because he was not yet prepared to meet the activists' demands to posit the Roman Question in radically new terms, which involved not only releasing the Catholic electorate but also allowing the organization of a Catholic political party.

Yet behind the pope's apparent intransigence and his rigid insistence upon the primary and decisive importance of the Roman Question, dramatic changes were developing. One of the most significant of these was the increasing appearance of Catholic voters at the polls in national elections. This began in 1904, when for the first time the ban on the electoral participation of Italian Catholics was lifted in districts where their votes helped defeat anticlerical and socialist candidates. His anxiety about socialism, which he considered a mortal threat, was leading Pius X into the gradual relaxation of the Non Expedit.

Not having a party of their own through which to channel their political efforts, by an ironic twist of fate Italian Catholics became spear-bearers for their traditional opponents, the liberals. The socialist menace drove the liberal bourgeoisie and the Catholics into an alliance between wealth and the altar that came to a denouement during the 1913 elections with the Gentiloni Pact.

Despite the fact that he allowed Catholic voters across the country to go to the polls in 1913, Pius X refused to yield to the activists' demand for autonomous political action, a Catholic party. The pope fought this demand with every weapon he could muster, including excommunication. The one-sided political orientation of the historiography of Italian Catholic Action probably originates in this conflict, which shows the Pope hurling anathema in connection with political matters. This tendency was further reinforced by the formidable success at the polls of the Partito Popolare a few years after Pius X beat down activists such as Sturzo, who, with the permission of Pius's successor, became the leaders of the Catholic political party. The appearance and importance of the Christian Democratic Party still later, after the collapse of the Fascist regime, accelerated the drift toward a political focus in the historiography of Italian Catholic Action.

Even those historians who represent this approach often admit that it was more than just political ideas and aims that set the activists on a collision course with the Vatican. There were social ideas as well as practices—such as their insistence upon the simple union—involved in the conflict between the pope and the activists. In fact, their inability to give a new political direction to Italian Catholic Action by organizing a Catholic party should direct the attention of historical research toward Catholic social theory and social action, for many activists turned toward social problems. The old leaders of Catholic Action were relieved to see Catholic youth turning away from politics, yet the flow of young enthusiasm and talent into social activities heightened the tension in Italian Catholic social action. The conflict between aged leaders and young followers, between custodians of ideals and activists—suppressed in the realm of politics—came to the surface with amazing verbal violence in debates about the social policies and aims of Catholic Action.

Quite early in my search for an understanding of this conflict, I discovered information printed in 1896 that pointed to what was to become the central theme of my work: the conflict over the mixed and the simple unions. In a short essay entitled *The Social Question and the Catholics,*[2] Salvatore Talamo, a leading Neo-Thomistic Catholic sociologist and social theorist, identified the organizational forms of labor, the *misto* and the *semplice,* as the key issues in the conflict between "conservatives" and "Christian Democrats." For the latter Talamo also used the words "Christian Socialists." In my work I avoided this term because clearly it did not catch on. Virtually all Christian Democrats refrained from using the word *So-*

cialist to describe their program. Only conservatives seem to have employed it on occasion and usually in underhanded attempts to discredit their activistic opponents by using a word with Marxist connotations. Talamo's perceptive essay also warned me of the problems that grew out of an overlap between social and political activisms. The term *Christian Democrat,* referring to both political and social programs, he cautioned, was rather vague. Indeed it was, as I discovered when I proceeded with my study. I attempted to clarify it by detailing its meaning insofar as social ideas and social action were concerned, in part because I hoped my work would become a modest corrective to previous studies, which, overly concerned with the political, failed to clear up the confusion Talamo noticed.

My personal experience as an intellectual of peasant background may account for my inclination toward social history involving the lives of working people. After finishing my studies at Hungarian and Italian universities, and before receiving my doctorate at the University of Rochester, I worked for several years in American factories. This experience also tended to place me on the side of the workers and not that of the *padroni,* the bosses.

The standards of my profession require that I point to my life experiences which, depending on one's point of view, may be seen as a source of an advantage or of a burden, or both, as I am inclined to perceive them. Hopefully, my awareness of these influences that affected the direction of my research and my *forma mentis,* which tended toward an empathy with those low in the social pyramid and scant sympathy toward figures of authority, whoever they may be, prevented me from abandoning the principle of scientific objectivity. Furthermore, I do not believe that this principle precludes negative judgments, although I anticipate some of my Catholic readers will be disturbed by my critical attitude toward one Giuseppe Sarto, whose earthly remains rest in Rome under one of the altars of Saint Peter's Basilica. He earned the highest honor that the church can bestow upon men, and is today venerated as a saint. In elevating him to the altar, the church proclaimed the judgment of God.

However, the acts of Saint Giuseppe Sarto were not played for the judgment of God alone. During the last years of his life, he was one of the most powerful of men. His influence ranged to the corners of the earth. The mighty and the poor alike bowed to him. Heads of state followed the humble peasants of his birthplace as they knelt before him. Hundreds of millions of people listened to his voice and pondered his judgments that came from the awesome height of the throne of Peter the Apostle. As God's deputy on earth and as a ruler of men, Pope Saint Pius X became a subject of history, and because he made history, the judgment of men, including mine, may also touch him.

1

Philosophy by Decree:
Leo XIII and the Thomistic Revival

During the papacy of Leo XIII (1878–1903), Neo-Thomism was fast becoming an official philosophy of the church. This must have come as a surprise to some, since at first Leo did not emphasize Aquinas's philosophy at the expense of other trends within the church's theological traditions. Although *Inscrutabili Dei consilio,* his first encyclical, issued on April 21, 1878, did point to the importance of Thomistic philosophy, the Angelic Doctor was mentioned as a member of a cast, together with the "great Augustine" and the "other teachers of Christian wisdom."[1] Even *Aeterni Patris,* Leo's "Thomistic" encyclical, published on August 4, 1879, listed several others within a review of the historical evolution of Christian doctrine, again reserving a place of honor for Augustine. Nevertheless, in *Aeterni Patris* Leo presented Aquinas's thought as the culmination in the development of theology and philosophy.[2]

Apparently Thomism was rapidly gaining an overwhelming importance in the new pope's outlook, for even before the publication of *Aeterni Patris* there were dismissals at the Gregorian University, then known as Collegio Romano. On May 16, 1879, a cleric well connected with the papal university reported to his superior in France that "during the last few days five professors have been dismissed from the Collegio Romano, among others the Fathers Palmieri, Caretti, and Zampieri. The wish of the holy father is the wish of God. They will not be teaching when the school reopens because they were not Thomists enough—but that is between us."

If there was a message here, by 1881 almost everyone in Rome seemed to have understood it. Thus a report written to the American bishop James Gibbons: "As Your Grace is aware, scholasticism's star is now in the ascent throughout the Eternal City. The majority of professors not bred up as Thomists have been forced to vacate their chairs in favor of the Napolitan schools of philosophy and theology; whilst every tongue has learned to lisp the new slang phrase in Rome: *Ut ait Sanctus Doctor.*"

That Thomism was an official theology of the church seems to have become history by 1898, and Leo's statement lends credence to this view:

> In our encyclical *Aeterni Patris,* we have sufficiently demonstrated the road to follow in the study of the superior sciences. To avoid the precepts of the Angelic Doctor is contrary to our wishes and is full of peril besides. . . . Those who wish to be real philosophers, and the religious must want that more than anything else, are obliged to establish the principles and the basis of their doctrine in Saint Thomas Aquinas['s teachings].[3]

However, the pope's attempt to center Catholic theology on the thought of Aquinas was less than a success on a worldwide basis. Although Thomism may have been declared *philosophia perennis* in Rome, the influence of Aquinas seems to have decreased the further away one was from the Vatican. Thus in France and Belgium, for instance, Thomism remained but one of several orientations in Catholic theology.[4] Even in Italy there was significant resistance to making Thomism *filosofia per decreto.* Telling a philosopher to follow in Aquinas's footsteps, some pointed out, was like asking a painter to paint like Michelangelo or telling a poet to write like Dante. But those taking the pope's side argued that what Leo XIII was doing was but pursuing a particular educational policy. At this point the arguments began to lean toward empty sophism, for although the papal instructions that followed the publication of *Aeterni Patris* did make Aquinas's philosophy an obligatory subject of studies in Italian seminaries, historical evidence shows that this was more than just a move to create a uniform system of philosophical education for the clergy.

Thomistic philosophy became decisive in shaping the intellectual outlook of Italian priests. Their pastoral activities, in turn, were

to give Thomistic ideas a degree of popularity among Catholic laymen.[5] This development explains the continual references to Thomistic notions in turn-of-the-century Italian Catholic thought.
While Catholic writers were directed to the philosophy of Aquinas
by so important a doctrinal statement as a papal encyclical, their
readers were prepared by their pastors to receive and understand
notions that grew out of Thomism.

The success of Thomism did not come suddenly. Rather, several
historical developments laid the foundations for the wide acceptance of Aquinas's ideas at the turn of the nineteenth century. In
fact, Leo did not initiate anything new but merely strengthened an
already existing interest in Thomism in Catholic theology. This interest, especially marked in Italy, had grown significantly during the
papacy of Leo's predecessor, Pius IX (1846–78), when intellectual
centers of Neo-Thomistic orientation appeared all over Catholic
Europe. Among the most significant in Italy was the semiofficial
church publication *Civiltà Cattolica* of Rome. Father Matteo Liberatore (1810–92), who with other Jesuits edited the publication,
was to play an important role in the drafting of *Aeterni Patris*. Per-
sonnel from the Thomistic Academia di Filosofia established in Naples, the "Napolitan school" mentioned in the letter to Monsignor
Gibbons, also played a role in carrying out the Thomistic initiatives
of Pope Leo XIII, who earlier, as the cardinal bishop of Perugia,
presided over yet another Thomistic intellectual center in that Italian town.[6]

These centers testify to the existence of Thomistic intellectual
traditions that apparently gained enough power during the second
half of the nineteenth century to become institutionalized in Rome,
Naples, and Perugia. Moreover, the writings of Aquinas were an
integral part of the intellectual heritage of the church for centuries.
Catholic priests studied the *Summa* long before papal instructions
made its reading obligatory. The printing office of the Seminary of
Padua, for instance, published the collected works of Aquinas as
early as 1698; and the biographers of Pius X tell how Giuseppe
Sarto, a young seminarian in Padua during the middle of the nineteenth century, moved with awe through the halls of the "mystical
and intellectual cathedral built by centuries of Catholic theology" as

he absorbed the *Summa* and acquired, according to one of his instructors, an "extensive and rare knowledge of the facts of medieval
history and their chronological order."[7]

The attention Sarto's instructors paid to medieval history and
Aquinas was a sign of the special importance Thomism gained after
the Revolution of 1789. During the Restoration Neo-Thomism became a refuge for the leaders of the church who rejected the Revolution and the intellectual and social changes it introduced. They
counterposed the philosophy of Aquinas to the ideology of the Revolution.[8] As the Italian historian Pietro Scoppola characterized it,
Neo-Thomism became a veritable "Catholic counter-revolution."
Even sympathetic observers of Pope Leo's Thomistic initiatives saw
Neo-Thomism as a "philosophical apology of tradition." The "return to the Middle Ages" involved in the adherence to Aquinas's
thought gave Catholic conservativism, as the French historian Jean-
Marie Mayeur was to observe, not only a theological but also a social and political coherence.[9] The vision of medieval society in the
works of Aquinas came to be upheld as the corrective for the conditions of modern society. Aquinas's ideas were pitted against the
ideology of bourgeois liberalism, particularly Hegel's, whose
thought reflected the new social, political, and intellectual conditions created by the Revolution.

Italian Neo-Thomism found its identity in a struggle against
Vincenzo Gioberti, the most important representative of Hegelian-
ism in mid-nineteenth-century Italy. The marked political and social
orientation of Giobertian philosophy imposed a similar emphasis
upon contemporary Thomists. Thus the Leonine generation of Neo-
Thomists carried on the earlier practice of applying Aquinas's philosophy to the social and political problems of the day. *Aeterni Patris* was part of this trend: from considerations of pure philosophy,
the encyclical moved on to social and political arguments in favor of
a Thomistic revival.

More specifically, *Aeterni Patris* stated that the philosophy of
Aquinas, because it admirably harmonized faith and reason, would
prepare Catholics for the defense of their faith against those who
opposed the dogmas of religion in the name of reason. For the pope,
however, the importance of Thomistic philosophy obviously went

beyond the defense of the principles of the Catholic religion, for he added that Thomism was also useful in combatting "perverse" modern political and social doctrines:

> For, the teachings of Aquinas on the true meaning of liberty, which at this time is running into licence, on the divine origin of all authority, on laws and their force, on the paternal and just rule of princes, on obedience to the higher powers, on mutual charity one toward another— on all of these and kindred subjects—have very great and invincible force to overturn those principles of the new order which are well known to be dangerous to the peaceful order of things and to public safety.[10]

2

The Right to Property
Sanctioned by Natural Law

The Defense of Private Property

Thomistic social philosophy was based upon the theological concept of *caritas,* Christian love. "The mistress and queen of virtues," according to Leo XIII,[1] charity was for Aquinas man's way of sharing God's essence, His very nature, which is love. Charity was the bond that united man with God and with his fellow men. For Aquinas *caritas* was the bond that made society a unit; it was the lifeblood of the social body, an indispensable means to social solidarity.[2]

Thomistic theology distinguished between spiritual and material expressions of charity. Spiritual forms, such as making an erring brother aware of his sins, were considered more important than acts of material charity, such as giving alms. Despite this, Aquinas stressed the need for both forms of charity in virtuous Christian life. The giving of alms was thus essential, and those Catholics who systematically avoided helping the "poor" with alms were committing a grave sin.[3]

The notion of charity as an instrument of social solidarity was supported in Neo-Thomistic theology by the concept of the "social function of property," which reaffirmed the traditional Christian principle of ownership as stewardship. This notion implied that the owners of wealth were "administrators" appointed by God to manage and dispense the bounty of earth, which was given by God to the whole of mankind. With property thus belonging in a sense to the community, all men were perceived to have the right to the basic necessities of life.[4]

Aquinas certainly would have been horrified at the sight of men hanged during the heyday of old-style liberalism because they stole a loaf of bread to save themselves from starvation. The English Car-

22

dinal Henry Edward Manning expressed the spirit of the *Summa* when he declared that "the natural right of every man to life and to the food necessary for the sustenance of life prevails over all positive laws," and "a starving man has a right to his neighbor's bread." For Aquinas indeed made it clear that in dire need for physical survival, taking someone else's property was not even stealing, but an exercise of "natural" rights.[5]

True as they may have been to the spirit of Saint Thomas, Manning's remarks apparently did not receive a wide response from Italian Thomists, whose writings came to be characterized by numerous references to another "natural" right: that of holding property as a private possession. Cardinal Alfonso Capecelatro (1824–1912), a leading member of the Italian episcopate and a very popular writer, stated that Aquinas "demonstrated" that "private property derived from man's very nature." But an intense and rather emotional debate among Thomists later turned up evidence to suggest that the Angelic Doctor was far from being as unequivocal as Capecelatro suggested. If he accepted private property as a "natural" right at all, Aquinas apparently qualified his acceptance. Statements have even been found in the *Summa* that suggest an outright rejection of the principle of private property as a "natural" right. And if private property did not derive from nature, then it would have to be included in some Thomistic category other than "natural law."[6]

We have here the explanation of the emotional intensity of the debate among Neo-Thomists, for in Aquinas's philosophy, "natural" law and "natural" rights imply permanence and immutability, as handiworks of God. "Civic" laws that could have provided an alternative category for property were enacted by states. If we concede that civic laws are relevant to private property, then as J. B. McLaughlin, one of the debaters, was to state, "We are to be prepared to accept schemes of social reorganization which abolish private property." And that would have been just as unacceptable to Italian Neo-Thomists as it was to McLaughlin, their conservative Irish counterpart. Since Aquinas said unequivocally that private property did not fall under the category of "natural law" and "civic" law was conceived of as representing a threat to private property, conservative Neo-Thomists took refuge in another category that

Aquinas also connected with property. According to the Angelic Doctor, this category, *jus gentium,* was established by human reason, but was not formally promulgated as were civic laws. Since reason was "natural," Neo-Thomists considered the particular *jus gentium* about property "natural" as well, which in turn led to the conclusion that private property could not be abolished without violating "nature."[7] As proof of the indispensability of private property, they usually referred to a passage in the *Summa* that argued that man should possess things as his own:

> First because every man is more careful to procure what is for himself alone than that which is common to many or to all: since each one would shirk the labour and leave to another that which concerns the community, as happens where there is a great number of servants. Secondly, because human affairs are conducted in more orderly fashion if each man is charged with taking care of some particular thing himself, whereas there would be confusion if everyone had to look after any one thing indeterminately. Thirdly, because a more peaceful state is ensured to man if each one is contented with his own. Hence it is to be observed that quarrels arise more frequently where there is no division of the things possessed.[8]

The Italian Bishop Geremia Bonomelli (1831–1914), like Capecelatro a prolific and popular writer and a major figure in the Italian church hierarchy, followed a pattern adopted by Catholic sociological treatises by referring to this passage and interpreting it as well. He stated that "not only nature, but the interests of society" too "demanded" the private ownership of property, since it was an incentive for work and, as such, promoted productivity and was thus instrumental in providing goods in abundance to fulfill human needs. A related argument presented private property as an "instrument of social peace." This was somewhat ironic in view of the fact that a Catholic handbill distributed in very large numbers in 1910 seems to have agreed with the Socialists in indicating "mine and thine" as a source of stress and contention, rather than of peace. Ironic or not, arguing that private property was a source of social peace was not contrary to the *Summa.* The same could hardly be said about another conclusion reached by Thomists at the turn of the century, namely, that society as such would not survive without private property, since, without it, men would degenerate into a pack of lazy savages, abandoning the path of virtue and salvation.[9]

This interpretation came to be questioned later,[10] however, as some Thomists argued that Aquinas did not declare private ownership absolutely necessary. According to some interpreters, the Angelic Doctor's preference for private property was conditional and valid only for societies in which the three reasons held valid. Although Aquinas might have been convinced that the common ownership of property was not practical, the impracticality of the ownership of property by governments did not necessarily follow. Furthermore, perceiving government ownership as the only alternative to private property was a rather one-sided, if not altogether forced, interpretation of Aquinas's arguments, since he usually spoke not of governments but of communities in connection with the social functions of property. It was a measure of the strength of a growing cult of the state that state property would be perceived by the leadership of the church at the turn of the century as the only possible alternative to private property. As opponents of the cult of the state, both Leo XIII and Pius X consistently argued in favor of private property. In fact, Catholic writers faithfully followed papal leads in presenting private ownership as something "natural" and as a civilizing influence.[11]

The Social Functions of Property

With its unhesitating acceptance of the principle of private ownership, arguing its necessity for the survival of society except in the state of perfection, such as man's condition was before the Fall, official Catholic social doctrine gave aid and comfort to the embattled liberals who defended private property against revolutionary socialists bent on its destruction. Although Neo-Thomist arguments seemed to coincide with the liberal conviction that private property was the universal sustaining principle of healthy social life, important differences on the subject of property remained between liberals and Thomistic Catholics. Unlike the liberals, Neo-Thomists saw in property only a means, not an end, in the life of society. For Catholics this was an important aspect of the principle of the social functions of property. By becoming instrumental in the practice of *caritas,* private property helped secure for its owner the most important gain of human life, salvation.

Traditions even older than Aquinas's thought came into play in connection with the social functions of property. In discussing these, Aquinas quoted patristic sources. Saint Augustine provided especially dramatic arguments: "Find out how much God has given you and take from it what is sufficient for yourself; the rest, which is superfluous, is necessary for others. The superfluities of the rich are the necessities of the poor; to possess what is superfluous is to possess what belongs to others."[12]

Quod superest date eleemosynam led to the very core of Christian doctrine, to the concept of *caritas.* In defining what constituted the superfluous wealth destined to be given by the "rich" to their "poor" brothers, Aquinas, and Catholic theology after him, recognized a threefold division among man's earthly possessions: goods necessary for one's physical survival, those necessary for properly maintaining one's social status, and finally the "superfluous." A fellow man's "extreme" material need, his lack of the bare necessities of life, obligated Catholics to share with him all their possessions but those necessary for their own physical survival. Thus the "common" need of a fellow citizen justified a share of the "superfluous" wealth of the rich.[13]

Modern popes repeatedly confirmed the importance of the diligent use of the "superfluous" in Christian life, and Catholic writers followed their lead in pointing out that the wealthy who kept their superfluous "robbed the poor." A Catholic handbill warned the rich that their possessions were not theirs alone but, through the charitable use of the superfluous, belonged as a birthright to the poor also.[14]

An emphatic warning, no doubt, but could the neatly defined medieval principles of charity fulfill the needs of twentieth-century society? The Italian upper classes were notorious for their *dolce vita,* their conspicuous consumption involving a massive waste of food, extravagant housing, and large staffs of servants as status symbols.[15]

With their category of goods necessary for the proper maintenance of one's social status, the Neo-Thomist champions of charity thus provided the rich with the theological and moral equivalent of the tax loopholes of which the wealthy so conveniently serve themselves while living within the confines of the modern state. Moreover, according to Thomistic theology, the rich had no obligation to give all of their superfluity away. Some of it could be held back to "further improve" their status. Besides, what constituted the superfluity of a modern businessman caught in fierce economic competition which forced him to assure the growth of his enterprise or go bankrupt?

Eventually Thomists generated a discussion about the productive development of the wealth one possessed: this was a way of talking about economic growth in general and the expansion of business in particular, an expansion sustained by using a part of the superfluous. So long as such practice served the interests of the community, it was to be perceived within the confines of Thomism.[16]

Arguments of this nature did appear in some Catholic treatises published in Italy during the papacy of Pius X. One of these, in fact, emphasized that "it was better to give work than it was to give alms, since people could have felt humiliated by alms, which often also led to laziness."[17] Characteristically, this pamphlet was a translation of a work from abroad: the reasoning it represented did not begin to prevail among Italian Catholics until after World War II. At the end of the nineteenth century, the typical Italian commentary about Aquinas's relevant arguments pointed not to providing jobs but to almsgiving as the way of fulfilling the obligations involved in the principle of the social functions of property.

Despite its emphasis on alms as the expression of the wealthy man's responsibility to his less fortunate brothers, Catholic social doctrine remained rather elastic insofar as the disposal of the superfluous was concerned. If there was a lack of precision in the law of *caritas* as it applied to property, it apparently originated with Aquinas. Turn-of-the-century Catholics were not alone in appearing somewhat elusive when discussing the superfluous. In fact, Thomists have continued to argue up to the present that it is impossible to "formulate precise rules for determining the magnitude of the obligations" connected with the disposal of the superfluous;[18] it all depends upon the circumstances. There are still no hard-and-fast rules, and there were certainly none at the turn of the century, save for such remarks as, "not every want obliges under strict obligation, but only that want which, if it were not relieved, the sufferer could not live. In such a case what happens is what St. Ambrose says, 'Feed him who is dying of hunger, if you do not you will kill him.' "[19]

In speaking of the social obligations that went with property, Bishop Bonomelli referred to these obligations as "voluntary socialism, daughter of Christian charity."[20] If, in everyday practice, the disposal of the superfluous represented anything but socialism, voluntary it certainly was! Thomistic theology left it to the wealthy man to decide not only what he was to give away as superfluous but also to whom he would give it. "The Gospel did not tell the poor to take from the rich, but the rich to give to the poor," warned the Jesuit Luigi Taparelli d'Azelio. So much for socialism!

The extreme individualism manifest in Taparelli's related arguments was to draw the attention of historians later as they tried to explain a strange twist in the outlooks of some Neo-Thomists who, showing the influence of liberal economic theory, emphasized individualism and tended to pay lip service to, if not to neglect altogether, the social functions of property. Somewhat paradoxically Taparelli, a lifelong fighter against liberalism, as well as Matteo Liberatore, a fellow Jesuit from the *Civiltà Cattolica,* appear to have prepared the ground several decades earlier for those Neo-Thomists who, driven by an obsessive fear of socialism at the turn of the nineteenth century, truncated Thomistic doctrine by giving it a liberal twist. But Aquinas's thought, it appears, could be all things to all men; and those who, like Taparelli, argued in favor of a "complete freedom" for the property owners in disposing of their superfluous could for once rely on Aquinas to provide support for their arguments, since he did state that "as there are many suffering wants, and it is impossible to relieve all with the same thing, so it is left to the good will of everyone, the distribution of his own to relieve with it those who suffer want."[21]

The "good will" manifest in the alms of the wealthy constituted part of the conceptual framework of nineteenth-century paternalism that was a world-wide phenomenon. But having developed in Italy under the sponsorship of Aquinas, paternalism acquired special, somewhat old-fashioned, tones. A perception of social reality according to which God had delegated some of His authority to the rich to run the lives of the working classes in the name of the Heavenly Father was part and parcel of paternalism everywhere. Yet in the writings of conservative Catholics in Italy, this notion took the form of an echo from the Middle Ages: the landlords as "kings" "ruling" over their "subjects," the people who worked their lands, became an idea much favored by Italian writers. After Marquis Achille Sassoli de' Bianchi presented this view at a Catholic congress in 1879, the image rapidly gained popularity.[22] Even the unusually forward-looking Bishop Bonomelli could not resist using it in a pastoral letter:

> In a large village located in a diocese near ours, a very wealthy gentleman lives with his family. Having worn the uniform with honors and after participating in hard-fought battles, he decided to leave his native town for the freedom of the fields. On holidays he is always on his bench in church, attending the mass and listening to the sermon. As for the peasants of the village, he makes sure they always have work. He visits the homes of the poor every month, and his hands reach out to those in need. He is a real father to the poor; that village loves him, adores him: we might say he is its king. Do you think that village would touch his property if a socialist wave ever washed over our countryside? Surely not, for the entire population would rise like a single man in his defense, his peasants were heard saying that! And here, my beloved, is the only efficacious way to counter subversive ideas, the way to arrest the socialist tide that rises menacingly in some countries! Here is a man who knows how to fight! If all the gentlemen would do as he does, socialism would not be possible.[23]

The Tutelage Extended to Working People
by the Upper Classes

As Bonomelli's little parable shows, aside from lording over the workers as their "king," there was yet another role for country squires to take on: that of the "father" to their employees. The noble landowners were not alone in fancying themselves in this role and, in

return, expecting gratitude and obedience from their "children."
Capitalists, those "divine instruments for the people," were also proclaimed by some of the Catholic writers as "fathers" to the workers
they employed.[24] This was also done under the auspices of Aquinas,
who had suggested that servants should be considered members of
their employer's family. Indeed, he perceived not only servants but
all the citizens of the state as members of a family. Thus writers
could claim with some justice to be within the magic circle of Thomism by presenting society as nothing but a large family under the
paternal care and "tutelage" of the upper classes.[25]

It was this attitude shared by many members of the church hierarchy that drew the angriest protest from young Catholic activists,
who argued that "the people will refuse to remain the brute anon-
ymous, gray force of society" as well as "the eternal child in perpetual need of guidance, unable to reach the age of majority, become *sui
juris* and govern itself." These words were written by Alessandro
Cantono in 1902, during the last full year of the papacy of Leo XIII.
They expressed the outlook of many of the young Christian Democratic activists. Emerging as their leader, Romolo Murri (1870–1944)
wrote an approving introduction to Cantono's volume. Several others had also been pressing similar arguments for years. By 1906 even
Bishop Bonomelli compared the "people" to a "youth who becomes
convinced that he does not need tutelage any more and demands to
be recognized as of age and able to act under his own responsibility."[26]

Bonomelli thus clearly broke ranks and took the side of the
Christian Democratic activists in a conflict between them and the
conservatively inclined majority within the church hierarchy. This
conflict, already smoldering during the last years of Leo's papacy,
flared up after Pius X became pope. The new pontiff insisted on
following his predecessor's directives to the letter, and therefore declared that Christian Democracy must remain *actio benefica in
populum,* "a form of charity," which effectively confined the role of
Christian Democratic activists to a social action coming from
above, a "tutelage" of the interests of the working people by the
"superior" classes.[27]

Frustrated by this limitation, the activists might have cited the biblical tale involving the rich, the camel, the needle, and the Kingdom of Heaven. Pointing out that the rich tended to evade the responsibilities of charity was not only admissible from the point of view of orthodoxy but became an almost obligatory part of related arguments in Catholic sociological literature. Thus a conservative pamphlet reflected the extreme difficulties of convincing the *padroni* that they had "obligations toward the workers in their employ."[28] Yet to draw the logical conclusion from this and then question charity's viability was to invite the ire of Pius X.

When he was a young priest, Giuseppe Sarto chose as his model Saint Vincenzo de' Paoli, whose acts of charity reached heroic dimensions. It was a model he followed faithfully, for Sarto's biographies abound with episodes demonstrating this. Eyewitnesses told how his firewood was not locked up so that those who needed it could help themselves; how his granary was almost always empty when he was a village priest; how his treasury was always open to the poor when he became a bishop and a prince of the church. As his testament stated, he always "lived poor" and reputedly had to borrow money for the train ride that took him to Rome and the papal throne. He is quoted as saying that his money was not his but belonged to the "poor." In another moving statement to his flock, he pleaded: "O rich, help the charity of your patriarch, give to his poor children. You will be giving to him. Nay, you will be giving to Christ."[29]

Sarto began his pastoral work in 1858 in Tombolo, a small northern Italian village where the misery of the few poor could be mitigated by the community. And it was; Sarto, the parish priest, made certain of that. This is one of the reasons the faithful venerate him today as a saint. However, his difficulty in coming to terms with the twentieth century adds a tragic tint to the saintly halo of Pope Pius X.

It seems the nineteenth century, or perhaps even the eighteenth, captured Sarto's mind. Or was it, as some of his biographers have suggested, that he remained throughout his whole life in a way a *prete di campagna,* a village priest? Whatever the reasons for his ways, the man who was to follow Leo XIII to the papal throne seemed tragically behind in his understanding of society. He failed to realize that the social world of the modern city was not the old-fashioned rural *Gemeinschaft* of Tombolo and Salzano, the villages that saw his first pastoral activities. A thorough conservative, he failed to see that there was a difference between eighteenth-century pauperism and twentieth-century social ills.[30]

Only a few years before he became pope, Sarto was reminiscing about his youth in mid-nineteenth-century Padua. He said that people complained even then

> about the ever-increasing number of poor and beggars in this town. A learned and saintly teacher who was a young boy during the eighteenth century repeatedly told us in school that there was no reason for such complaints in those times because without the luxury of public assistance . . . charity took care of all. . . . The substitution of official alms for private alms amounts to the destruction of Christianity, and it is an attempt on the principle of property. . . . If aid comes [to the poor] through laws and alms are not motivated by the heart because they are not free any more, they lose their merit before God; alms [then] cease to be channels of grace and safe instruments of health; right is substituted for alms and work; the tie of love that alone can unite the poor and the rich is broken, the sentiments of gratitude and of recognition vanish, and poverty becomes a public function, a public office, a public occupation.[31]

This argument against public welfare measures must have drawn some astonished looks from the audience, for Sarto was speaking to a gathering of Catholic social scientists. At least some of them must already have been enough attuned to modern reality to break with the intellectual traditions established by the Neo-Thomists of the *Civiltà Cattolica,* especially by Taparelli, who argued in favor of the property owners' rights to dispense their superfluous as they saw fit, and who linked these arguments with broadsides against welfare measures by public authorities.

By 1896 even some of the conservatively inclined Catholics, Salvatore Talamo among them, came to understand the need for public welfare measures. In arguing in favor of them, they would point to the *Rerum novarum* of Leo XIII. In a few years' time, even Cardinal Capecelatro, though he agreed with Sarto that "without alms there was no Christianity" and that a "pact of charity" tied the rich and poor within society into a single community, was driven into admitting that more often than not the rich "evaded" the obligations of charity. The logical solution to this dilemma was to call upon the public authorities to assume the "tutelage" of the interests of the poor, and Capecelatro eventually reached that conclusion. In turn, this solution led to the need for extra taxes, and consequently the state had to violate the sacrosanct realm of the superfluous, which was to be profanely called profit and therefore taxed. But because of their mistrust of the post-Unification state, which, they felt, threatened the very existence of the church, such a suggestion was not easy for Italian Catholic conservatives to accept.[32]

Cardinal Sarto's objection to public welfare measures was certainly sustained by this mistrust. But there was more to it: his rejection of "official alms," like that of Taparelli decades before, was motivated by a strict adherence to the Neo-Thomistic principle of charity as a means of social solidarity. By creating a system of mutual dependence among different social strata, charity and alms became vital in establishing unity among the faithful. The poor depended upon alms for their physical survival; and the very existence of the rich as Christians (and their salvation) was conditioned by their providing the poor with at least the basic necessities of life. This symbiosis that united the rich and the poor within the fold apparently came to be seen by Sarto as an essential condition for a Christian community and hence indispensable to the survival of the church as an institution.[33]

3

Inequality of Rights and Power Proceeds from the Very Author of Nature

The Hierarchical Ordering of Society

The symbiosis that tied various social strata into a unit through the practice of *caritas* was an aspect of a social organicism that characterized Catholic thought. The perception of society as an organism went back to medieval, and specifically Thomistic, trends in philosophy.[1] These were reinforced during the nineteenth century by Romantic thought, which also emphasized the organic nature of society. However, the body analogy, the centerpiece of Catholic social organicism, was, in fact, a carryover of traditions even older than the thought of Aquinas, for the church had traditionally been called a "mystical body." This perception of the community of the faithful was transformed into an image of society as a "body."[2] In turn, this analogy suggested a division of society into "arms"—those who performed the manual tasks—and a "mind" that directed the activities of the other "members" of the social body, with all contributing according to their "natural" capacities.

The organic analogy per se was not hierarchical because it stressed the indispensability of all the members, the dependence of the whole on the parts. It was a paradigm expressing the need for social solidarity, and had, in fact, a pull toward egalitarianism. But Catholic sociologists at the turn of the century tended to disregard the implications of egalitarianism in the organic analogy.[3] Rather, it was more consistent with the hierarchical notions manifest in Catholic theology to argue that certain groups performed functions of a higher order than others. Thus Count Stanislao Medolago Albani (1850–1921) suggested that there was a division of labor of a particular kind within the organically ordered social body, and that there were the "hands to do the [physical] work" and the "mind to provide

34

direction." Not surprisingly, the count considered his own kind, the landowner, the "mind."[4]

This major division of society, as reflected by Medolago, was the most important element of Catholic social thought at the turn of the century. Writers used a variety of terms to define the two basic social groups of this division. Theological treatises on charity recognized them as the "rich" and the "poor," whereas Catholic sociological and political literature referred to them as the "superior" and "inferior" classes (or "low people" [*basso popolo*]). In Catholic sociology the "people," the socially "inferior," were the working classes employed in agriculture and industry. It was indicative of the influence of Thomistic theology that the terms poor and inferior classes were used interchangeably, just as rich and superior classes were.[5]

The identification of the poor with the inferior classes, the people, characterized the outlook of Giuseppe Toniolo (1845–1918), the major Italian Catholic sociologist of the era, whose theoretical works contributed substantially to the social outlook of Catholics.[6] With the warm approval of the future Pope Pius X, then Cardinal Sarto, Toniolo announced during the 1890s that the "elevation" of the inferior classes could not be entrusted to the people alone. Working people, Toniolo argued, could take care of their own problems only in exceptional cases. Their "salvation" was to come through the upper classes, which had "the natural historical mandate for the initiatives and the normal direction of civic life."[7]

The "tutelage" of the interests of the inferior social stratum by the superior classes remained the keynote of Catholic social action after Cardinal Sarto became Pope Pius X. He followed the Leonine tradition in sending Catholic activists "to the people" and urging them to endeavor "to dry their tears, to alleviate their sufferings and to improve their economic condition by wise measures." And like his predecessor, he never failed to emphasize that the problems of the inferior classes were primarily religious and moral, and not material ones.[8]

For their part, Catholic publications faithfully followed the arguments of Pius X. *L'Osservatore Romano,* for instance, pointed out that Catholic activists cannot approach the people "with empty hands, but [they] do not have to go with hands exuberantly and exclusively full of earthly goods and material advantages." The "moderation of the [people's] intemperance" and the mitigation of their "excesses" was the task of Catholic activists as well. A Catholic handbill became still more specific about the tutelage of the people by warning the rich to be sure to "teach [the people] Christian resignation, teach them the love of work, teach them the love of saving [*risparmio*], help them in their need. Speak to them . . . of their duties toward themselves, their families, their companions, their neighbors, toward God." A Catholic pamphlet published in 1911 went so far as to suggest that the "surveillance" of the conversations of the workers was the duty of the *padrone,* the owner of industrial enterprises. If he heard talk against priests, religion, or morality, he was to "impose silence" on the workers.[9]

Another writer, the Jesuit Father Giuseppe Biederlack, was even more to the point, charging the *padroni* in the name of *caritas* with the obligation to "prevent the sins of the workers." The idea that the obligations of charity, supposedly mutual, may impose on the workers the duty of preventing the sins of the capitalists did not occur to either Biederlack or any other Catholic writer. It went with the hierarchical understanding of the social order that an overwhelming share of responsibility was attributed to the superior classes. They were responsible not only for their own but also for the working classes' sins and omissions. Thus Medolago:

> Who taught the people to love idleness and to avoid work? From whom did they learn those principles which now show their logical and terrible consequences? Who planted in the people the seeds of insubordination, the germs of revolt? From whom did they learn to scorn authority, to sneer at the law, to jeer at the greatness of priesthood, the sacredness of the sacraments, and the majesty of God? Oh, gentlemen, let us beat our breasts and confess in shame: every one of us who belongs to the educated class, to the high class, to the rich class can repeat with the poet, *me, me adsum qui feci.*[10]

Such a low estimate was typical of many Catholic writers, for they often viewed the people as so irresponsible that they apparently could not even sin on their own, and had to be told even about duties toward themselves. Some writers like Salvatore Talamo pointed out how Christianity honored manual work through the example of the Carpenter's Son. This was to show that the church ennobled the role of the workingman. Still, Catholic intellectuals were rather slow in extending this honor to the workers who were their contemporaries. Even Toniolo, who sincerely believed that the elevation of the people to a "major participation in the benefits of civilization" had to be the aim of Catholic Action, consistently betrayed a low estimate of the workingman. For him the people were an impassive, gray mass, waiting for the superior classes to "descend" to them and "conquer" them for the church.[11] The social and political initiatives belonged to the upper stratum of society, to a hierarchy, which according to Toniolo was "instituted immediately and positively by God."[12]

Elsewhere Toniolo called the hierarchical ordering of society "natural," applying the Thomistic theological principle that equated with "nature" the immutable laws that God, "the Author of the social order," built into His Creation.[13] Characteristically the defense of the hierarchical social order by conservatives like Toniolo often trailed off into a defense of the church's own hierarchical ordering. These intertwining series of arguments, which appeared both in sociological treatises and in papal encyclicals,[14] gave an important clue to the persistence in Catholic thought of the hierarchical understanding of society. Obviously challenges to hierarchical social order hit a raw nerve because they were thought to represent the initial stage of an eventual challenge to the hierarchical principle governing the church leadership.

Because of this threat to the very existence of Catholic Christianity, the principle of a hierarchical ordering of society manifest in the thought of Aquinas[15] struck an especially receptive cord in the minds of orthodox Catholics at the turn of the nineteenth century. At that time the leadership of the church felt under siege by waves of anticlericalism, secularism, and modernism. But even without these challenges, the hierarchical understanding of society was expected to die hard, if ever, among Catholics. In the church they have as perfect a model of hierarchy as any. Especially when it came to churchmen, how could their perception of society not be influenced, if not overwhelmed, by this model? But this transference of a religious idea into the social realm involved more than just churchmen. Toniolo, for instance, insisted throughout his life that the social order was a "pyramid with its top pointing to God" and never seemed to have given up the principle of *gerarchia,* the hierarchical ordering of society.[16]

With the hierarchical perception of society went the notion of a hierarchy of obligations for the well-being of society. In this way the hierarchy of duties sustained a hierarchical understanding of moral responsibility that charged the rich with the sins of the poor. Thus the paternalism implied in the Thomistic social symbiosis took on a full dimension, for the greater one's wealth, the greater his responsibility for the well-being of his fellow men. A heavy burden fell on the rich, who, according to Toniolo, owed a "special tutelage and aid" to "the weak, the poor, the have-nothings."[17] Toniolo connected the tutelage of the lower classes' interests with the upper classes' higher education; in doing so, he made a claim for society's leadership by the superior, the educated class. He seems to have assumed that better education gave superior qualifications in the social, political, and even moral realms of life, qualifying the upper classes as tutors in ethics to the poorly educated masses. Thus Toniolo often described the need for the tutelage of the inferior classes by their social superiors as the moral education of the people, their elevation to "Christian consciousness" by those who had the benefits of a superior education.

To some extent this educational elitism was shared by the Christian Democratic activists. Although they increasingly rejected the other provisions implied in tutelage, they too tended to see their own role in the moral elevation of the people, a form of tutelage with the activists sharing the fruits of their advantages in education with the working classes. The activists parted company from social conservatives in that they expected the people eventually to reach intellectual maturity and free themselves from the tutelage of the upper classes. Of course, conservatives like Toniolo considered tutelage a perpetual arrangement in the life of society.[18]

The Rejection of the Principle of Equality

Suggesting that the poor constituted a permanent element of the social landscape was another way of saying there always had been and always will be inequality in society; or, as Medolago put it, society in every historical period naturally came to be divided into superior and inferior classes.[19] Catholic writers defended this position with vehemence.[20] Bishop Bonomelli's was a typical argument: in 1886 he pointed out in a pastoral letter that

> insofar as bodily strength and spiritual gifts are concerned we are unequal: there are those who are robust in body and those who are weak, those who are healthy and those who are sickly, those who are smart and those slow-witted, those who are strong-willed and those who are weak, those who thrive on fatigue and those who detest it, the prudent and the reckless, the frugal and the intemperate, the thrifty and the spendthrift and so on. The consequence of all this is a diversity in attitudes, physical strength, intelligence, will, and moral conduct, which in turn leads to a diversity in work, production, and property as different causes bring on different effects.[21]

Undoubtedly relying upon notions assumed to be commonplace, Cardinal Capecelatro too stated in 1901 that there exist among men "three inequalities: physical, intellectual, and moral. From these derive inequalities in possessions."[22] It was thought that Aquinas's wisdom formed the basis for this prevailing attitude, for he was quoted as saying that equality in possessions "is in contradiction with the order of nature, according to which providentially, a certain inequality exists among created things, either with regard to nature or as regards capacity: consequently, to admit equality in temporal goods, such as possessions, is to destroy order in things, which, according to St. Augustine, results from inequality. For order is nothing else than the setting of equal and unequal things in their proper place."[23]

Later research was to throw serious doubt upon these particular lines. But the questioning of the authorship of the fourth book of Aquinas's *De Regimine,* from which the above quotation was taken,[24] did not invalidate the claim of Thomistic support by late-nineteenth-century theologians. Other works of Aquinas, especially his *Summa contra Gentiles,* provided ample evidence to suggest that he did indeed think that a basic inequality among men existed.[25] Whether this inequality was in the material realm of life or elsewhere later became the subject of debate. But at the turn of the nineteenth century, Italian theologians were not yet in the mood to question the permanence of the poor upon the social landscape by suggesting that Aquinas may have talked of spiritual and moral attributes and not of material possessions when he discussed "natural" inequality. Still, the debate among Aquinas's interpreters[26] indicated that he just might have been too good a philosopher to violate logic, as his late-nineteenth-century followers did by establishing a causal relationship between differences in physical strength, intellectual dexterity, inclination toward sinning, and a necessary and "natural" inequality in the possession of things material.

Italian Catholic Neo-Thomists called upon Aquinas once again to be their star witness when they put the idea of democracy on trial. In arguing that differences in physical, mental, and moral attributes preempted the possibility of democracy as a sound political system,[27] Neo-Thomists executed the same leap over logic as they did in connection with economic inequality. Indeed, Thomistic Catholics tended to tie these two clearly separate issues into a single bundle of arguments; and in their writings, they fired broadsides against the principle of democracy alternating with shots fired in anger against economic equality. They saw not two targets but rather a single one, and this was socialism, which pressed for both political and economic equality. As a program of action, socialism did not become a serious issue in Italy until after 1900; but the more foresighted churchmen, Leo XIII among them, had identified it earlier as a threat to the church and all it stood for. Bishop Bonomelli addressed these issues as early as 1886 in his pastoral letter *Proprietà e socialismo.* The title as well as the range of the arguments presented in the *pastorale* were indicative of the Catholics' concerns about socialism. Aside from its godlessness, the idea of abolishing private property agitated Catholics more than anything else in Socialist doctrine. The vehemence of their trying to press home the "natural" inequality among men clearly masked a deep anxiety about the survival of private property as an institution. Thus Bonomelli skillfully employed the argumentative apparatus of Thomistic Catholic social philosophy:

> There always will be rich and poor, there always will be material inequality because such is a natural necessity. If that was not the case, where would be charity, the queen of all virtues and fulfillment of the law of the Gospel? There have to be rich and poor, but in such a way that the rich improve a bit the lot of the poor and the poor accept the rich as their masters, their benefactors, their loving fathers; and rich and poor are held together by the sweet ties of Christian charity, which alone can give us the real and only possible equality. The head does not oppress the body upon which it rests but guides it and gives life to it, and the body does not rebel against the head but serves it, and through a harmonious relationship [between the body and the head] comes a shared well-being. The same thing happens in social life: you workers are the body and those of property, capital, and intelligence are the head.[28]

The argument that "equality of earthly goods and enjoyments" is against nature and the well-being of society reoccurred in Bonomelli's pastoral letter. One might add that this theme was repeated endlessly in other Catholic treatises as well. Should economic equality be established "through a frightful upheaval," Bonomelli said,

> it would not last, and would disappear in a few years. But there is another equality that is possible to establish, at least to a point. It is not the equality of rights and duties, of talents and wealth, but an equality that springs from the great law of charity promulgated by Jesus Christ: "that which remaineth, give alms." Such is the judgment pronounced by Jesus Christ. Commenting on this, Paul the Apostle writes, "Let your abundance supply their want [so] that there may be an equality."

It was a measure of the influence of Aquinas at the turn of the century that most Catholic writers on social subjects agreed with Bonomelli that the judicious use of the superfluous and the law of charity were useful means of social leveling, and a way of ending social tension. In spite of this agreement, Thomist Catholics eventually split over the issue. This difference was not in substance as much as it was in emphasis. Some like Bonomelli took up positions on one end of the polarity, but agreed with those on the other end that there was a natural inequality among men, and that complete equality, if anything, remained an aspiration. However, instead of considering the idea of equality a human folly, as their conservatively inclined colleagues did, people like Bonomelli usually granted to such an aspiration a legitimacy not only in the eyes of men but even of God. Bonomelli certainly did this in his 1886 pastoral letter, which, addressed to the working classes, was also a dramatic appeal to the wealthy:

> O proprietors, o rich, o gentlemen, do not disdain to lower yourselves and yield to those who suffer and work for you. *Ut fiat aequalitas:* "that there may be an equality." If you refuse to do it voluntarily today, soon you may be forced to do it. If you do not concede now spontaneously, perhaps some day it will be snatched from your hands and you will not get credit for having granted it. The more the two classes, the rich and the poor, are separated by a cleavage, the more terrible the clash will be some day. But if the two classes are fused by Christian charity and come together as brothers, no clash at all will occur. If we think about the current state not only of Italy but the whole of Europe, if we consider the road we have traveled during the last fifty years, if we contemplate historical developments that accelerate as rapidly as falling bodies governed by the law of gravity, we are left with the conviction that the current movement toward equality is as necessary as it is irresistible, that there is no force strong enough to arrest it: monarchs cannot do that; neither can republics, nor politicians, nor armies, nor all the erudites of the world. The wisest thing to do is to regulate the course of this impetuous river so that it will continue to run within its banks. In its essentials the movement toward equality is good and holy: it comes from God who made man perfectible. . . . But it would be a disaster if this movement rushed ahead out of control and breached its banks. If they were not shortsighted, those living in France could have observed from 1750 on a nationwide social movement that pressed for the abolition of iniquitous and intolerable privileges, a movement that pressed for a radical transformation, for equality. An immense disaster could have been very much reduced in size if not completely avoided, if, instead of denied and resisted in often unwise ways, this movement

toward equality was given a smooth run to follow, if this river was channeled, this universal movement regulated. But this was not recognized in time because it was thought that changes could be prevented. What happened instead was that the river overflowed its banks, rivers of blood ran, and mountains of dead bodies were built. A transformation that could have been slow and natural turned into a frightful revolution that was an immense crime and a tremendous justice at the same time.[29]

With its lack of distinction between political and socioeconomic equalities, Bonomelli's argument was typical of Catholic treatises on the subject. At the end, though, it showed the writer as adrift, moving away from social conservatives. After stating that the French Revolution of 1789 had done "justice," Bonomelli turned in the direction of separating the political from the socioeconomic. At the time he wrote the pastoral letter, a clear distinction was beginning to emerge between these categories. This was due in part to the division that was developing in social science, with groups of scholars claiming and studying distinct spheres of life. But this division of scholarly labor and the subsequent distinctions between economic, political, and social areas can also be seen as a response to particular needs in society. Political egalitarianism was gaining wide acceptance all across Europe at the turn of the century, but those who were willing to concede to the masses the right to vote were not necessarily interested in economic equality. Quite the contrary, the introduction of nearly universal manhood suffrage, a major breakthrough toward democracy, represented in Italy an attempt by liberal statesmen to take the wind out of Socialist sails.[30]

The Catholics' animosity toward the Italian state and the liberal statesmen who led it certainly had to do with their unwillingness to separate the issues of socioeconomic and political equality and to consider the acceptance of democracy and, with it, the political reality of contemporary Italy. Characteristically, those who drifted in the direction of considering those issues separately eventually also showed an inclination to accept the principle of political equality. This willingness to take up political and socioeconomic equality as separate topics of discussion eventually became the divide between

Catholic social and political conservatives and the Christian Democratic activists. The activists, along with their supporters in the church hierarchy, inevitably reached the conclusion that the march of political equality and the coming of democracy was inevitable. They also talked of reducing socioeconomic inequality, but usually stopped short of even considering economic equality.

As his pastoral letter showed, Bonomelli considered an attack on inequality not only a possibility but a necessity. From this position he eventually moved toward supporting the Christian Democratic activists' aim of pressing for political equality and, simultaneously, exposed himself to the ire of Pius X by suggesting, as most of the activists were inclined to do, that the time had come for settling the Roman Question. His despair over the pope's rejection of these suggestions is evident in a private letter he wrote in 1911 to Cardinal Capecelatro:

> It is horrible! The motherland and the Church in conflict. . . . I go crazy (*divento pazzo*) if I think about it. . . . Eminence, where are we heading? I wrote to Agliardi and Rampolla and others, begging them to say and do something: they deplore the situation, they think as I do, they did what I asked them to do, they tried, but all in vain. Maybe, as happened in 1848, God will let the river of flames run its course in order to break up and sweep away the old structure and let the Church emerge reborn. Maybe the Vatican too will sink. I don't know anymore what to say, what to pray for.[31]

This *cri de coeur,* with its focus on political problems, is a perfect mirror of the reality of Italian life. The obsession of the Vatican with the Roman Question and the anguish of those who wanted to settle that conflict in order to focus the attention of the faithful on the problems of contemporary society are painfully evident. The letter also echoes Bonomelli's 1886 *pastorale,* which suggested that refusing to yield to mounting pressures for greater equality was to court disaster. However, this conviction, then based on evidence drawn from the past, had become by 1911 an expectation of a frightful deluge. What despair in an old man's heart, after struggling in vain with conservatives who insisted that bowing to pressures for equality was an invitation to disaster! To social conservatives, changes in the direction of equality were more than disastrous: they were sins, since inequality was the handiwork of God. Certain principles, the Jesuit Gaetano Zocchi declared, were "eternal, necessary, indisputable, and indestructible." Among these "facts," "dependent on a superior will, on Providence," Zocchi listed the "miseries of life, the wickedness of instincts because of Original Sin, . . . the inequality among men and consequently the difference in intellectual, moral, and physical abilities, exingencies and needs that all require different satisfaction."[32]

So deeply ingrained was the objection to the doctrine of equality among Catholics that even Medolago, who was to spend his life improving the lot of the working classes, insisted that men were unequal by nature, some being physically strong and others weak; some "more inclined toward manual work" and others "toward the highest speculative endeavors." It was the dream of "demented minds" to expect equality to materialize in the way the socialists did, said the count, who then added liberty and fraternity to those dreams of demented minds. Medolago argued that inequality was established "by God, Creator and Ruler. He so ordained that there be those who command and those who obey, masters and servants, poor and rich: one like the other, the work of the Lord: *utriusque operator est Dominus.*"[33]

The Permanence of Classes on the Social Landscape and the Paradoxical Objection to Conflict among Classes

Those who, like Medolago, affirmed an innate inequality in society apparently did so with the support of the highest authority of the church. In his *motu proprio* "Fin dalla prima," one of the first documents he released after his assumption of the papacy, Pius X went on record to state that:

1. Society as established by God is composed of unequal elements as the members of the human body are unequal. To make them equal would be impossible and would amount to the destruction of society itself.

2. Equality among the various members of the social [body] exists only insofar as all men trace their origins to God, the Creator, they all

have been redeemed by Jesus Christ, and will be judged, rewarded or punished according to their merits or demerits.

3. From this it follows that it is according to the order established by God that in society there be princes and subjects, capitalists [*padroni*] and proletarians, rich and poor, learned and ignorant, nobles and plebians, who, united by the tie of love, are to aid each other to reach their final destination in Heaven and, here on earth, their material and moral well being.[34]

These statements constituted the first three of nineteen propositions advanced in "Fin dalla prima," propositions that were identified as "norms" to be followed "religiously" on pain of interdict by church authorities. The importance of these propositions was further emphasized by the fact that under each of them was a reference to a document released by Pius's predecessor Leo XIII. In connection with the statements, according to which society was class-divided by divine arrangement, a reference could also have been made to Cardinal Sarto, who lectured in 1896 to a gathering of social scientists about the "inexplicable mystery of inequality among men on earth that is as necessary as it is inevitable, and that would return the day after a generous dreamer would think of abolishing it because it is the law of this world destined to perish."[35] In 1903, as pope, Sarto talked of society as "the work of God, Who Himself wanted a diversity of conditions." And as late as 1910 he stated that "to maintain the diversity of classes, which clearly is a characteristic of a well-constituted community, means to preserve the form and character God, its Author, gave to society." The statement again was Leonine—in fact, a direct quote from the encyclical *Graves de communi* issued in 1901.[36]

When he condemned class conflict, Sarto's consistency was also the consistency of the church's official doctrine. Even the thought of it was a sin: "Language which might inspire aversion for the higher classes is, and can only be regarded as, altogether contrary to the true spirit of Christian charity."[37] Since an equation had been established by the leadership of the church between class struggle and violence, the doctrine of Christian love dictated that the church condemn class conflict, as indeed she does to our own days.[38]

Yet another equation connected strikes with class struggle and violence. Thus Pius X remained consistent throughout his life in condemning strikes. As late as 1913, he declared that strikes were "against the well-being of the workers and the quiet life of the citizen".[39] This statement repeated almost word for word what Leo XIII argued in *Rerum novarum*. Utilizing the social paradigm of the body analogy, that encyclical presented harmony among classes as "natural" and conflict as "unnatural," and stated further that the strike "not only affects the masters and their work people alike, but is extremely injurious to trade and to the general interests of the public; moreover, on such occasions, violence and disorder are generally not far distant and thus it frequently happens that the public peace is imperiled."[40]

Thus the Catholic labor movement had to carry the burden of a paradox manifest in Catholic social philosophy, which insisted upon distinct social classes but condemned conflict among them and looked upon such manifestations of class struggle as strikes as anything but desirable. When the central office sent out a questionnaire about the activities of Catholic organizations of labor, to the question "Did the members take any part in strikes?" the president of the local in Bagolino, in the Brescia province, responded: "No, they all behaved." In maintaining *buona condotta,* good behavior, by staying away from strikes (in fact, by organizing a protest against one called by another organization of labor), the Catholic unions conformed to the expectations of the leadership. This happened in 1891. But the mentality that, in the words of the historian Antonio Fappani, made a person guilty of the "worst possible conduct" even to think of a strike[41] was to remain with the Catholic labor movement during the decades to come.

The obsession with the avoidance of social conflict and strikes that colored the attitude of the church leadership led to a marked aversion toward urban society and the industrial working class, which was seen as hostile toward the "superior classes" and, because of that, as a threat to social peace. Unlike the urban industrial workers, the rural population was perceived as respectful of law and order, deeply religious, and willing to accept the guidance of the church. Giovanni Spadolini noted the preference of Catholics for rural society "with its advantages of solidity, wholesomeness, and continuity."[42] This view was motivated by Thomistic theology with its emphasis upon a symbiotic relationship among various social strata, a relationship that Catholics thought was dead in the urban environment but alive and well among the peasants. This idealization of the countryside as the "height of moral life" ran uninterrupted throughout the history of Italian Catholic Action. In 1874, at the first congress of the Opera dei congressi e comitati cattolici, the umbrella organization of Catholic Action, Alfonso Rubbiani, the general secretary, set the tone by referring to the

> sweet quietness of the countryside [which] turns out to be always the height of order and morality. In the genesis of the city, we find the remorse of man the sinner who trembles from the fright of rebellion, turned pale seeing Creation and thinks to be able to forget God the Vindicator [*Dio vindice*] by surrounding himself with artifacts that do not directly carry the sign of that creating hand, that [man] the sinner sees armed with lightning and scourge. Man in the state of sin necessarily had to build the city, and it is not accidental that we encounter in the Genesis Cain, the first murderer, the first among men to be cursed by God, as the first who builds a city. The innocent man, by contrast, was placed by God in a garden among flowers and plants, and here is the explanation of why the just, who have a clear conscience, prefer the silence of the countryside and the delinquents need to find cover, hide, circumscribe and limit the horizon.[43]

Rubbiani was not alone in praising the peasant for being

> robustness personified. [The peasants] breathed the air of the fields and hills, pure and rich in oxygen, left adolescence vigorous, bloomed in youth, were hardy during virility and preserved their strength during old age, which mitigated decrepitude. Work increased their vigor, they converted frugal nourishment into good blood, they needed less than the industrial worker, and their need could be satisfied at little expense. They maintained an affection for their families, who in most cases shared work, and it was habitual for them to observe the sacred laws of decency and morality. Their cheerful songs, often resounding in the valleys and mountains, showed that they went through their days tranquil and satisfied.[44]

The striking thing about this idealization of the countryside and its people as God-fearing and respectful of the priests as they were of the social order, in contrast to city-dwellers, who constituted *civitas diaboli,* a community of Satan, is that upon examination it turns out to be utterly against the spirit of Thomism. Detailing the social philosophy of Aquinas, Ernst Troeltsch makes "the remarkable discovery, that in contrast to the inclination of modern Catholicism toward the rural population and its specific Ethos, it is solely the city that St. Thomas takes into account. In his view, man is naturally a town dweller, and regards rural life as the result of misfortune or of want."

Aquinas's writings, like those of his mentor Aristotle, did include a rural-urban contrast. But this, very much unlike the late-nineteenth-century Catholic conservatives' comparison, showed agriculture as "dirty and miserable" and life in the countryside, then ravaged by feudal barons, as anything but the scene of a good life. Instead, the Angelic Doctor idealized "the medieval town, with its principles of peace, with its basis of free labour, and corporate labour groups, with its stronger intellectual interests and its care and protection through its administration for everyone, which provided a fertile soil for Christian ideals."[45]

In their use and abuse of the ideas of Aquinas, Italian Neo-Thomists failed to notice his aversion to rural society. The idealization of the countryside and its people continued, but along with it went the idealization of life in medieval towns where there was no "antagonism between the superior and inferior classes," but an "admirable harmony with which the world was governed by Divine Providence." The words were Medolago's.[46] Together with Toniolo he will be our guide as we follow Italian Catholics in their quest for the magic formula that they hoped would allow them to make class struggle, that modern sin of sins, disappear from the face of the earth. This journey by time machine to the Middle Ages, Aquinas's world, produced an Italian version of the corporative doctrine, whose development constituted the first chapter in the history of the Italian Catholic labor movement.

4

Fraternity and Angelic Charity

Catholic Corporative Doctrine

The Catholic conservatives' traditional aversion to social conflict sent them in search of an alternative to the liberal-capitalistic system that they considered the breeding ground of class struggle. In working out the details of the alternative, known as the corporative system, during the last three decades of the nineteenth century, Catholic conservative attitudes underwent a transformation from traditionalism into a full-fledged ideology of conservativism.

In making the distinction between traditionalism and conservativism, Karl Mannheim describes the first as a psychological attitude that, dissatisfied with the present, tends to "cling to the past." Conservativism, which according to Mannheim is "traditionalism become conscious," is more than a reactive reflex. Unlike traditionalism, which usually exhausts itself in endless grudges, conservativism combines the objections to basic aspects of the human condition with the working out of an alternative.[1]

The emergence of the corporativist alternative, which made Catholic conservativism into a full-fledged ideology, was clearly a response to the threat posed by the emergence of the industrial working class. The bourgeoisie was also very much on Catholic conservative minds, but, characteristically, objections to it, severe as they might have been, tended to be grudges,[2] fitting into the pattern of what Mannheim defines as traditionalism. But when the industrial working class began to flex its muscles as an autonomous force during the last three decades of the nineteenth century, traditionalism fast consolidated into a conservative ideology, and the corporativist doctrine was forged.

Jean-Claude Poulain, a French Catholic historian, was to talk of corporativism as "demobilizing."[3] The thrust of the corporativist doctrine was to neutralize the industrial working class and prevent it from becoming a vital social and political force. In searching for the Italian version of this ideological demobilization, we have to look to Giuseppe Toniolo. He served as the chief Italian theoretician of Catholic corporativism, and his contribution to the attempt to eliminate class struggle was very substantial. Toniolo presented the social class as "a moral fact, a historical and necessary fact" and not only conceded to classes a degree of autonomy but also recognized the phenomenon of class-consciousness.[4] Nevertheless, what Toniolo gave in social theory with one hand he took back with the other. If classes were for him "natural" and "historical," so was a hierarchical ordering of society.[5] Thus he allowed only a limited claim of social and political importance to the "inferior classes" by declaring that social and political initiatives constituted by and large the rights and duties of the "superior classes."

He was, however, a good enough social scientist to suggest that "in certain historical periods" ruling classes did not measure up to their tasks and by necessity were replaced. But if he ever suggested that a new "superior class" would emerge from among the workers of Turin and the landless peasants of the Po Valley, this possibility was pushed out into the infinite future. All he had for them was a hint of a rejuvenated elite, a "young hierarchy" possibly emerging through the circulation of the elites.[6] This was a notion that Vilfredo Pareto was to develop in his *Trattato di sociologia generale,* published in 1916, into a full-fledged theory, promising to lower-class elements the possibility of rising into the ruling class on an individual basis.

It was not that Toniolo did not allow for the inferior classes' gains in the material conditions of life and even in social importance. However, he drew the line on politics; and when in 1913 the right to vote was extended to the working classes, he deplored this as a Masonic plot to "dechristianize Italy en masse."[7] Furthermore, whatever gains he may have allowed the working classes, limits were to be set to these by the hierarchical ordering of society, which Toniolo, like Sarto, conceived as divinely ordained. That notion and the reference to the working classes as "inferior" remained with Toniolo throughout his life, as did the perception that the industrial working class represented a threat to society by its very existence.[8] His obsessive interest in the medieval guilds was due to that perception. Toniolo turned to the medieval *corporazione* because he hoped it would provide an organizational form to neutralize the threat by submitting working people to the "tutelage," and by implication the control, of the "superior" classes.

A particular understanding of the nature of social classes gave him an opening into the corporative theory. The more the Marxist notion of classes based on the ownership of the means of production became known and accepted, the more the Catholics tended to drift away from their old understanding of society which, somewhat like the Marxists', distinguished between the "rich"and the "poor." Toniolo, following this drift, argued that the possession of wealth was only one, and probably not the most important one, of the defining characteristics of classes. A class, he declared, "results from the most intimate rapproachment of ideas, of sentiments, of mutual services, of a common finality that is dependent on an affinity of education, of profession, of civic interests, and of habits of life."[9]

Thus Toniolo produced a striking definition of social class that combined in a way both Max Weber's perception of status groups, conceived as communities based on shared interests and life-styles, and Emile Durkheim's professional-occupational groups as the basic elements of social organization. Whether such was the case with Weber and Durkheim is debatable, but Toniolo's concept of class surely represented an attempt to deny the validity of Marxian social analysis by calling into question the meaning of the central Marxian concept of classes. Luigi Sturzo (1871–1959), who also based his social theory on the perception of classes as professional-occupational groups, characteristically concluded that the professional-occupational organization of the working class was "per se contrary to socialism."[10]

Durkheim's theoretical position was also relevant to the development of the corporativist doctrine. When published, his theory *volere nolere* gave aid and comfort to the advocates of corporativism. Durkheim's work, like Toniolo's, provided the social "scientific" proof for the validity of the conservatives' argument that class consciousness, as perceived by the Marxists, should be and could be replaced by professional-occupational consciousness.[11] This was to unite into meaningful social groups all those who contributed to particular lines of production. Thus instead of the proletarians of the world uniting, those who produced steel, for instance, were to be united in social awareness and aims—united from the capitalist who owned the factory down to the lowliest cleaner of the workers' washroom.

It was an integral part of the corporativist doctrine to "conquer the people," as the French Catholic conservative Albert de Mun put it, by instilling in the proletariat a professional-occupational consciousness, or, as yet another French conservative was to say, by "substituting the professions for classes as the basis of social life."[12] This mention of Frenchmen is not accidental in connection with the need for the corporativist restructuring of society and the revival of the medieval corporations. French Catholic conservatives, especially de Mun, produced the first articulate and concrete arguments, and thus gave a final stimulus for the development of *corporativismo* in Italy. That Toniolo joined in the search for "durable" institutions to replace contemporary ones and, like the French conservatives, found these in the medieval corporations was a foregone conclusion given his training, his focus, and his methodology as a sociologist. Toniolo's method was intensely historical, in that he was like virtually all the other giants of modern social science. But unlike Pareto, Mosca, Weber, and Durkheim, Toniolo's approach tended to remain permanently focused on the remote past. With this fixation his work fits into the traditionalist pattern of the rejection of the present and the cult of the past. The time machine that took Toniolo on his trips into the past often landed in the Middle Ages because that was where he expected to find fellow conservatives from other European countries on a journey similar to his own. Particular Italian traditions also entered into play in connection with Toniolo's preference for the Middle Ages; many of these traditions no doubt represented rather wishful thinking. Those were the days for Toniolo and his friends, the days on which to base a conservative and very Italian utopia: during the Middle Ages, religion was solidly entrenched as a vital force; the papacy was strong and, in confrontations with weak states, inevitably victorious. Oh, the thought of Victor Emmanuel at Canossa![13] Then there were the *corporazioni,* guided by *caritas,* and no class conflict.

Toniolo was not a fool to turn sociology into science fiction. He was a good enough social scientist to sense what historical research would turn up decades later: that the medieval guilds eventually developed into complex organisms with inner tensions that frequently exploded into class struggles between lower guildsmen and the rich ones who were the forerunners of modern capitalists. Even Stanislao Medolago Albani, who had much less claim to a scientific method in spite of efforts to acquire it, noticed that the medieval guilds "naturally carried in themselves the marks of an institution in part decayed and decadent." But such conditions came later.[14] If only the time machine were set for very early, the earliest possible period, the scene of the eventual destruction of the guild system could be avoided.

Perhaps someone finally saw the folly of moving farther and farther into the past until pure and unadulterated feudalism was reached. A resolution was duly debated and passed at the 1877 congress of the Opera dei Congressi e comitati cattolici, the umbrella organization of Italian Catholic Action, pointing out the need to study the medieval corporations "before their degeneration," "during the period in which they were inspired by Faith and Christian Charity" in order to put them to proper use "in the benefit of the industrial classes and of social harmony." And yet the resolution was left out of the *Acts* of the congress.[15] In spite of this mishap, intended or unintended, the time travel not only continued but intensified. The idealized image of medieval corporations was necessary in order to maintain the integrity of the Catholic utopia of social restoration that was to lead the world back to that providentially arranged harmony built on the superior classes' superior role in the life of society.[16]

Italian Catholic Congresses and the Mixed Union

The mixed union, modeled on the medieval corporation, thus became central to the consolidation of the traditionalist rejection of modern society into a full-fledged conservative ideology. The very first congress of the Opera, convened in 1874, upheld as models of social organization "the ancient corporations, which were especially flourishing in Italy under the guidance of the Church and were animated by real sentiments of fraternity and angelic charity."[17]

At the fourth congress of the Opera, held in 1877, the themes of "fraternity and angelic charity" were expanded into that of the solidarity of producers, a "direct and loving relationship" between the captains of industry and the workers that would emerge through the revival and adaptation to modern times of the medieval guilds. Marquis Achille Sassoli de' Bianchi, who gave the keynote address and drafted the resolutions, along with other speakers, executed a frontal attack on the liberal social and economic system, rejecting the laissez-faire economy and the principle of supply and demand. One after another, speakers decried the social "isolation" of the individual and the "damaging individualism" that was being perpetuated since the Revolution of 1789 had abolished the system of corporations and created conditions that destroyed the small industrial enterprise. The consequences were pauperism and the proletarianization of the working class, social disequilibrium, and class struggle.

These arguments were reflected in the resolution, accepted by the congress, which pointed out that "the worker does not feel anymore either loved or protected, but irritated by social inequality, which, since the explanations provided for it by religion and faith are suppressed, he does not accept anymore." The work of the clergy, particularly the services of nuns, was deemed useful in leading the workers to the "spirit of Christian brotherhood." But in the return of the "reign of solidarity to the kingdom of work," the corporations were also indispensable because they would "bring together" the capitalist and the workers. Expected to revive "spontaneously" and freely, the guilds were to allow for a "legitimate independence" on the part of the workers, thus responding "perfectly to the sincere aspirations that arose in the world of work."[18]

Information was soon forthcoming as to the precise nature and limits of these aspirations. Sassoli, like Medolago on other occasions, suggested to the 1879 Catholic congress the establishment of a school of "Christian social economy"; and his suggestion eventually trailed off into talk about a "great social movement" that would bring the *padroni* together with their "brothers," the workers, in an organizational form aimed at combatting the socialist labor movement. Socialism based on the autonomy of the working classes was, according to Sassoli, "the root cause of [social] dissolution and conflict." Thus the concept of the mixed union emerged during the ten years following the 1877 congress in the speeches and writings of Sassoli and others. That this organizational form was to place the inferior classes under the angelic guidance and care of the superior classes was not stated with the clarity that hindsight gives the historian. There certainly was no mention yet of the "demobilization" of the proletariat. Rather, there was a steady stream of talk about social solidarity and the need to eliminate class struggle as the term *mixed corporation* appeared increasingly in the writings and private correspondence of Catholic spokesmen.[19] The leaders of Italian Catholic Action reflected and debated, and in doing so drew heavily upon information from abroad. Count Medolago's aristocratic income allowed what Toniolo could not afford on a professorial salary: travel abroad. Hoping to contribute a presentation, Medolago went to an international symposium held in 1885 and asked Toniolo to coach him in preparing the speech. But he came back with the report that because of the overcrowding of the schedule his presentation was left out. A sense of inferiority is evident in the letter he wrote to Toniolo as he reported about having been in the presence of greats, like de Mun, at the conference. The two revived earlier ideas about "establishing among us little by little a real school of Catholic economy like the one that exists in France and Germany."[20]

Medolago felt an especially pressing need for a theoretical elaboration. As the president of the second session of the Opera, it fell upon him to implement the idea of the mixed union, which, during the 1880s, was viewed increasingly as the form the revived guilds should take. In attempting to work out the statutes for such an organization, Medolago wrote in a letter to Toniolo of a "great embarrassment": he simply could not find in the land of Italy one organization that could serve as a model. There were several organizations of Catholic labor, but he found that "only rarely did the *padroni,* indispensable for the corporations, join these." The upper classes tended to congregate in charitable organizations, another type under Medolago's direction; but given all the talk about the workers' "legitimate independence," he was disinclined to accept organizations of charity as the models for the revived guilds.

Eventually, as luck would have it, in Sicily "a workers' association with excellent statutes, approved by His Eminence the archbishop of Palermo," was discovered. But Medolago had to report to Toniolo that a close inspection by the Comitato Permanente of the Opera found these statutes "too prolix" and gave the Jesuit Father Alfonso Casoli, a close associate and eventually the biographer of Medolago, the task of studying in a hurry "some of the statutes of the ancient corporations" in order to harmonize the rules governing the Sicilian organization with these. This solved two problems: the elimination of extreme verbosity and the "adaptation" of medieval organizations to modern conditions. As for the results of this quest, they were much less than satisfying to Medolago, who wrote Toniolo that given the utter ignorance of Catholics (meaning his colleagues on the Permanent Committee?) in sociology and economy, it was "pure folly" to throw together the statutes of the modern corporation with such haste, but "my colleagues were really in love with those statutes, and I had to accommodate them."[21]

Foreign Models and the Italians' Choice

Thus the leadership of the Opera rushed through the statutes of the mixed union against the better judgment of Medolago, who wanted more time to consider how to base the organizational form of Catholic labor on concrete social and economic conditions. Yet his colleagues were in a hurry, in part to catch up with the development of the corporativist doctrine abroad. The theoretical groundwork laid no less hurriedly a few years earlier by the French aristocrat R. La Tour du Pin, and in just as much ignorance of concrete social and economic conditions, reassured the Italians of the righteousness of their course. La Tour, in fact, went beyond just stressing the need for the medieval guilds' revival in the form of mixed unions. He argued that in their modern form the corporations, organized in each line of production, should be obligatory. He talked about them as "states within the state" and intended to give them the power to deliberate and vote upon the issues of the economy. The catch was that the vote was to be taken not by counting the hands raised but by category: one for the owner of the factory, one for all the workers, a tie! In completing the blueprint for the "restoration of the Christian state," La Tour even designed a "Great Council of the Corporations," a senate of a kind that was to hold consultative power within a "social monarchy."[22]

The brave men of central Europe's aristocracy were not going to be beaten in the international race for the development of old-fashioned traditionalism into a full-scale ideology, complete with a political system to replace the hated bourgeois regimes. This is not to say that the system presided over by the old Emperor Franz Joseph could be called, by any stretch of the imagination, a rule of the bourgeoisie. Such was not a problem in central Europe, and was not what bothered the neo-feudal aristocrats like Karl von Vogelsang (1818–90). What was on his mind, though, was also in the thoughts of La Tour and his Italian followers. By reinstating the medieval guilds, Vogelsang, a solid Thomist, hoped to do away with class struggle. What a *coup de main* it was to be: *Entproletarisierung des Proletariats,* the deproletarianizing of the proletariat, which, reordered into the revived corporations, was to disappear. And rightly so, according to Vogelsang, in whose judgment "justice to the proletariat cannot be anything else but the disappearance of the working class, following its absorption into the class of property owners."[23] Vogelsang's blueprint was complete with plans for the reorganization of the state into one based on a professional-occupational representation that was to replace the parliamentary system.

Vogelsang's proposals were published at the same time as Medolago's colleagues had so hurriedly worked out the *statuto* for the mixed union. Thus the Italian Catholics had at least two models to choose from when, in 1887, they considered the problems related to the industrial working class at the seventh congress of the Opera.

Marquis Lorenzo Bottini provided the principal address, entitled *La questione operaia e la corporazione cristiana.* Shortly before the congress opened, the marquis confided to Toniolo that he simply had too much to say in the time allowed; hence, *noblesse oblige,* he decided to print and distribute his presentation at his own expense.

The first part of his address, dealing with the *operaio,* the industrial worker, was like a replay of speeches at previous Catholic congresses. It was a catalog of the horrors introduced by the capitalist system, whose immediate origins Bottini dated to the passing of the French law that abolished the corporations after the Revolution of 1789. What followed, according to the marquis, was a free reign of individualism, the destruction of social solidarity, and the moral degeneration of human beings into factory workers, concentrated in enormous numbers in conditions that bred drunkenness, sexual promiscuity, and prostitution. Bottini claimed the capitalist system deprived the woman of her womanhood, since a working woman "was not a woman anymore." It also deprived the families of mothers by forcing them into work because inadequate pay did not allow the fathers to support their families by themselves. Worse than that, periodic unemployment left the workers without any income whatsoever; and while they worked, a merciless exploitation instilled hatred in their hearts toward their exploiters. If the legal system allowed "the *padrone* the freedom to oppress the worker," Bottini ventured to say, "logic and justice demanded that the worker be given the freedom to defend himself." He did hurriedly add that he did not believe the "*questione operaia* had to be resolved through a struggle between the *padroni* and the workers."

Thus the readers of Bottini's presentation arrived at the second part of his arguments, in which, by the reintroduction of the *corporazione cristiana,* he proposed to resolve the social issues connected with the appearance of the industrial working class. Quoting the German Bishop Emmanuel Ketteler, the marquis declared these issues to be "primarily religious in nature." He defined the corporation as "an association permanently established in a hierarchical form [including both] the entrepreneurs and the workers engaged in particular areas of production, with the aim to sustain cooperation toward common goals of a religious, moral, civic, and economic nature." Bottini promised that this "hierarchical union between the diverse social classes of the members" "will be suitable to mitigate the suffering of the workers, make the position of the capitalists more secure, to extinguish the fire of discord that blazes between [the workers and the capitalists] and to make for the reign of order and consequently of peace instead." Who could want more than that! Well, it would have been nice if the workers were offered a few shares, but the Italian aristocrats were not inclined to be as generous as Vogelsang, who held out the promise of eventual co-ownership of the means of production.

Other speakers at the congress spoke of sharecropping, *mezzadria,* as the ideal condition in agriculture, ignoring the suggestions of land reform, the breakup of large landed estates into small holdings by some central European aristocrats in a self-flagellating mood. As for Bottini, he talked of experimental models of the corporation developed somewhere in the Dual Monarchy, only to reject them because, he said, these did not allow the workers a proper share in the direction of the organization. In addition, their membership was obligatory. The marquis mentioned that there was a third type, not obligatory, "developing in France and England" that, unlike the Austrian models, did not "destroy" or even "offend" the principle of freedom, and thus responded well (as, presumably, his own proposal did too) "to the needs of large-scale industry, to the spirit of the times, to the nature and traditions of Italy, and finally to the base foundation of our corporation which is the Christian and Catholic religion." Bottini suggested that the mutual aid societies, of which a large number existed in Italy, be used during the first phase of the buildup of the new corporations. He added as a second thought that the corporative system, when it was fully developed, would be useful in reducing on a national, and even on an international, level the excesses of competition that were damaging to the social fabric.[24]

It was proper to hold out the hope of developing neat little monopolies, after offering the capitalists the mixed union, a means of control over the workers and an institution to be empowered, one presumes, to determine not only the "just price," as La Tour suggested, but also equally just wages. Characteristically, in a series of letters exchanged with the industrialist Alessandro Rossi during the spring of 1888, Toniolo discussed both an "alliance of the superior classes with the enlightened and active clergy, [an alliance] guided by the common and inexhaustible inspiration of Faith and Charity." As for the *corporazione,* he called it a concept "just and obtainable in the sense of a collective representation of similar class interests." After the passing of "so many democratic waves," Toniolo expected the concept of "free, moral, and charitable patronage" exercised by the superior classes over the inferior ones "will be proved valid in no less measure than the [concept of] fraternity."[25]

The 1887 Catholic congress thus held out a hand toward the bourgeoisie. This was done in a very Catholic manner, by demanding, "Recognize your sins and repent, or you will burn." First there was a long list of sins, including that of exploitation and the class hatred that grew out of it. But there was salvation for repentant sinners, at least, in the form of the corporativist program that offered a cure for class struggle by confining the workers within a hierarchically ordered social structure; in other words, under the paternalistic care of the *padroni,* guided by old-fashioned angelic charity.

As for the workers, from here on they would be told that the corporation would save them from exploitation. Thus Andrea Cappellazzi, speaking in 1890 of the unfair power of the *padrone* over the worker: "The real and reasonable vindication of the worker is in the reestablishment of the corporations of the Middle Ages and not in strikes."[26] Toniolo eventually outdid this promise in 1901:

By reordering itself [*ordinandosi*] into corporations, the proletariat acquires the exigency and dignity of a class, and we can talk with a scientific rigor of the genesis of a fourth estate as the providential law of the current moment. And the relevance of today's social transformation does not end here, since the corporative reordering of the people, by provoking the joining into the corporation also of the superior strata, promises to accelerate the corporative legal reordering into classes of the entire society and thus to correct from its roots up the leveling individualism that is the greatest vice of contemporary society.[27]

Thus those workers who were somewhat theoretically oriented could feel reassured that if they joined the corporation, they would not only be saved from exploitation but their social nature, stolen by the wicked capitalists, would also be restored to them. The atomization of society—or as Ketteler referred to the theme, the *Polverisierung des Menschengeschlechtes,* the "pulverizing of mankind."[28]— was a recurring theme of the Catholic complaints about the liberal-capitalistic system. As Taparelli's works show, objection to atomization became standard in Neo-Thomistic social analyses and often came paired with the objection to the principle of equality and the insistence upon the hierarchical nature of the social order.

The concern about atomization led to an emphasis on the need for "intermediary" institutions to protect the individual against abuses. In continuing to argue this need toward the end of the nineteenth century,[29] aside from going back to Taparelli, Italian conservatives also began to draw heavily on arguments developed abroad. In this connection French Catholic conservative thought, for which the notion of "intermediary" institution was central since the times of Restoration, was of particular importance.[30] The search for such institutions drew Frenchmen as well as Italians toward the medieval corporations and the urging of their revival as the cure for the modern atomization of society.[31]

The State as Moderator of the Affairs of Society

In Germany, where the need for such revival was voiced as early as in 1837, the arguments in its favor were fully developed by Ketteler by 1877, when he declared himself in favor of the organization of the working class along professional-occupational lines. This coincided with the suggestions of his close associate Abbot Franz Hitze, who in 1880 listed the corporation with the family and local civic community as intermediary institutions. Based on professional-occupational interests, the corporative organizations were to be obligatory according to Hitze. This led to protest on the part of a good many conservative German Catholics who, like their Italian counterparts in 1887, asserted the principle of freedom when it came to the organization of labor. Hitze's scheme did not win the approval of Ketteler either because the bishop feared an undue influence on the part of the state, which, according to Hitze's scheme, was to be called upon to enforce obligatory participation in the corporative organization. The position taken by Ketteler in 1877 probably reflected the immediate experience of the *Kulturkampf,* a conflict between German Catholics and the government, for Ketteler had already shown himself attuned to the particular German traditions that placed a strong emphasis upon the role of the state in social life. In connection with the organizations of labor, for instance, he insisted that the state not only guarantee their existence through legislative means but also that laws protect the working class from abuses.[32]

The Italians were even more emphatic than Ketteler about "freedom," and against an obligatory membership in connection with the corporations, and they too were motivated by immediate historical experiences. It became an Italian Catholic tradition to oppose the rise of state power because this implied that the other major institution, the church, ended up in a weaker position. The arguments about the unnecessary and dangerous growth in the power of the modern state were embedded in Taparelli's discussion of modern society. The denouement of the Risorgimento, which set the church into a deadly conflict with the state, imposed upon conservative Catholics in a still more aggravated form the traditional hostility toward the state. This hostility, in fact, sustained their drive to work out the details of an alternative to the liberal-capitalistic system, a drive that can be seen as concluding in 1887 with the appearance of the mixed union. The obsession of the Catholic leadership with that organization, and their hurry to institute it, was a telltale sign of their understanding that the mixed union was the last missing piece to complete the development of Italian traditionalism into a full-fledged ideology, an alternative to the existing system.

The mixed organizations of workers and *padroni* were to constitute the initial, seminal developmental stage toward an eventual reorganization of society along professional-occupational lines. The mixed unions—*corporazioni* as they were often called, evoking their medieval origins—were to become "states within the state" when they fully developed into nationwide organizations, gathering all within occupations, such as mining, steelmaking, railroading, teaching, and the like. These corporations in turn were to send representatives to a central institution that was to replace the parliament.[33]

Visions of such a complete transformation of both the social and
political realms of life began to appear in the writings of Italian Catholics after 1887 when the mixed union as a concept was fully developed in Italy.

The force of the corporativist vision was such that it held under
its sway even many of the activists, who tended to be just as critical
of the liberal system as their older and more socially conservative
coreligionists were. The corporativist alternative offered an outlet
for the radicalism of some of the activists, the Turinese Luigi Caissotti di Chiusano, for instance. In 1896 he developed a proposal for a
full-fledged corporative political system to replace the current one,
which he considered a political expression of the liberal-capitalistic
atomization of society. During the last years of the nineteenth century, the talk about replacing the parliament with an institution
based on professional-occupational groups intensified. Filippo
Meda, who soon would become a member of parliament and two
decades later would be the first Catholic member of a government in
post-Unification Italy, registered a dissenting voice that was rare
then among Catholics, even those of activistic orientation. In 1896
Meda suggested in a typically reformist fashion that instead of doing
away with the parliamentary system, it should be democratized by
enlarging the then very limited suffrage.[34]

It might be argued that the idea of the corporativist reorganization of the political system was an empty threat on the part of Italian
Catholics. How much this was not the case may be shown by the fact
that the plan for a corporativist reorganization of the state constituted a part of the 1919 program of the Partito Popolare. The survival of the corporativist doctrine, albeit in a much truncated form,[35]
in this program was ensured by the hold of corporativism over the
minds of the Catholic activists of the prewar decade, Sturzo among
them, who had a massive input into the Popular Party's program.

If, on the other hand, some Catholics at the turn of the century
had reservations about the idea of the corporative state, this was
mostly because of their hostility to the notion of the state as moderator in the affairs of society, an idea that was implied in corporative
political doctrine. Catholics, especially the orthodox kind like To-

niolo, assigned the role of moderator to the church and the pope.[36] Furthermore, information from abroad did nothing to affirm the political aspects of the corporative doctrine and pointed to initiatives that were no more than intellectual constructs utterly divorced from reality. The blueprint produced by Hitze, for example, was nothing but an exercise in applied logic.

In 1880 Hitze brought to a logical conclusion the criticism of the liberal system and advanced a proposal for the transformation of the state into a corporative one, with political representation based on professional-occupational groups. But after drawing up this blueprint, Hitze made no effort to find support for it, letting it die of neglect while he became intensely involved with reform legislation, activities in line with the ideas of his master and teacher, Ketteler, whose criticism of liberalism provided the basis for Hitze's corporativist plans, but who never moved himself in that direction.[37]

La Tour, obsessed with the idea of the corporation as a "state within the state," convinced himself that the time was ripe to begin the buildup of a corporativist political system in France. He initiated what he thought was to become a movement by calling a series of meetings that eventually culminated in 1889 in a general assembly of delegates from eighteen provinces, claiming to represent "corporativist" institutions abolished by the Revolution, but now revived. The assembly, which was to precede the Estates General of the Counterrevolution, became a sideshow to the celebration of the centenary of the Revolution held in France during the year 1889. As much as the actors enjoyed the show, it soon exhausted itself, hardly noticed by the public,[38] especially by the working classes, of whose aspirations the French aristocrats had shown no more awareness than their Italian counterparts, carried away as they were with utopian plans of their own.

The Italians were selective when it came to absorbing the foreign experiences and criticisms related to the corporativist doctrine. They responded to the objections to increasing the state's power in regulating society, since they realized with the foreign critics of corporative political theory that this implied laws that would have taxed away the superfluous and thus would have diminished the role played by private charity, so important for conservatives like Sarto. Like Taparelli they perceived the progressive income tax as a perversion, "masked communism according to which the government takes from the rich to give to the poor." A dialectician in the tradition of Thomism, Taparelli counterposed to this the "reasonable communism of giving the superfluous to the poor, which is not only reasonable but evangelical also." The thesis and antithesis were resolved by concluding that "the Gospels do not tell the poor to take from the rich, but the rich to give to the poor."[39]

Thus supported by local Neo-Thomistic traditions, Italian Catholic conservatives agreed with the foreign critics of the increased power of the state. At the same time, they ignored a chorus of voices heard abroad that pointed to the folly of expecting the corporation, a medieval organizational form, to play a vital role in modern life.[40] The idea of the mixed corporation, uniting the workers and the capitalists within the structure of large-scale industrial enterprises, was fast becoming a laughingstock among people even moderately attuned to reality at the same time Italians discovered the concept and began to push it with all their might. Hence, one of the crucial foreign developments was lost on the Italian Catholic leadership. In Italy both Catholic labor theory and organizational practices remained behind because of the desperate need of the Catholic leadership to maintain the integrity of a social utopia of which the mixed union was a necessary part. As a result decades were to pass with frustrated experiments to prove that the mixed organization of labor was not a valid proposition.

As for the "revival" of the *corporazione,* there was local and relatively recent evidence to suggest that it was condemned to fail. But in the need to prove the validity of this crucial element of the Catholic social utopia, Bottini chose to present these failures as roaring successes. Thus, not surprisingly, the suggestion of the "revival" of the corporations was based on an earlier "revival," which Bottini mentioned in his speech. In 1852 Pope Pius IX authorized "the establishment in the city of Rome of universities and corporations," which, according to the relevant papal document, "were suppressed and abolished by the *motu proprio* of Pius VII, our predecessor of sacred memory." Taparelli expressed high hopes on the pages of the newly founded *Civiltà Cattolica*. The corporations, he argued, represented a natural human right to association. He predicted they would acquire great "dignity and social influence" by perfecting not only methods of production (*arte*) but also the worker himself. The public would experience "a new life-style, not that of the barricades and turmoil, but that of loyalty and proper service. This loyalty and service is the goal to be pursued, since the workers, corrupt and libertine, are inclined [to pursue their goals] by the use of violence and by taking advantage."[41]

If anything survived of the spirit of the ancient corporations into modern times to support the hopes of Bottini, Medolago, and the other leaders of the Opera, it was in the form of mutual aid societies. They knew this; that was why at the 1887 congress they declared these the organizational base upon which the new corporations were to be built. As for the ones revived thirty years before in Rome, they disappeared without a trace after the government banned them with a law passed in 1864. This act contributed to the illusion that the ending of their rather undistinguished existence, like that of their French counterparts before the Revolution of 1789, was due to a bourgeois-liberal conspiracy. Thus the Catholic conservatives had yet another thing to blame on the bourgeoisie: the denial to society of the beneficial effects of the renewed corporations.

The suggestion that it was feasible to revive the *corporazione* was out of touch with reality. This was shown by the fact that the proposals of the 1887 congress faced a conspiracy as well: a conspiracy of silence. The local police chief used the word "indifference" in a report that described the public reaction to the congress. He reassured his superiors in Rome that the "haranguing" at the congress was not heard "outside the walls of the meeting hall." That indeed something like that was the case is shown by the fact that a month after the events Medolago complained that the press was still ignoring the Bottini speech, the *pièce de résistance* offered by his Second Session at the congress. Bottini himself registered something of a shock. The time, trouble, and money spent on gathering and printing what he had to say seemed to have been wasted, as he told Toniolo in a letter: "The papers are silent about my little work;" "My little work is asleep because nobody wants it."[42]

5

The Spirit of Revolutionary Change

The Encyclical *Rerum Novarum* and the
Appearance of the Concept of the Simple Union

The conspiracy of silence that enveloped Bottini's report to the 1887 congress of the Opera ran high and wide. In fact, with a little stretching of the imagination, even the editors of the *Civiltà Cattolica* could be included among those who conspired to kill the marquis's proposals for the revival of the *corporazione* by ignoring them. The semiofficial church publication usually followed what happened in Italian Catholic Action with a hawk's eye; but sixteen months were to pass before the periodical picked up the theme of the 1887 congress, and even then somebody was clearly playing for time. Instead of discussing the details of Bottini's presentation, the *Civiltà* expressed generalities, such as the need to "lead the working classes, and with them the whole society to the mistakenly abandoned principles of Christianity."

It was another year before Father Liberatore, who during the 1870s aided the pope in composing the Thomistic encyclical *Aeterni Patris,* addressed the problem of the revival of the medieval guilds in the pages of the *Civiltà Cattolica.* In its broad outlines, Liberatore's treatment of the problem, including his definition of the corporation to be revived as a mixed union, seemed to coincide with Bottini's presentation and the resolutions accepted by the 1887 congress.[1] But if the coincidence led to a sigh of relief on the part of Bottini and his taskmaster Medolago, it was somewhat premature. Unbeknown to them, the position taken by the aged Liberatore, reflecting in some of its details the approaches to modern social problems advocated by "neo-feudals" like Vogelsang, was deemed inadequate by the holy father himself.

Leo XIII followed with intense interest the worldwide debate among Catholics about the social issues of the age, but he withheld judgment until his thoughts could be finalized in the form of an encyclical. Liberatore, whom the pope charged with providing a draft of the encyclical to be promulgated, presented a schemata in 1890 that was apparently a version of his arguments in the *Civiltà Cattolica* two years earlier. In pròposing a program of corporative revival, Liberatore, like the leaders of the Opera earlier, disregarded the foreign criticism of the corporative doctrine. By 1890 the very term *corporative* was discredited outside Italy. A Catholic congress held at Liège that year duly debated and accepted the proposal to drop the word henceforth and refer to the Catholic organizations of labor by using the term *professional.* Although Leo XIII did not insist on this new terminology, which took some time to catch on, by ordering a revision of Liberatore's first draft the pope in effect rejected the proposal for a corporative transformation. As the historian Bruno Malinverni was to put it, in his new encyclical *Rerum novarum,* the pope "speaks of corporations, but not of a corporative regime."[2] In its final form, the encyclical clearly opted for a reformist pattern instead of the basic restructuring implied in the corporative doctrine. The word *corporation* did appear in the encyclical; Leo argued that the destruction of the corporations made the workers defenseless. As for remedies, the pope was gratified to know "that there are actually in existence not a few associations . . . consisting either of workmen alone, or of workmen and employers together, but it were greatly to be desired that they should become more numerous and more efficient."

"Workmen alone," a reference to what came to be known as the "simple" union, represented a revolutionary change in Catholic labor theory and amounted in effect to a modification of the basic thrust of the decision of the 1887 Italian Catholic congress, which was insistent upon the mixed organization as the sole form of Catholic labor. Not only Liberatore but all the others who contributed to the successive drafts of *Rerum novarum* followed that approach. The reference allowing for the existence of the simple union was added at the pope's insistence just before the encyclical's publica-

tion. In adding the clause that implied the recognition of the working classes' right to organizational and social autonomy, the pope
was guided by the international experience of the church. For years
he had resisted conservative demands that he condemn experiments
with autonomous working class movements such as the Knights of
Labor in the United States. By stating in *Rerum novarum* that, although the mixed organizations were preferable, autonomous ones
were also acceptable, he expressed an essentially positive conclusion
to those experiments.[3]

In other aspects *Rerum novarum* continued the tradition of defending the principle of private property, but it clearly deviated from
tradition in one sense: it carried none of the old hostility toward the
industrial working class. In fact, like Bonomelli's 1886 pastoral letter, which was in some ways a remarkable forerunner, Leo's "labor
encyclical" went a long way in trying to understand the workers'
discontent; but even beyond that, it sought concrete remedies. And
if the Italian Catholics needed evidence of the importance of such an
approach to their war on socialism, this was forthcoming shortly
after the publication of *Rerum novarum* in 1891.

In 1892 labor unions called *fasci* were organized all over Sicily
by miners and agricultural laborers, and strikes broke out in
numbers unknown in the history of the island. The massive wave of
labor unrest was linked, somewhat unjustifiably, to the Socialist
party, formally established during the same year. The panic that
ensued among the Italian upper classes led to the fall of the government. Francesco Crispi, the new prime minister, sent an army of
occupation to the island and broke up the *fasci* by the brutal use of
arms and legal means.[4] The aftershocks of these events were severe
in Italian Catholic minds. The most jolting was the realization that
the supposed religiosity and conservativism of rural society and its
resistance to innovations, social conflict, and socialism was illusory.

The Catholics' attempts to explain the explosion of social unrest
among an essentially agricultural population at first covered the usual arguments, according to which religion had declined and the
workers had forgotten that poverty was forever a divinely ordained
attribute of their lives. Inevitably, however, Catholic attention

would eventually rivet on the Socialists, those "outside agitators" to whom was attributed an unduly large share of blame for the troubles caused by the *fasci*. And those who fixed their attention on the Socialists were often struck by their own ignorance of the motivations and sustaining ideas of the socialist movement. Caricatures and secondhand notions did not suffice to explain the great success attributed to Socialists. And given the rural nature of the people involved, the old Catholic critique of the industrial working class was irrelevant. Thus Toniolo, who was by then intensely involved with the study of socialism as a historical phenomenon, received one request for information after another.[5]

Toniolo's realization that the Catholics' war on socialism was still nothing more than a war of words led him to produce the "Program of Catholics in Confronting Socialism" in 1894.[6] The document, known as the "Programma di Milano" after a meeting of the Catholic Union for Social Studies debated and approved it, carried the signatures of the members of the *presidenza* of the union, including Toniolo, Medolago, and Bottini. It was Toniolo, though, who argued the case and arranged the arguments.

The events in Sicily were clearly on his mind, for the very first lines of the "Programma" register the shock of witnessing the success of socialism in a nation as "little predisposed" to it as Italy and even among the "rural classes," so "little ready" to "allow access" to socialism. As for the explanation, the document points to the anguish and suffering of the working classes, which was "a real malaise . . . produced by a series of prolonged violations of the Christian social order based on justice and charity." The explanation carries the usual solution of Catholic conservatives: it is the "restoration and predominance of Christian consciousness" in the affairs of society, the "reconstruction of the fabulous and stable edifice of the Christian social order."

> The most solid guarantee of a restoration rests with the reconstitution of professional unions or corporations among the civic population and in the countryside, where in separate trades the large and the small would find solidarity of interests and of affection for everything which

touches the common ends of civilized living and where in particular the working classes would recover tutelage and decorum. Professional unions which therefore not only have an economic scope but look toward the single result of the organic composition of society, today pulverized by a diffuse and ruined individualism . . . that if the superior classes of property owners and capitalists find it repugnant to enter into mixed organizations with the inferior classes (which represents the ideal of the organizations proposed by Catholics), in that case the Catholics would accept that the workers join in exclusively worker professional unions and proceed by way of a legal resistance in the pursuit of their own rights, without however, as a rule closing entry to welcome classes now reluctant and opposed to their organization in the future. In other words, espousing the cause of the workers, we never lose sight of the entire society and its normal balance.[7]

Finally, two years after *Rerum novarum* mentioned it, the simple union entered Italian Catholic labor theory. But by the time Toniolo and his colleagues got through with incorporating it into the program of Catholic Action, instead of a normal alternative to the mixed, as it was in *Rerum novarum,* the simple union became a threat, a sword of Damocles hung over the heads of the capitalists and landowners. If they did not see their sins and mend their sinful ways, if they continued to resist joining the mixed unions and assuming the paternalistic care of their workers, then, and only then, they would have the simple union imposed on them by the Catholics.

The "Milan Program" arguably was not a step forward in Catholic labor theory,[8] but at least it acknowledged the simple union as a theoretical possibility. In adding the *semplice* to the repertoire of the Catholic labor movement, Leo XIII allowed himself to be guided by the international experience of the church. But for some time after the publication of *Rerum novarum,* the conservative leadership of Italian Catholic Action seem to have refused to be guided by the pope. Resolutions passed by both the 1891 and 1892 congresses of the Opera appear to have omitted the simple union as an alternative to the *misto.*[9] Toniolo at least was not inclined to put on the incredible performance of ignoring the pope's suggestion. He was also acutely and rather painfully aware of what the resolution of the 1892 congress called "an almost universal apathy of the superior classes" toward any organization that included the "inferior classes." Toniolo had shown a clear awareness of this apathy, which he called "the neglect and abuse of the conserving and directing role of the superior classes."[10] The *padroni* simply refused to carry out the paternalistic obligations that Neo-Thomistic Catholic theology attempted to impose on them through the mixed union.

Thus Toniolo added the simple union to the traditional threats of revolution and the demise of private property that would visit the upper classes if they did not mend their sinful ways. By 1894, as his signature on the "Milan Program" shows, Medolago too was frustrated enough with the refusal of the *padroni* to join the mixed union to threaten them with the simple union. This frustration was clearly reflected in his speech to the congress of the Opera held in Rome during February of 1894: "Unfortunately the *padroni,* bound to the carriage of liberal economy, see in every concession made to the workers an attempt on their rights, in every organization of which the workers are members, a *diminutio capitis* [a reduction in leadership role]."

Monsignor Giorgio Gusmini, a local observer and colleague, described what those who organized labor encountered:

> The Count Medolago knew from experience that when in the Bergamo region strikes by cotton and silk workers and peasants broke out, the *padroni,* scared by the strikes and coming to us with the idea of the mixed union in which they would have had an overbearance [*la miglior parte*] were smiling at us, but when the fear of the strikes was gone, and through our work of pacification, they graciously turned their backs on us and did not want to see us anymore.[11]

So the *padroni,* at least the capitalists among them, were getting what they deserved; for the February, 1894, Rome congress declared the simple union legitimate in industry, and the factory owners' resistance to the improvement of the workers' conditions was mentioned as the justification of this momentous change in the practice of Catholic social action.[12] It was, in fact, no other than Medolago who drafted the resolution that was guaranteed to rankle some conservatives.

What followed was like a replay of the response to Hitze's similar proposal in Germany a decade earlier. Like their German coreligionists, Italian conservatives saw the specter of class struggle raising its ugly head when the simple union was recognized as legitimate. The conservatives, led by G. Battista Paganuzzi, called a new congress within a few months and mounted a counterattack aimed at reinstating the mixed union as the prevalent institution of Catholic labor. At least as far as rural organizations were concerned, the resolution of the September, 1894, Pavia congress insisted upon *misto*. Only "if exceptional circumstances did not permit composing them in that manner could, in a transitory way, [separate] organizations of landowners and laborers be formed. These must not prevent with their statutes the other parties from joining, and they will eventually be asked to enter. In the meanwhile, activities have to be regulated in such a way as to exclude every suspicion of class struggle."[13]

The rural aristocracy, heavily represented in the leadership of the Opera, broadcast to the world with the resolutions of the Pavia congress that they would not tolerate even the thought of the rural working classes imposing demands on them. The working people would receive improvements handed down in the form of charity, if and when the landlords felt like granting it. The rural aristocracy announced that it had confidence in the survival of paternalism in the countryside, and that they would do what the bourgeoisie had failed to do: assume paternalistic control over their "subjects."

Six years later when the 1900 congress of the Opera convened in Rome, the irritation of the Catholic leadership with the capitalists seems to have abated somewhat. But a resolution still threatened them, declaring that both the simple and the mixed union might be useful for the "reconstruction of the representation of the industrial working class." But the simple union as an alternative was submerged within a vast plan involving a corporativist reorganization of society. In fact, rarely mentioned by name in the resolution, the *semplice* was buried in a list of other organizational forms such as banks and credit unions, all including both *padroni* and workers.[14] The talk about the representation of working-class interests was meaningless, not only because of the insistence upon the mixed nature of Catholic organizations, but also because the resolutions of the Rome congress showed an understanding of classes as professional-occupational groups that by definition included both capitalists and workers, landlords and landless peasants. The term *professional* used in connection with Catholic organizations of labor had been invented abroad years earlier in order to get away from the discredited "corporativist" label. But at the Rome congress, corporativism carried the day in the spirit of the resolutions if not in name.

The advocacy of the mixed union, which was very much a part of the corporativist scheme, and the resistance to the *semplice* apparently did not coincide with Toniolo's convictions. As early as 1898, he recognized the "historical and factual necessity" for the simple union.[15] To make the inevitable palatable to the conservatives, Toniolo came up with a peculiar definition of the simple union. He first hit on the formula in the "Milan Program," and it then found its way into the resolution of the 1894 Rome congress. The definition was a marvel of simplicity, presenting the *semplice* as a temporary means needed because of the failure of the *padroni* to fulfill the obligations of the law of charity. Thus conceived as something abnormal, the simple unions would eventually disappear, absorbed into the corporative system as society was restored and once again took the shape God wanted it to have.[16]

Because this formulation referred to salvation in return for the admission of sins and the mending of sinful ways, it was within the mainstream of Catholic tradition. It was bound to appeal to the conservative aristocrats, since it was a message of hope framed by the corporativist social utopia. But those who were inclined to activism could live with it too, since it allowed for the simple union for which the social reality of Italy called. The *Rerum novarum* had recognized the *semplice* as legitimate. The last-minute decision to include the simple union in the encyclical may not have been preceded by full consideration of the new organizational form's implications, such as the social autonomy of the working classes; but it certainly was not an impulsive act. For years Leo XIII had observed the international labor scene, including a large-scale application of the concept and massive confrontations between the propertied classes and unions, which certainly did not fit into the pattern Italian Catholic conservatives had in mind in connection with the mixed union. It is likely that Leo added the simple unions to the repertoire of Catholic Action because, after some hesitation, he decided there was a need for them.

If such was the case, many of the Italian clergy saw eye to eye with the pope. After the publication of the encyclical, the Italian synods, the periodic meetings of the diocesan clergy, turned to such themes as "commutative" and "distributive justice," the relationship between capital and labor, and the right of the workers to organize and to strike in order to protect their interests. These discussions, which in the words of the historian Angelo Gambasin "echoed the main points of *Rerum novarum*," showed that at least to some of the Italian clergy the simple union appeared to be an idea whose time had come.[17]

However, the full meaning of the social autonomy of the working classes implied by the simple union did not become clear immediately. In time the conservatives' fears that the *semplice* would be linked to class conflict proved to be justified. Furthermore, as strikes inevitably followed the birth of simple unions, the clergymen active in organizing them had no choice but to take the side of the workers.

The Fasci Movement in Sicily and the Social Activism of the Clergy

The social activism of the clergy brought with it consequences unforeseen when it began on a large scale during the last decade of the papacy of Leo XIII. It took a major social upheaval—the movement of the Sicilian *fasci* during 1892–93—to move the pope in the direction of a hesitant but increasing commitment of priests to social action. Leo XIII, according to Toniolo, was "embittered by the pitiful state of the rural masses in some regions of the peninsula and the insidious Socialist propaganda among them, and by the recent agitations and violent repressions in Sicily," and wanted the conflict resolved through the intervention of the Catholics. This call spoke of the Catholics in general terms and did not specifically point to priests. But the traditional role of priests always included that of the peacemaker, the mediator in disputes, and eventually they were encouraged to perform these functions in labor disputes: "Do try to accomplish the greatest good possible with the maximum of prudence, but also with the greatest of freedom." Such was the response by the Vatican in 1894 to a query about whether priests may take a leading role in establishing rural credit unions. That same year permission was also given to priests to take a hand in establishing "rural unions." This initiative, which turned out to be a failure, was to draw into rural cooperatives both the landowners and the agricultural laborers. The statutes for these organizations adopted in 1894 made the village priest a member of the local directing office with a power of veto about matters concerning morality and faith.[18]

Thus old and new came to be mixed. The emphasis on the traditional role of the priest as religious and moral guide disguised new functions that the leadership of the church allowed priests to undertake. Beginning a bold experiment with social activism, a "social apostolate" of the clergy, the church moved somewhat hesitantly, expanding outward the perimeters set by *Rerum novarum* within a few years of its publication. The encyclical did call upon "each to put his hand to work," but the work assigned to the clergy was to remain within traditional bounds: the "inculcation" of Christian morality "in all classes" and the establishment in society of the rule of the laws of "charity, the mistress and queen of virtues."[19] The signal to go beyond this role came from the pope in a somewhat casual remark he made in an audience with Leon Harmel, a French Catholic social activist: "The clergy has to leave the vestry and live with the people. The parish priest does not have to limit himself to be the minister of the cult and guardian of faith; but has to be the friend and adviser of the people in their earthly interests also."[20]

The pope's remark was evidently timely. *Prete fuori dalla sacrestia*, "Priest, out of the vestry," soon resounded in the words of bishops who were becoming desperate about the massive social crises involving their flocks, and anxious to respond to the call of their leader. "It is not enough to hide in a corner of the church and mumble Hail Marys and the Lord's Prayer and there bewail the past, hoping that an angel coming from heaven will save society," Monsignor Blandini, the bishop of Noto, told the Sicilian congress of

Catholic Action held in 1895. If this meeting could be said to have adopted a slogan, it was "Priest, the pope wants you out of the vestry."

This call for social action by the clergy had such an overwhelming response that between 1895 and 1904 virtually all the positions of leadership within Sicilian Catholic Action were filled by priests.[21] With some notable exceptions, these activist priests, Sturzo among them, were almost all young. It was ironic that these young idealistic clergymen were more attuned to reality than their experienced older colleagues, who, in Italy as elsewhere in Europe, were too attached to "the old pastoral-charitable model" of priesthood, in the words of the German historian Emil Ritter.[22] In other words, they adhered to notions of Catholic conservativism that confined the role of the priest to preaching and disdained involvement in social action.

The misgivings of the traditionalists were not unjustified, for the activist priests often failed to maintain the neutrality that the universal nature of their ministry demanded.[23] Presumably poised between social groups, they sometimes found it impossible to play the role of mediator and peacemaker. The casual nature of the pope's remark, instrumental in triggering the movement of priests into social action, suggests that Leo XIII himself was to face unforeseen consequences once again. The social apostolate he demanded inevitably involved class conflicts, since some of the bitterest feuds among Christians at the turn of the nineteenth century were about wages and working hours. And their sense of charity led some priests to understand that the workers' demands were not only justified but reasonable, and that their fulfillment was feasible within an economic system driven by the profit motive. The priests had to learn that the road of charity sometimes led them to the picket lines. Among them was Father Giulio Rusconi, a *cappellano del lavoro* (workers' chaplain) in the town of Rho. Cardinal Ferrari, the archbishop of Milan, who gave the title to Rusconi and two other young priests, acted out of concern for the increasing success Socialists had shown in organizing labor in his diocese. The task of the workers' chaplains was to counter Socialist propaganda and organizational work. In initiating a new approach to the social mission of priests, Ferrari continued to show a social concern that earned him a reputation as a "social bishop."

When Catholic conservatives attacked him, labeling him a "subversive bishop," Leo XIII decided to intervene by expressing his support and approval in an 1898 letter to Ferrari.[24]

Soon after being sent to the town of Rho during the summer of 1900, Father Rusconi realized that the Socialists' success was due in good measure to the scandalously bad living and working conditions of the agricultural laborers and industrial workers. The working class listened to the Socialist agitators because they pointed out the workers' ruthless exploitation. They joined the Socialist labor organizations because they promised to improve their conditions. Only a few months after his arrival in Rho, and with the approval of his archbishop, Rusconi set out to introduce "social reform." Although Catholic mutual aid societies came in the wake of this reform drive, its most important element became the appearance of a Catholic labor union in Rho.

After a study commission of sociologists sent by Cardinal Ferrari pointed out in vain that the salaries of the industrial workers had to be, and could be, improved and their working hours reduced, a strike was called by Rusconi's organization. It took only five days for the owners of industrial enterprises to change their minds about the feasibility of the "social reform" of Father Rusconi. The new contracts they signed with the union reduced working hours from twelve to ten and considerably increased the daily wages of the workers. The landless peasants of the zone who tilled the large holdings (one owned by a religious order) were quick to learn from the success of the factory workers. Soon they were in Father Rusconi's unions too, and went on strike after their demands for improved land rental conditions were rejected. The landowners, like the industrialists, gave in one by one.

The story of Father Rusconi's doings in Rho led to a chapter in the political history of Italian Catholic Action. The people who felt the benefits of Rusconi's "social reform" went on to break the vicious circle of conservative political bossism by the landowners, who traditionally represented Rho in the Provincial Council and the Parliament. As electoral reforms extended suffrage to an ever widening segment of the population and the papal ban on the electoral participation of Catholics was gradually lifted, the factory workers and agricultural laborers led by Rusconi insisted on electing a Catholic representative. Thus began the political career of Filippo Meda, who was sent by the people of Rho first to the Provincial Council and later to the Parliament. Meda eventually became the first Italian Catholic politician since Unification to become a minister in a government.[25]

A similar chapter in the class struggles of Italy, also culminating in Catholic participation in Italian political life, was written in Bishop Bonomelli's diocese. After a wave of Socialist-led strikes stirred up the people in 1900, at Bonomelli's "advice and stimulation" the priests of the Cremona diocese established study groups to figure out how to combat the penetration of socialism. Drawing the only possible conclusion from their discussions, the priests decided to set up Catholic labor organizations to rival the Socialists'. For lack of lay leaders, the priests ended up heading these organizations; and by the summer of 1901, several of them were facing the landowners with demands in the name of their parishioners, whom they had organized into unions. If they held any illusion about the "fraternal and angelic charity" of the *padroni,* this experience was enough to disabuse them of it, for they received flat refusals. So much for the "Christian solidarity among the *padroni* and the workers," heralded by the Catholic congress that urged the revival of medieval corporations.

Thus the priests reported back to their bishop that the Catholic labor organizations had to be simple, and that they had to stage strikes in order to register any material gains for their members, gains that made the peasants turn to the Catholic unions instead of the labor leagues inspired by the Socialists. Since some of the priests heading the Catholic unions were willing to call strikes and sustain them long enough to wring concessions from the landlords, the Catholic organizations of labor made impressive headway within a few years.[26]

Experiences such as these went a long way to disprove the notion of paternalism, by showing the capitalists and landowners utterly unwilling to offer economic gains to the workers. Gaining improvements in wages and living and working conditions through a confrontation with the *padroni* led to a growth of class consciousness, a sense among the workers of their own strength. Demands for autonomous organizations and the rejection of the paternalistic mixed union grew out of these experiences, as did the view that class conflict was a fact of life and strikes were an unavoidable aspect of this conflict. As the workers became aware of all this, so did their organizers, the activist priests. For many Christian Democratic activists, this merely confirmed a longstanding conviction.

Class Conflict as a Fact of Life

With a remarkably sharp eye for an emerging reality, Salvatore Talamo described as early as 1896 how the Christian Democrats were convinced that class conflict and strikes were as unavoidable as the gathering of the working class into organizations of their own if the workers ever wanted to improve their lot.[27] *La Democrazia Cristiana,* a Turin publication, wrote in 1897:

> Charity based on balls and dinners at which the rich stuff themselves with food . . . is a real insult to the people who are dying from starvation in hovels. Let us establish a basic truth: the strike is a sacrosanct right of the worker, and also of the workers united in associations. It will be an *ultima ratio,* it will be a two-edged weapon, it will be more ruinous for the worker than the *padrone,* be it what you want, but it is a sacrosanct right in the name of real liberty, of that individual and human liberty that comes from God and has nothing to do with that aborted tyrant called liberalism.[28]

A programmatic meeting of Christian Democracy, held in Milan during May, 1901, declared the confrontation and struggle between classes "an abnormal and painful fact," but a fact of life nevertheless, as was the need for the extreme measure of the strike.[29]

The evolution of Sturzo's outlook demonstrates the Christian Democratic priest-activists' radicalization in response to Leo's call to "go to the people." Intensely involved in the social apostolate the pope demanded, Sturzo declared in 1898: "We Catholics do not want class struggle, nor can we allow the stronger to overcome the weaker; thus we gather together the weakest, and we join them so that they may be able to perform their moral functions, so that they would not be taken for helots, slaves, or serfs, but for brothers in Jesus Christ, and with their work they may perform honorably the mission assigned to them by the Lord."[30]

In a 1901 essay about the organization of labor, Sturzo presented the theme of class struggle as a fact of life, imposed upon society by the prevailing sociopolitical system. According to Sturzo, the consequence of the hostility between social groups was that the mixed organization of labor, which might be desirable and even obtainable in the long range, was impractical at present because the relationship between labor and capital was characterized by mutual diffidence. Thus Sturzo, who by then subscribed to notions of consciousness reminiscent of those developed by Marxists, argued in effect that the liberation of the working classes had to be a job for the working classes. Citing the motto *Tout pour le peuple et tout par le peuple,* he talked of the "vindication of the working class" as coming necessarily through the efforts of workers. Paternalistic tutelage by the upper classes was so far removed from his thinking that he did not even find it necessary to refute it: he simply did not mention it.

Yet Sturzo's reasoning remained in the mainstream of Catholic thought in more than one way. Like Toniolo he presented classes as essentially professional-occupational groups. Furthermore, he talked of a basic hierarchy in society, a theme that he developed by pointing to a natural inequality among men, which on a societal scale emerged as a hierarchy of classes. This inequality necessitated the Catholics' throwing their support behind the working classes, whom the individualism of the liberal capitalist system left weak. Thus through the back door and unannounced, the old theme of tutelage found its way into Sturzo's sociology, taking the form of aid, comfort, and organizational efforts to be extended to the working classes through Christian Democratic activism, within which Sturzo assigned an important role to priests. He deplored the fact that the clergy, because of old habits and the limitations imposed by the prevailing political system, were secluded in the vestry and were thus neglecting the workers. But in Sturzo's words, the priest's new role, that of the "father and defender of the workers," involved basically moral and religious functions. This was a somewhat ironic statement considering that by 1901 Father Sturzo himself was a veteran of several years of social action,[31] and must have had very little time for preaching.

The moral and religious tasks Sturzo assigned to priests in 1901 were superceded by a new conception of the priestly role in an essay Sturzo wrote the next year. Its title, "Social Conflict, the Law of Progress," gave away the moral dilemmas it presented to priests. In a jarring, bold application of social Darwinism, Sturzo declared that struggle was the "natural" condition of man in society, as was a perennial disequilibrium and conflict among social classes.[32]

One reads Sturzo's essay with a degree of disbelief, yet it bespeaks the overwhelming influence of social Darwinism at the turn of the century that the historical literature does not register any particular shock on the part of the audiences to which Sturzo read the essay before its publication. He held no less than three readings, one of them in the palace of the archbishop of Milan, of all places. That such a thing could happen gives a sense of the freedom Leo XIII allowed.

Writing about the wide range of Catholic social action that developed abroad in response to *Rerum novarum,* Sturzo decried the relative scarcity of such a response in Italy. He explained this by pointing to the prevalence of conservativism, which he connected with the overbearance of the *Questione Romana* in Italy. Nine years after its publication, many Italian Catholics had not yet read Leo's labor encyclical, he said. But Sturzo's essays seem to suggest he had not read *Rerum novarum* himself. First, there was the argument about struggle as the "natural" state of society: in Leo's encyclical the word *natural* was used in connection with social harmony, and class conflict was presented as against nature. Second, there was the matter of classes. The way *Rerum novarum* defined them[33] was certainly closer to the Marxian notion of classes as social units related to the ownership of the means of production than to Sturzo's concept, which was strictly professional-occupational.

That Sturzo conceived of classes in this way shows the hold of the corporativist doctrine over Italian Catholic minds, an influence that clearly did not affect Leo. In fact, some claim that Sturzo deemphasized the concept of social classes, declaring them "secondary forms" only, much less important than such societal units as the family, the church, and political formations.[34] This perception must have appeared later in Sturzo's sociology, for the essays reviewed here do not evidence it. If true, though, the denial of the importance of social class, even in its functional-occupational form, would be an interesting extension of a social activism that was insistent on conflict while denying the existence of the social framework within which it was conceived to evolve. Sturzo's early drift into a rather crude form of social Darwinism, which saw conflict as universal in man's social nature, could have been a preparatory step toward a theoretical position that insisted on conflict but denied the existence of classes.

The 1901 Wave of Strikes and the Reaction of Leo XIII

Sturzo's 1902 essay, which declared social conflict "the law of progress," was a close reflection of the realities of Italy. The unionization of the labor force was relatively low in Italy compared with other European countries.[35] Yet at the beginning of the century, Italy experienced a massive increase in strikes. Annual government statistics add up to a total of 2,555 strikes, with 676,669 workers participating during the fourteen years ending in 1900. The fourteen years that ended with 1914 register a total of 16,841 strikes with 4,291,059 participants, a 559 percent increase in the number of strikes and 534 percent increase in the number of participants. Even more dramatic than these aggregate figures is the increase of strikes in agriculture, which registered 178 strikes with 84,022 participants during the period 1887–1900, and 2,978 strikes with 1,500,300 participants during the years 1901–14, a 1,579 percent increase in the number of strikes and a 1,686 percent increase in the number of participants. After adding up his data about Italy, the American economist Alexander Gerschenkron had to conclude that "between 1901 and 1913 there was only one year when the number of days lost by strikes remained below the one million mark; in some years of the period it exceeded three and was just under four million."

Those who attempt to verify statistical information such as Gerschenkron's through other sources often remark that the agencies that collected statistical data usually undercounted. Thus, although not fully reported, strikes in 1901 led to a loss of 3 million workdays in agriculture alone, constituting a dramatic backdrop to Sturzo's argument that conflict was indeed a part of social life. During 1901 the number of workers involved in agricultural strikes—222,985— exceeded the number of strikers in goods-producing industries and services, which was 196,540. In 1899 there were only 268 strikes (16 percent of the 1901 total), 259 in goods-producing industries and services and 9 in agriculture, involving a total of 45,089 workers. In 1900 a total of 93,375 workers participated in 387 strikes in industry and services and 27 in agriculture. The 1901 explosion brought 1,671 strikes with 419,525 workers involved.[36]

The pope's comments on the 1901 explosion of strikes followed the traditional approach that tended to inculpate the upper classes for social disturbances.[37] There was something ironic in this continued Catholic inclination to blame class conflict on the moral shortcomings of the *padroni*. Because it gave personal foci to conflicts this was conducive to violence by the workers, who were inclined to play the role of avenging angels. Thus Catholic intentions once more produced results very contrary to those intended. In the south at least, as the historian Francesco Renda observed, strikes by Catholic unions had a somewhat greater tendency to degenerate into violent turmoil and disorder than those led by the Socialists, who focused attention and working class anger on the "system" rather than on individuals.

What Leo XIII had to say about the 1901 wave of strikes, nevertheless, reaffirmed the need for moral regeneration, involving the "mission of the Church in defending justice, [defending] the weak, the widows, and the oppressed." But the pope could not be seen taking the side of one social segment in a conflict for the same reason priests could ill afford to confront the *padroni* in strikes while maintaining the universal nature of their ministry. Thus Leo's 1901 encyclical *Graves de communi* emphasized the need "to unite the rich and the poor in the bonds of fraternal charity," and failed to mention strikes, a conspicuous omission in Leo's last "social" encyclical.[38] But something more than silence was forthcoming from the Vatican in connection with the theme of class struggle. The publication of *Graves de communi* coincided with the appearance of a series of articles in *Civiltà Cattolica*. The flurry of activities in the editorial offices of the *Civiltà* could not be accidental, and the information that flowed in unusual volume could be seen as supplementing *Graves de communi*. Less authoritatively, with less finality, the *Civiltà Cattolica* appeared to say to Italian Catholic Action what the pope did not want to state in *Graves de communi,* which was addressed to the universal church. But the message was unmistakably clear, as was the style of Catholic conservativism, and it conveyed a broad interpretation of the needs of society rent by labor conflict and the needs of the working classes in particular.

Working people, in the considered opinion of the Jesuit editors of the *Civiltà,* needed more old-fashioned religion, more "spiritual" than "corporeal nourishment." The *questione operaia,* the problems of the industrial working classes, were presented by *Civiltà Cattolica* as primarily moral and religious in nature, rooted in the working classes' lack of proper Christian virtue that would lead them to respect the ruling class as such and accept the deprivations that went with their own status. This chain of thought extended the argument that the *Civiltà* had voiced earlier, according to which "as long as the world exists, the people, Christian or not, will have to sweat and put up with hardship: as long as the world exists, the people will invariably remain what they are, that is a mass born not to govern but to be governed." The *Civiltà* also suggested that, in order to reduce social conflicts, Catholic activists had to cease "throwing insults constantly at the superior classes" and desist from inculpating the capitalists, thus making the workers even less inclined to accept their fate and whatever they were making per hour at the moment.

The contrast between the pope's statement that inculpated the "superior" classes and the opinion expressed by *Civiltà Cattolica* seems to invalidate the notion that there was a central coordination behind the latter. The contrast may reflect the tolerance during Leo's papacy of a wide range of opinions while a search was on for practical alternatives to guide Catholic Action. If he allowed Christian Democratic activists to express opinions that almost denied his own statements, Leo probably saw no reason why conservatives too could not state their case even on the pages of *Civiltà Cattolica*.

Another possible interpretation—like the previous, subject to confirmation by archival research—is that during his last years Leo was becoming more conservative. *Graves de communi,* which clearly attempted to dampen some of the fires the pope generated with his demand for social activism, points to such an interpretation.

So does another suggestion made in the *Civiltà Cattolica* articles in connection with strikes, a suggestion that was critically important in view of Leo's silence on the subject. The stance taken by the Jesuit editors was overwhelmingly negative, and strikes were shown as highly impractical as means employed by Catholic Action: "Speculatively speaking, one is disinclined to refute the idea that the Catholics organized by Christian Democracy may honestly resort [to strikes . . . but] in practice the danger is too great and too close that the strike becomes transformed into something else: thus Catholic writers and the authoritative leaders of Catholic Action had been generally in agreement advising against it in Italy."[39]

But strikes were increasingly becoming a reality. The response of the September, 1901, congress of the Opera, held in Taranto, to the massive wave of strikes that year was to recognize the strike as a weapon for Catholic organizations of labor, a last resort to be used "with the greatest caution and prudence," but legitimate nevertheless.[40] Catholic Action was apparently no less opportunistic than the *padroni,* who, to Medolago's chagrin, turned to the mixed union when pressures built up but did not want to hear about it when the strikes abated. The organization Medolago headed used the simple union and even strikes in times of stress only to downplay both when things had calmed down.

The acceptance of the strike as legitimate was partially explained by the appearance on a significant scale of the simple union, which by its very existence carried the potential of strikes. The number of simple organizations of labor under Catholic direction could not have been very large in 1900, since it was apparently a major event when in Bergamo, the center of Catholic social action, one was founded on June 23, 1901. But by the end of that year, there were fifty-four, and twelve months later, eighty-four. The enthusiasm was unbounded: even the archconservative Paganuzzi talked of

popolarismo cattolico at Taranto, and the *Civiltà Cattolica* edito-
rialized during May, 1901, in favor of the Christian Democrats and
the simple unions they went out to organize. Behind all this enthusiasm was a letter by Cardinal Mariano Rampolla, the papal secretary
of state, that, although insistent upon respect for the authority and
rights of the *padroni,* accepted the principle of the simple union with
the proviso that mixed commissions of workers and *padroni,* as well
as permanent arbitration boards, be set up.[41] And behind the cardinal's letter and the sudden enthusiasm for Christian Democracy on
the part of the leadership of the Opera was the threat of socialism
that reached a peak in 1901.

The resolution of the Taranto congress spoke of the strike as a
"weapon of defense." And so it was, rarely used by Catholics against
the *padroni,* but certainly useful, like the simple union against the
Socialists. Study after study of specific organizations and localities
had shown that in organizing simple unions, Catholics, even the activists, were assuming a typical posture of defense, reacting to the
Socialists' presence on the scene,[42] rather than acting out their own
vaunted ideals. The Italian Catholics' acceptance of the simple
union was nothing but an act of opportunism. And because it was an
act of expediency, the mixed union returned to the center of their
attention every time the Socialist menace had abated.

Toniolo and the Ascendancy of the Simple Union

Toniolo's effort to provide an intellectual justification for the
changes that came in response to the 1901 wave of the "Socialist
menace" grew into a major advance in the development of Catholic
labor theory. At first it incurred the resistance of the conservative
leaders of the Opera, who did not want tactical moves made permanent. Led by Paganuzzi, they objected when, at the April meeting
of the Permanent Committee, Toniolo observed that the mixed
union had proved itself impractical and that Catholic organizational
efforts had to concentrate on the *semplice.* But Paganuzzi and his
colleagues got the message in the form of Rampolla's letter the next
month, and Toniolo was allowed to proceed.

Toniolo's arguments appeared in a series of articles published in the *Rivista internazionale di scienze sociali* in 1901 and 1902.[43] Describing the "historical moment," he presented a panorama of massive social unrest,

> the spectacle of popular agitation under the forms of coalitions, of strikes, of private and public violence, . . . [which are] nothing but the products of brutal avenging passions, of the invading spirit of revolution, Socialist propaganda. . . . Today the demands of the inferior social strata are indiscreet and bold, involve even the benefits of the rich gained through the increase in production, and extend even to those who are blameless and shake the very basis of [private] property.

Because the "intemperate pretensions assault even the honest and generous among the rich," Toniolo noticed among the *padroni* an inclination to resist the demands of the working classes. But it should not be forgetten, he warned, that

> the lowest of the low too have to be elevated by civilization to an honest life, that the issue is not always about bread, but about moral offenses committed against the dignity of the poor worker. The landowners and the capitalists really benefited from an immense increase in production, but the workers did not receive an equitable share. While the worker continues to languish and, in fact, sees his conditions worsen, he also sees, since his own hands are responsible for it, a very rapid multiplication of wealth in mighty factories and on the regenerated countryside.

Reminding the "rich" that "Christian labor" was "the source of the material and moral" elevation of society, Toniolo recalled them to the duties their wealth imposed on them. These duties included responding in proper Christian manner to the demands of the workers, however bothersome these might have been, since, Toniolo argued, the rise of those demands represented nothing less than the will of God, the culmination of a providential design. The *ammaestramento,* the "teaching" that the professor derived from the study of the last hundred years, was that God in His infinite wisdom wanted a change in social relationships, a change that involved the "vindication of manual labor," the "legitimate elevation of the working class, of its compensations, of its social respectability" to the "dignity of a class."

In return for the acceptance of God's will manifest in history— *nota bene* of the last hundred years, not of the medieval centuries— Toniolo offered to the rich the control over the change that Providence prescribed for humankind. Another *ammaestramento* he drew was that "this great providential task has to be principally accomplished by the superior classes through generously following, amplifying, and perfecting the work that had already begun. Thus [the task involved the superior classes'] normal obligations inherent in their economic and social superiority."

A somewhat oversimplified statement about what follows in Toniolo's argument would be that the superior classes may accomplish their "providential task" by accepting the simple union. The professor knew only too well how unpalatable this was to the *padroni,* who avoided even the mixed union. With the carrot in one hand and the stick in the other, Toniolo argued that if the *padroni* did not take on the responsibility involved in the change ordained by the Lord, if they refused the Catholic "corporation," the "rich" would have the revolution. For Toniolo this was an either/or proposition, since in yet another *ammaestramento* he argued that the choice was between the Catholic program and socialism.

The use of the word *corporazione* was another way of trying to make an unpleasant truth acceptable. By 1901 the term for Catholic organizations of labor was *professional.* By going back to the language of corporativism, Toniolo was clearly catering to the sensitivities of the upper classes by serving up new wine in an old bottle. The mixed union, of which the term *corporation* was a re-evocation, was mentioned in his essays as an alternative to the simple organization of labor, like the simple union was earlier in treatises favoring the mixed.

The main thrust of Toniolo's arguments was clearly that the time had come for the *semplice.* In attempting to justify the need for the simple union as the basic organizational form of labor, and the social autonomy of the proletariat that it implied, Toniolo pointed to the reality of the breakup of society into two distinct and antagonistic segments: "Economically, because such is the nature of things, within industrial and agricultural enterprises the *padroni* continue to direct and pay the workers, but socially, outside the landed estates and the factories, the capitalists and the workers form, or tend to form by now, two classes that are more than independent: they are autonomous." These two classes, which were not defined on the basis of occupation along the lines of the corporativist doctrine but in the Marxian sense, as based on possessions, "will probably never be rejoined," according to Toniolo. The events of 1901 apparently were enough to leave doubt in his mind as to the feasibility of the social "restoration" of the corporativist utopia. This makes it all the stranger that he referred with the word *corporation* to the growing union movement, toward which he said all things "converge." Surely he could not be talking of the mixed union: he numbered four million members worldwide and pointed to Great Britain as the country where the movement was the strongest. But impressive as these numbers were, Toniolo apparently felt that he had to take on the "objections" raised in connection with the "recomposition of the proletariat into a class" that the growing labor movement brought about. First he turned to the "objections of liberal economy," such as the alleged violation of "personal liberty" and "the equality of citizens." After disposing of these, he moved on to the "more delicate and graver doubts raised in connection with the new corporative institutions, not on account of a violation of doctrinairism, but in connection with justice and charity, the basis and guarantee of the Christian order, which is civilization."

Among these doubts he dealt with class struggle and the connected issue of the selfishness of pressing for the rights and interests of the working people without ascertaining their awareness of the limits imposed by their duties toward fellow men. As for the problem of class struggle, he argued that boards of arbitration "or better yet, mixed commissions with permanent power to arbitrate" in conflicts would have to be created. Further, he pointed out that labor unions can become, as they did in England, the means of social peace rather than the source of an *incendio sociale,* a social conflagration. As the ultimate guarantee of this, he pointed out that the organizations of labor will remain, and have to remain religious in orientation, and he argued throughout against those who would want the unions to become "neutral," that is, nonreligious, in character.

Although stating forcefully that "there are moments when it is not enough to do things, but it is necessary to say," to preach "from high that the church always had been a special friend of the people," he also renewed the offer of an alliance between the clergy and the propertied classes, which he mentioned during the 1880s in his correspondence with the industrialist Alessandro Rossi. "The ruling classes," Toniolo said, "carried on for over a century a calculated and obstinate struggle against the Catholic church." They could still save themselves from the extinction socialism would visit upon them if, "not for other reasons, to make amends for their past sins and for the sake of their own and the common salvation, they do not oppose, but cooperate with this elevation of the proletariat to an autonomy in the corporations." What Toniolo offered to the "superior stratum" in return for mending their sinful ways was more than just the promise of their continued social superiority. He also offered the services of the church in keeping the working masses within the limits traditionally imposed by religion, thus minimizing the economic and social cost to the propertied classes of the change warranted by Providence. For such was the practical meaning of the principle of *confessionalità* that Toniolo so adamantly defended. If the Catholic labor organizations were to remain strictly religious in nature, they must avoid class struggle like a plague. Strikes, manifestations of that disease, could not be very high on their list of priorities: strikes were to be a last resort, used, if ever, "with the greatest caution and prudence."

The November, 1903, congress of the Opera sustained the principle of *confessionalità* with only a minor modification.[44] Previous congresses insisted upon the religious orthodoxy and dogmatic trustworthiness of the members of Catholic organizations. The 1903 congress, held in Bologna, reaffirmed the religious orientation of the labor unions; nevertheless, the resolution it adopted allowed, at the discretion of local leaders, the membership of persons "not quite secure, as long as they will not damage [the religious beliefs of] others, but these will be able to persuade them in fact to mend their ways."

If this change in the traditional principle of *confessionalità* pointed toward working-class solidarity, so did the plan of the resolution to unite the craft union locals into provincial and eventually national confederations, with all these making up a single "great National Federation that represents the unity of the working class of the whole country." Thus in Bologna the corporativist grand design was transformed into a vision of a single Catholic organizational framework that incorporated the entire Italian working class. Since it left out of consideration the Socialist opposition, the plan was not much less utopian than the conservatives' corporativist plans of two decades earlier.

In line with the turn away from corporativism, the resolution of the Bologna congress for all practical purpose abandoned the pursuit of the mixed union, recognizing

> that in the present historical conditions the mixed unions, composed of *padroni* and workers, will constitute exceptions, the Congress determines (*fa voti*) that the simple unions, composed of workers only shall gradually aim at establishing the autonomous and complete organization of this class. . . . This does not mean that we cannot and should not aim at the mixed union, uniting the two elements of the class, the workers and the *padroni*. This, in fact, will be the ultimate of means because more than anything else it will bring order, harmony, and the well-being of society. For that reason even the simple union will not be based on the principle of class struggle, but by coordinating the interests of singular elements with the general interests of the class, and of the whole society, it will always aim at a harmony among classes.

In order to keep friction between *padroni* and workers at a minimum, the congress took up Cardinal Rampolla's (and Toniolo's) suggestion to establish mixed commissions that were to arbitrate conflicts.

The language of the resolutions was not without ambiguity. It used the term *class* to refer to both the working class as a separate entity and to professional-occupational groups, which traditionally included both the workers and the *padroni.* Yet in spite of this contradiction in terminology that pointed to the mixed union, by 1903 the *misto,* as Ernesto Vercesi pointed out, became an "academic" issue as far as the activists were concerned. The way Sturzo, for example, saw it, "To believe in the mixed organizations, which sustain the interests of the *padroni* and of the workers in a homogeneous manner (*in funzione omogenea*), is to believe that utopia is possible."[45]

Giorgio Gusmini's remarks were typical of the activists' discontent with the mixed union that exploded in Bologna. He argued that trying to unite the *padroni* and the workers within a single organization ran

> against the modern attitude of the working class. If the *padroni* show a great reluctance to associate with their workers because they feel this would debase them, we must say that there is no great inclination toward it in the working class either, since the workers would rather go into a camp in which they can breathe with freedom. . . . Our inability to adapt the ancient corporation to the exingencies of modern times . . . led to so many and so severe difficulties that not only acting in a practical manner was prevented but theoretical studies and votes [at congresses] too that were nothing but expressions of ideals were insisted upon.[46]

Reality prevailed over utopia in Bologna, and the historians of Italian Catholic Action usually mark the 1903 congress as the event that concluded the debate over the usefulness of the mixed union.[47]

6

To Restore All Things in Christ

The Reorganization of Catholic Action under Pius X
and the Suppression of Democratic Tendencies

The debate about the usefulness of the mixed union may have been over in 1903, as the historians of Italian Catholic Action claim, but the victory of the activists in Bologna proved to be short-lived. Far from convincing the conservatives that the insistence upon the *misto* was leading Catholic Action into a dead-end street, the activists aroused conservative outrage. It was not that conflict between the activists and the conservatives was new. Leo XIII noticed, and spoke up against, a "sterile discord" within Italian Catholic Action.[1] In fact, *Graves de communi* was an effort on his part to settle disagreement by defining the meaning of Christian Democracy and the aims of Catholic activism. But Leo XIII did not go beyond declaring general principles, apparently expecting that the details of a blueprint for Catholic social action would emerge from the clash of opinions.

Even if he shared his predecessor's tolerance for conflict, Pius X, who followed Leo XIII to the papal throne in 1903, had to act. The "discord" in Italian Catholic Action reached an impasse during the last years of Leo's papacy. By the time Sarto became pope, both sides had shown themselves utterly resistant to compromise, and the clash of conservatives and Christian Democrats became an either/or proposition. When the apparent victory of the activists came in Bologna and a conservative sabotage threatened to immobilize Catholic Action, Pius X made his move. He was, in fact, asked to step in and settle the conflict by a resolution that received a majority vote at the July 2, 1904, meeting of the Permanent Committee of the Opera.[2] The pope decided to dissolve the Opera and reorganize Italian Catholic Action.

A year later, in the encyclical *Il fermo proposito,* Pius X etched out a blueprint for the organized activities of Italian Catholics. According to the encyclical, the authority of the church covered everything that "touched upon conscience in any manner."[3] Thus the pope asserted the right to speak with authority binding on all Italian Catholics not only on religious matters but on political, social, and economic issues as well. As the new organizations began to take shape, he made it clear that he was "imposing" the tasks on Italian Catholic Action and demanded "unconditional" obedience in connection with these tasks.[4] The historian Arturo Jemolo aptly noted that Pius X insisted on telling his Italian followers "not only what they had to believe, but also what they had to do."[5]

Under the pope's watchful eyes, the new organizations of Italian Catholic Action appeared one by one: the Unione Popolare to direct propaganda and the Unione Elettorale to coordinate political action. Although the Second Section of the Opera, which after the reorganization took the name of the Unione Economico Sociale, was specifically exempted from the dissolution, the activities it directed suffered from the shock and disruption that followed the dissolution of the Opera. Labor organization was especially hard hit and appears to have gone into a nosedive. In 1903 there were 229 Catholic unions. Their numbers went down to 170 in 1904, and to 135 by 1907. In the uncertainty that followed the dissolution of the Opera, the Economic Social Union apparently turned to safer and less controversial activities such as banks and credit unions, which registered a greater growth than the labor movement even after it recovered from the massive decline experienced during the years 1903–1907.[6]

The decline and disarray, including the collapse of a large number of union locals, left the Catholic labor movement weak and ill prepared to compete with the Socialists during a new wave of labor unrest similar in magnitude to the one in 1901. It began in 1906 and peaked in 1907, when there were 377 strikes in agriculture involving 254,131 workers, and a staggering 1,881 in industry and services with 321,499 participants.[7] The pope, of course, could not have foreseen the confusion and uncertainty that was to overtake Catholic Action following the dissolution of the Opera. Even if he had, however, it is questionable whether he would have opted for a less drastic action given the paralyzing conflict within the organization.

In breaking up the Opera, Pius X probably intended to create conditions for rebuilding Italian Catholic Action by disabling both contending sides, which had worn each other down into an impasse. But the new pope's reputation for othodoxy and conservativism created the immediate impression that, rather than condemning the conservatives, he wanted to censor the activists and their drive to gain social autonomy for the working classes. Pius X was in fact clearly irritated by the tendency of the activists to talk of not only social but also political autonomy, and by their inclination to push the meaning of Christian Democracy beyond the Leonine definition as *actio benefica in populum,* a social action "in favor of the people," by giving the concept a political meaning. The word *democracy* meant to them the active participation of the people in the government. The direct implication of such a position was that Italy's Catholic citizens should gain a share in the political life of the country. The pressure for the lifting of the Non Expedit and for permission to organize a Catholic political party was setting the Christian Democrats on a collision course with the pope.

Yet the implications of the activists' concept of democracy went beyond the demand for Catholic political participation and a political party. It countered the hierarchical concept of society that subjected the lower classes to the perpetual tutelage of their presumed social superiors. Authentic democracy, Murri argued, was inconceivable without "the direct, effective, and organic participation of the people in the government of their affairs." He added that rather than being "generously granted by the superior classes," the participation of the people "will have to be conquered by the people themselves." He indicated as the task of Christian Democracy the awakening of the people to their rights as well as to their strengths, so that they could "conquer" their rightful place in society.[8] Murri was not alone with such opinions. Many young Christian Democrats shared his view that the "people," the working classes, were the "arbiters of tomorrow" and that the idea of democracy should be reconciled with Christianity.[9]

The pope's response to such proposals was overwhelmingly negative. The Lega Democratica Nazionale, a group organized in 1905 under Murri's informal leadership to promote democratic ideals, was pursued by a papal anathema. The Lega's conspicuous failure in recruitment was at least in part the consequence of the continuous objections of ecclesiastical authorities to its ideals and of their bans on the attendance of Christian Democrats, especially priests, at its meetings.

The aversion of Pius X to the Lega was motivated by several considerations; clearly one of these was that the Lega was a rival of the official church-sponsored organization the Unione Popolare.[10] Another cause of the pope's hostility toward the Lega involved its claim to "autonomy," independence from ecclesiastical authorities, on the grounds that its aims involved not religious but social and political matters. Pius X also objected to the orientation of the Lega toward political action. Its political involvement tied the fate of the Lega Democratica Nazionale to the Roman Question and the Non Expedit. The pope's objection to the aims of the Lega and of the young Christian Democrats in general came to be connected with his refusal to allow the unconditional and full political participation of Italian Catholics until the church's claims involved in the *Questione Romana* were settled. Consequently, it could appear that the pope's objection to the proposals of Christian Democrats was primarily due to practical considerations concerning the Roman Question.[11]

This might have been the case; yet a difference in social and political philosophies was also involved in the conflict between the pope and the young Christian Democratic activists. If we want to fully examine this conflict of social and political ideas, we have to take advantage of the fact that nascent Christian Democracy was not restricted to Italy. In France, for instance, there was no ban on the political activities of Catholics. The Sillon, a loose organization of French Christian Democrats similar to the Lega Democratica Nazionale, was free from the restrictions the Roman Question imposed upon the activities of Italian Catholics. Yet the Sillon shared the fate of the Lega: the severe disapproval of Pius X.[12]

It would be easy to line up statements by the Sillonists that would match almost word for word those made by Murri, who in

1901 told a regional Catholic congress: "The hour of democracy is here, a new force, the class of the humble surges forth to claim justice. . . . We must prevent our adversaries from gaining a monopoly over the vindication of the people['s rights]: we must prevent that the call of the church finds us again unprepared. Let us make common cause with the people, because the vindication of freedom is a cause we share with the people." As he observed the conservative leadership of Catholic Action calling for something other than an alliance with the working people, Murri criticized the conservatives' mentality "that considered the worker and the peasant natural subjects of their masters" and, with a warning tinged with regret, began to talk of the social policy of the church as "unfair toward the popular classes" and consequently "ruinous for the interests of the church and of Catholicism in Italy." As the initiatives represented by the Lega Democratica Nazionale were grinding down to a sad failure, leaving behind broken hopes and destroyed clerical careers, one of the *legisti* remarked with bitter sarcasm that instead of an alliance between the church and the working people, a *connubio,* "a loving union between a pseudo-religious conservatism and the pseudo-constitutional vestry" was taking place.[13]

The Ban on the Social Activism of the Clergy

The withdrawal of the priests from active involvement in the labor movement, which the pope ordered, was an aspect of the union of political conservatism and the church, the alliance between wealth and the altar, that increasingly became a reality during the papacy of Pius X. As he saw it, the priests who were active in organizing labor would inevitably get caught in strikes. The involvement of the clergy in social conflicts jeopardized the universality of their ministry and threatened their effectiveness as priests. It also violated the principles of *caritas,* which the pope considered absolutely essential in the life of the Christian community. Even though he saw challenges to the "superior classes" as an offense against the very spirit of Christianity, Pius X moved slowly on the issue of priests leading labor unions and actively participating in strikes, showing caution that was quintessentially his own. It was not until 1905 that he stated clearly that priests had no place on the picket lines: "The priest, raised above all men in order to accomplish the mission he has from God, must also remain above all human interests, all conflicts, all classes of society."[14] Once he got going, Pius X moved in a style that was as much his own as was caution, with a Byzantinism that gave a basic characteristic to his papacy. This style involved secret investigations and condemnations without trials that were aimed at stamping out the modernist heresy, with which taking the side of the workers came to be associated under the code name of "social modernism."

After the experiment with the workers' chaplains was quietly terminated, Father Dalmazio Minoretti fell under the suspicion of modernist heresy. Minoretti was the theologian-turned-sociologist who suggested it to Cardinal Ferrari, providing theoretical arguments in favor of instituting *cappellani del lavoro*. But the historian trying to unravel the story of Minoretti's heresy found only insinuations about the "negativism" of his work as a sociologist. His social criticism, according to some, did "more damage than good." The apostolic visitor sent to his diocese by the pope denounced Minoretti as "not as securely papal and scholastic as he should be."

The accusation, with its innuendos and guilt established without trial, was typical of the antimodernist campaign under Pius X.[15] The fact that Minoretti publicly accepted class conflict as a fact of life and strikes as extreme but nevertheless employable and unavoidable weapons to be utilized in *actio benefica in populum* was not mentioned. Opinions such as Minoretti's—who incidentally was doctrinally sound enough to eventually become an archbishop—were demonstrably the cause of antimodernist persecution dealt out by the Vatican to other priests in a style similar to the one that pursued Minoretti. During the papacy of Pius X, advocating strikes and supporting the side of the working classes in them—even the thought of it—became a capital sin for priests.

The nightmarish quality of another series of events during the era of Pius X is due exactly to the fact that they involved not so much action as thought. Lorenzo Bedeschi told this story, documented so as to make it unquestionable.[16] It involved a group of young priests from Cesena, not far from Rho. These priests were not involved in the labor movement themselves; they followed the letter of papal instructions and stayed out of labor conflict. They merely expressed thoughts about it; and in expressing their thoughts, they followed the lead of their young bishop, Giovanni Cazzani, who was intensely interested in social problems. Among Cazzani's papers in the diocesan archives, Bedeschi found a long, unsigned essay about the genesis of labor organizations. The unknown "sociologist," probably one of his priests, told Bishop Cazzani that the local labor organizations were developing under the leadership of the Republican party, which was radical and anticlerical like the Socialist party. Lack of Catholic initiative in organizing unions left the Catholic workers no choice but to join the locals led by the Republicans. They had to unite not only because the spirit of class solidarity was strong among them but also because the landowners who confronted them had united.

The young bishop evidently stated the facts of life in 1906 when he reaffirmed in a pastoral letter the right of the "working classes" to organize in the defense of their "common interests." The workers' rights to their own organizations had been confirmed by Pope Leo XIII more than a decade before. Hence Bishop Cazzani's arguments appeared safely within the confines of the official social doctrine of the church. Toniolo printed Cazzani's pastoral letter as one of the publications of the Unione Popolare. Even Pope Pius X seemed to have agreed with it: through his secretary he sent a message to Monsignor Cazzani that appeared to include "comforting expressions."[17] It would have been a happy ending for a story about a bishop if the story had ended there, but it did not.

Catholic laborers, who sent to Cazzani letters of moving gratitude for "vindicating" their "rights," read the pastoral letter as lifting the long-standing ban of the church upon their membership in Republican-led labor leagues. Even some of the diocesan clergy came to similar conclusions and encouraged the workers to join these organizations.[18]

The Cesena episode illustrates a problem of leadership that became acute in Italian Catholic social action during the papacy of Pius X. The tight central control over Catholic Action by the church hierarchy discouraged the development of a lay leadership that would have replaced the aging aristocratic leaders. Even if these had not yet reached the age of retirement, they could not be successful labor organizers because the workers detested their paternalistic attitude of superiority toward the working classes. Under the benevolent eye of Pope Leo XIII, a group of young Catholics were readying themselves for just this eventuality. An intense and realistic discussion of social problems prepared these young Christian Democrats for successful leadership of the labor movement. But they were to be disappointed after Cardinal Sarto was elected pope. Rather than giving them new places in leadership when Italian Catholic Action was reorganized, Pope Pius X forced them out of the positions they already occupied.[19] The papal ban on the participation of priests in the labor movement gave the final blow to the hopes of young Christian Democrats, for many of them were priests who hoped to become workers' chaplains, like Rusconi, if they were not already. But during the papacy of Pius X, their concern with the misery of their flocks increasingly had to find expression not in action but in worried thoughts, expressed in occasional writings.

The young Christian Democratic priests of Cesena poured out these thoughts on the pages of a local Catholic paper, *Il Savio*. Their acknowledged leader, Canon Giovanni Ravaglia, one of the close associates of Bishop Cazzani and an instructor of theology in the local seminary, expressed especially strong concern about the working class. As he explored the problem of class conflict, often by commenting on short pieces written by Catholic activists from Germany, Belgium, and the United States, he stressed the need to elevate "the proletariat to the dignity of a class." He seemed to consider confrontations between the workers and the *padroni* inevitable, and did not hide the opinion that those priests who took the side of the landowners "betrayed the people." He was also one of the priests who, in the silence of the bishop, interpreted the pastoral letter as suggesting that Catholic workers could join non-Catholic organizations. If the outrage of local landowners and their pressure through the conservative cardinals in the Vatican was not enough to bring a papal investigator to Cesena, the suggestion of Ravaglia obviously was.[20]

Ravaglia's personal troubles were, by a superb irony, those of Neo-Thomism, for he was a convinced Thomist who accepted

Aquinas as teacher and leader, as Pius X wanted him to do. He was one of those who responded to Pope Leo's call about renewing social science and society through the study of the works of Aquinas. But he had too good a mind and too much intellectual independence to do what became the practice of "safe" Thomists during the papacy of Pius X, which was to mouth what the pope had to say about Aquinas's wisdom and quote the sayings of the Angelic Doctor the pope quoted. Ravaglia struck out on his own and achieved a reputation by a bold application of the Thomistic principles to modern society. In so doing he reached conclusions that went beyond his original inspirations, Leo's *Aeterni Patris* and *Rerum novarum.*

Taking off from the Thomistic theme of the social function of property, he pushed on toward asserting that the workers' right to the necessities of life was just that, a right, and not the subject of the charitable acts of the *padroni,* which they may or may not grant, depending on how far they were willing to go in alienating their superfluous. What followed logically, and Ravaglia stated this openly, was the workers' right to gather in organizations of their own and to strike if they felt they were shortchanged for their labor. Certainly this went a long way to focus the anger of the local landlords on him, especially since they were trying to prevent local Christian Democratic laymen from organizing simple unions. The mixed model was, one can safely assume, nonexistent in the area, nothing but a figment of the imagination of conservative minds bent on maintaining old-style paternalism intact.[21] The apostolic visitor sent by the pope in response to the local landowners' pleas noted in his report that they were "cold" toward religion and "not one of them" was inclined toward "Christian zeal manifest in concrete action." The *Visitatore Apostolico* was a Dominican monk by the name of Tommaso Pio Boggiani, who, according to one of the witnesses he examined, "instilled fear with his looks and left his audience cold and terrorized." The Dominican, it seemed, went after heretics with the zeal of the "bloodhounds of God" of olden days.

His presence frightened the young Christian Democratic priests, but he obviously consoled the local landowners who managed to get his ear. They seem to have convinced him that Bishop Cazzani's pastoral letter was the "spark that ignited the fire" of strikes in Cesena, in spite of the fact that the zone was notorious for strikes even before the bishop set his foot in Cesena. The *Visitatore Apostolico* also reported back to Rome that the condition of agricultural laborers was "fairly good," and he seemed to suggest that there would probably not have been strikes if it were not for Cazzani, the "Socialist bishop." Boggiani faithfully quoted the title that the local landlords had given to Monsignor Cazzani, together with their opinion that the bishop incited hatred against them "among the inferior classes." He was also accused of being a failure for not "censoring" *Il Savio* and the Christian Democratic priests who wrote for it.

As for the priests, and Ravaglia specifically, the major charge against them was that of *murrismo,* which was by then equated with the modernist heresy. Although Ravaglia was declared by the apostolic visitor *di ottima condotta morale,* "not wanting in moral conduct," since he could not be accused of the kind of rebellion against the church authorities that Murri was by then drifting into, he was nevertheless a *murriano* in that he viewed the proletariat as an autonomous social force. His and the other priests' approval of the previous year's strikes by agricultural laborers thus became an indictment in connection with *murrismo* and *modernismo.* According to Boggiani's report, they "proclaimed the [religious] neutrality and non-confessional nature of labor organizations as the condition of the success of their action in favor of the people. They [the Christian Democratic priests] are intolerant of any opposition to their views and go as far as to pass a low judgment even on the supreme church authorities when these take positions contrary to their ideals."

Father Boggiani had apparently forgotten the Leonine call to the priests to "get out of the vestry," for he seemed to have held against the Christian Democratic priests that they created a conflict with their conservative colleagues, "who are content to be simple ministers of the cult and do nothing for the people." Another recurring point of the apostolic visitor's report was the dislike of the upper classes, especially of the landlords, by the Christian Democratic priests, who were referred to throughout the report as "modernists."

The use of this term to brand those who expressed opinions about action in favor of the people and hostility toward propertied interests was a typical doctrinal aspect of the antimodernist witch hunt conducted during the papacy of Pius X. Also typical was the sentence of guilt by association and without a proper trial, such as a detailed examination of the doctrinal outlook of the accused. The studied distortion of the workers' material conditions in the report left little doubt as to whose side Boggiani took in the labor conflict of Cesena. All the available evidence seems to suggest that Pius X let himself be guided by Boggiani's report, as he personally supervised the disciplinary action taken against the priests of Cesena. The secrecy in which Pius X shrouded the action can probably be ascribed to a bit of bad conscience about the whole affair on the pope's part. If his feelings were not equivocal, this obviously did not mitigate the severity of the pope's reaction.

The purge that followed among the diocesan clergy of Cesena hit Canon Ravaglia the hardest. If the main point of accusation against Ravaglia seems to have been that he was a friend of Romolo Murri, this was for the pope the worst that could be said against anyone. The name of Murri was by 1907 already firmly connected in the pope's mind with the modernist heresy. This was especially true when—as in the apostolic visitor's report on Ravaglia—the suspicion of *murrismo* appeared together with the questioning of the validity of the pope's judgments concerning social issues.[22]

Pius X ordered that Ravaglia resign from his position as instructor of theology, but Ravaglia had to keep the real reasons for his resignation secret. The pope's personal letter to Cazzani about this was little short of being bizarre, for he told the bishop that Ravaglia's resignation had to occur "spontaneously and without anybody discovering or even suspecting who desired it."[23] As for Bishop Cazzani, his humiliation was complete. Not only did he undergo the ignominy of an inquisition but he ended up denouncing the young priests with whom he obviously once felt a basic sympathy. He reported in a letter to Pius X that the papal order about Ravaglia had been carried out, but he made a last, moving attempt to defend him. The closing sentence of the letter should have been engraved on the bishop's tombstone as his epitaph and as a testimony to his quality as a churchman. But Cazzani's words were also a commentary on the style of leadership established in the church by Pius X, for Monsignor Cazzani declared himself the Pope's *strumento senza ragione e senza volontà:* his "instrument without reason and without will."[24]

For another tale involving a strike and a bishop, one may quote no less an authority than Pope John XXIII, who as a young priest was personally involved in the strike that was called by Catholics in Ranica near Bergamo in 1909. Another protagonist was Monsignor Giacomo Radini Tedeschi, a close associate of Leo XIII and his adviser on social matters. When the local bishop died in 1905, Pius X picked Radini—against the advice of curial prelates—to fill the episcopal see of Bergamo, which the Pope called the "first diocese of Italy." To emphasize this decision, Pius X personally consecrated the new bishop, who asked Father Angelo Roncalli, the future Pope John XXIII, to become his personal secretary.

It is safe to assume that Radini's social activism had to do with the aversion of the pope's conservative advisers towards him. His arguments about the social mission of the clergy must have been particularly irksome, for he unequivocally stated in 1896 that "the priest absolutely has to enter into social life" and in so doing he "carries out his mission as Jesus Christ did." He referred to the seclusion of the priest in the vestry and the restriction of his work as nothing but preaching a "false notion of priesthood" that liberalism propagated, in its hostility to the church, in order to confine the role of religion in the life of society. The French edition of Radini's 1896 speech carried a preface by Chanoine Dehon, the Catholic sociologist, who informed the readers that Pope Leo highly approved of what Radini said, adding that the text "expresses [Leo's] thought and describes the action priests have to undertake and the organization of Catholic Action as the pope wants it."[25]

On the basis of the information currently available, the insistence of Pius X on appointing Radini to the bishopric of Bergamo, the center of Italian Catholic social action, remains an enigma. The statements he made as bishop show Radini insistent upon retaining a role in social activism.[26] And this was precisely what he did in 1909 in a very striking and, by then for the clergy, very unusual way. During that year workers employed in Ranica, near Bergamo, asked for the right to organize a union while simultaneously demanding the reduction of the work week from six days and ten and a half hours a day, as well as a wage increase. When these demands were refused, a strike broke out, apparently led by Niccolo Rezzara, a layman and close associate of Medolago.

What outraged the *padroni* even more than the involvement of the Unione Economico Sociale in a strike was that Bishop Radini also openly supported the strike in words and deeds. The long strike, "sustained by the solidarity of the Christian proletariat of Italy," in the words of Mario Chiri, another functionary of the Economic Social Union, ended with a victory for the workers. Angelo Roncalli, yet another *rapporteur* of the event, actively participated in bringing the conflict to a victorious end by rounding up material support. He reflected some years later:

> It was good to see that the cause of workers was defended by the bishop, not only from the heights of the episcopal pulpit but openly in the public square, in capital-labor conflicts, and in the workshops. Monsignor Radini felt that it was his duty to give an example and he had the courage to do it.
>
> When the strike began, Radini was among the first to put on the list to help the workers; and he was among those who gave generous sums to assure the daily bread of the striking workers. Then from all sides this was called a scandal; unfriendly reports were sent to higher authorities. . . .
>
> At Ranica it was not a problem of wages or persons that was at stake but a principle: the fundamental question of freedom of the Christian organization of labor, as opposed to the powerful organization of capital. He resolutely took the side of the striking workers because in doing so he fulfilled a highly Christian duty and acted for justice, charity and social peace. He let the shouters go on shouting and went calmly on his own way, taking an active part on behalf of the striking workers.

Roncalli, who clearly never had any doubt about the righteousness of Bishop Radini's or his own action, reported that, when the strike was over, his bishop received a note from Pius X: "We cannot disapprove of what you have thought prudent to do since you were fully acquainted with the place, with the persons involved, and with the circumstances." Yet in spite of this reassuring letter and the pope's continuous declaration of the bishops' right and duty to take a directive role in Catholic Action, a strange and disconcerting fact crept into Roncalli's tale, giving it anything but a happy ending. The future Pope John XXIII reported that after the strike Bishop Radini "found himself in a state of uncertitude and doubt as to whether he still deserved the complete confidence of the Holy Father."[27]

Thus the historian is left once more with a personal tragedy and a series of questions as well. How much of Bishop Radini's self-doubt and anguish was due to those "unfriendly reports sent to higher authorities"? Was the Bishop made to feel guilty for siding with the workers through a reflex reaction that was clearly out of style during the papacy of Pius X? Was the suspicion of modernism that hung over Angelo Roncalli for some time connected with his support of the striking workers? The answer to these questions awaits the examination of materials in the Vatican Archives. In the meantime, the only thing one can do is to search for parallel occurrences in the life of Pius X, the most important of the *dramatis personae*. The only biography of the pope that may be called official, since it was written by a close associate in 1905, and read and "corrected" by Pius X before its publication, offers a description of an act strikingly similar to Radini's, yet at the same time utterly dissimilar as to the role Sarto, then the patriarch of Venice, played in it. It happened only two years before his elevation to the papal throne; thus what he did cannot be ascribed to either youthful folly or to an impulsive act. This is the way Angelo Marchesan, the biographer reported the episode:

A real friend of the people, for whom he sacrificed himself always and everywhere, he trembled with sacred indignation when he saw that under the disguise of false economic advantages, the usual trouble-makers inspired the workers to rebellion and anticlericalism. Thus when in August, 1901, a group of comrades, announcing a public meeting, tried to draw the women workers at the tobacco processing plant into the federation of state employees, of which the workers at the arsenal were also members, the patriarch, convinced that such meetings are held with discontent and strike in mind, to prevent from happening in Venice what had been deplored in other localities following such meetings, he thought that the office of charity demanded and it was also part of his duty to prevent these poor women from accepting the invitation to attend such meetings, or even worse, give their names to an association about which they knew nothing. To this end, with the permission of the director, he himself went to the plant and with his good and persuasive words exhorted the working women to establish a league only among themselves and without getting mixed up with public meetings where perverse instigators, instead of improving their conditions, could only worsen them. And if they desired something justifiably, as in the past, now too they should come to him who would be ready for the tutelage of their interests.[28]

We clearly cannot say that the cardinal was trying to prevent the women workers from joining the union, for he suggested to them to form one of their own, presumably a Catholic one. But he certainly did his best to persuade them not to join an unspecified nationwide organization that one may presume was a Socialist-inspired one, although this is not clear from the narrative. If indeed it was, then the case throws more light on what happened to Ravaglia than on Radini's troubles. At the same time, we cannot see Sarto's act of paternalism as a manifestation of neutrality, of staying above all classes and conflicts, as he later demanded clergymen do.

Ambivalence remains in the case, since a degree of uncertainty about the issue of class conflict involving Catholic unions continued even after Sarto became pope. He was clearly determined to keep the clergy out of it. Eventually, they were enjoined from participating not only in organizing unions or giving their names to employers' associations but even from taking a leading role in credit unions,[29] an activity that was first opened to the clergy by Leo XIII, who told them to act there "with the greatest of freedom." Ironically the withdrawal of priests from the labor movement aided the Socialists because it deprived Catholic Action of the enthusiasm, talents, and leaders badly needed to stem the tide of socialism. Even the ban on leading economic institutions such as credit unions was apparently harmful. Pointing to the lack of trained laymen to take over the positions occupied by priests, the Unione Economico Sociale had to beg the Concistorial Congregation, which issued the relevant decree, for a period of grace before it was put into effect.

The withdrawal of priests from social action, clearly damaging to the prospects of Catholic Action, has to be considered part of the decline of Catholic labor organizations that set in following the dissolution of the Opera. Yet the withdrawal cannot be said to have been complete, for the figure of the *assistente ecclesiastico,* the clergyman advisor to Catholic organizations, became a standard feature during the leadership of Pius X. But the advisers, unlike Pope Leo's priest activists who were told to act "with the greatest of freedom," were appointed by the bishops to whom they were directly responsible for their activities, which presumably involved the traditional guardianship over morality and religion. Hence the ecclesiastic assistants represented a control over Catholic Action rather than action itself.

Doctrinal Adjustments

Thus Pius X nailed down some of the matters left loose by his predecessor in the practice of Italian Catholic Action. But he was determined to tie up the loose ends of Catholic social doctrine as well. In connection with this move, however, for lack of written evidence, we must often interpret the pope's acts in order to arrive at some tentative conclusions about his intentions, which, contrasting with Leo's attitude, the historian Bruno Malinverni described as "applying brakes, rather than innovating."[30] Freezing into solid ice what was in a state of liquidity and flux under Leo is probably a better way to describe what Pius X did.[31] The changes introduced in the instruction of sociology at the Scuola Sociale of Bergamo are illustrative of this.

The institution came into being in 1910, after years of preparation that followed receipt of a "password" from the newly elected pope in 1904. It was first received by the Bergamasque lawyer Amilcare Martinelli, who reported that Pius X asked him to create "urgently" a center for social studies that would relate to the Holy See in a way of "absolute obedience." Originally intended for both the clergy and laymen, the school, eventually raised to the rank of a Catholic university by Pius X because of the pope's preoccupation with the indoctrination of clergy, had very few laymen among its first graduates. Its establishment in the "first diocese of Italy" was obviously one of the tasks expected of Bishop Radini, who called on Father Giuseppe Biederlack to teach sociology at the Scuola.

Biederlack, a former rector of the Gregorian University in Rome, had an international reputation and carried elements of a German theoretical outlook and experience with the organization of labor. This was rather ill-suited to the doctrinal perceptions of Italian Catholic conservatives, who often railed against the *Tedescheria* ("Germanism") Biederlack represented, since this included the unequivocal acceptance not only of the simple union but also of strikes. Although rejecting the principle of class struggle as such, Ketteler, for instance, accepted "the usefulness of the strike" as early as in 1869.[32]

In the lectures he delivered during the first academic year of the Social School, Biederlack not only advocated the legitimacy of the simple union but blasted away at those who resisted it by insisting on the mixed form of organization: "There are many rich, who associate with others in order to enrich themselves, but do not want the corporations of arts and crafts introduced and thus resist the rightful association of the lower classes and . . . [the] rights of their workers to autonomous organizations of labor [*sindacati*]." There was even more to come, as the students attending Biederlack's lectures heard him speak of the usefulness of the strike weapon for Catholic labor as well. Although he condemned class struggle as such, and restricted the use of strikes to contract negotiations, that is, to occasions when there was no binding contract in effect, he made no bones about strikes being needed in order to make economic gains: "A strike can generally improve the conditions of the worker since it arouses in the *padroni* the fear that their workers too may strike, and it is the fear of strike that prompts the *padroni* to accept the proposals of the workers."[33]

The apostolic visitor did not come at this time because the pope decided to intervene personally. After a revision of the curriculum and the reassignment of the faculty in 1912, probably adding substantially to Bishop Radini's self-doubt, the teaching of Biederlack's old course went to Giulio Monetti. Pius X found Monetti's lectures "of secure doctrine and indispensable utility."[34] What the pope deemed doctrinally safe was certainly different from Biederlack's opinions, so much so as to induce the historian Bruno Malinverni to talk of *bestemmie,* "swearing," as he related what Monetti might have thought of Biederlack's propositions. Father Monetti also proved himself useful to the pope by detailing for the students of the Scuola Sociale "the modernist errors in the practice of Catholic Action."[35]

Monetti was a firm believer in the "reestablishment of the Kingdom of God on earth." As expected, bringing back the golden age of the Middle Ages implied for him the revival of the medieval *corporazioni.* The trouble was that, by the second decade of the twentieth century, expectations that the mixed union could work had become utopian. Monetti described how the mixed union could morally unite the "rich and the poor," with the workers always maintaining proper "respect" toward the *padroni.* But he had to ask, somewhat pathetically, Why was it that, if the mixed union was so good, it did not work? In attempting to answer the question "why the mixed union failed to spread," he pointed to the diffidence not of the workers but of the *padroni.* According to Monetti, the *padroni,* "embittered by socialist violence," did not see fit to grace the mixed unions with their presence, preferring to establish organizations of their own. The mixed unions, when possible "always preferable," were deemed by this sociologist somewhat impractical "in large-scale industry where thousands of workers are under the command of a single capitalist."[36] The angelic charity of the *padrone* may have been immense, but this was clearly spreading it a bit too thin.

Properly entitled *digressione,* a digression, Monetti's treatment of the organization of labor was matched by a similarly old-fashioned perception of class conflict and strikes, which he considered absolutely unnecessary. Outside agitators, the sinful inclination of the workers to "substitute brute force for rights," and the lack of mutually binding charity emerged as the major elements in another digression, which implied that strikes and class conflict, a "sword of Damocles that hangs as a continued menace over contemporary society,"[37] would just go away if there were no outside agitators, if charity reigned and superfluous were distributed as the law of *caritas* required.

Neutrality in Labor Conflict

Monetti's lectures and the two volumes that reported them could have been perceived as an exercise in wishful thinking about the old Catholic utopia if it were not for the fact that they included the texts of circulars Medolago sent out to the member organizations of the Unione Economico Sociale.[38] These documents clearly contrasted with lectures delivered by Biederlack at the Scuola Sociale. Pius X replaced Biederlack with Monetti because the pope expected the latter to say what he wanted said. Monetti's lectures were indeed "of indispensable utility" because they expressed what the pope wanted to establish as the official policy of the church. As Pius X formulated this policy, it seems to have demanded the avoidance of strikes and strict neutrality when they arose. This might be expected in connection with the role priests played, but the pope seems to have extended the demand for neutrality to Catholic labor organizations as well.

Thus one step taken forward in Catholic labor theory and practice during the papacy of Leo XIII—the recognition of working class autonomy—was followed by two steps backward by Pius X, who insisted on the mixed union and neutrality in labor conflict. And doing just what the pope appears to have demanded, articles in *Azione Sociale*—the official publication of the Unione Economico Sociale—reviewing a series of strikes that occurred in the Parma region in 1908 described how the Catholics adopted an attitude of neutrality in the clash of "two armies, organized solidly, those of the *padroni* and of the workers."[39]

Neutrality in a conflict involving revolutionary syndicalists, as was the case in Parma, was one thing, but to declare neutrality as a principle for a movement that intended to reach the workers was something else. Clearly, the Unione Economico Sociale was to be involved in conflicts and strikes. This, as the events in Ranica showed, was unavoidable; and here was a conflict between ideals and reality, between directives coming from above and the demands of life imposed on the activists of the Economic Social Union. They tried their best to compromise. G. Molteni, who wrote on the subject of strikes in *Azione Sociale,* argued that "probably the country where there are no strikes is the island of Utopia." Yet he echoed the words of Sarto as well with the "heartfelt and spontaneous wish that workers and *padroni,* proletarians and capitalists, rich and poor learn the way to live in harmony, brotherhood, and economic and social solidarity, sustained by a strong sentiment of Christian charity."

In trying to bridge the unpleasant reality of strikes, which Molteni said often were not only "legitimate but necessary," and a utopia that defined them as both unnecessary and against God's order, Molteni not unexpectedly turned to those who had traditionally been the mediators not only between men and God but also between men in conflict with each other:

> The clergy, especially the parish priests, can contribute in a conclusive way to the good outcome of workers' agitations by preparing, promoting, and favoring professional organizations without which the masses of workers go to war, as a rule, to be defeated. . . .
>
> The parish priest can and has to be of help in strikes, attempting to induce the entrepreneurs, who by chance are deferential to him, to recognize as their obligation to listen to and discuss with them what the strikers have to say. . . . Nobody . . . can deny the obligation and convenience for the priest, and especially the priest in charge of souls, of getting involved in such controversies.[40]

The involvement of the priests in putting pressure on the *padroni* was a role not only tolerated but demanded by Pope Leo. But during the papacy of Pius X, it became other than a "convenience" for priests, especially since *L'Osservatore Romano* was less than complimentary toward strikers. In reacting to the 1906 wave of strikes, the word *hooligans* (*teppisti*) was one of the milder ones used by the paper to describe strikers. The terms *mob* (*plebaglia*), and *scoundrels* (*barabba*) were also employed in reference to the "social substratum" (*sub-strato sociale*) involved in labor unrest. Strikers were also compared to the *brigands* (*briganti*) of decades past.[41] The editorial writers of *L'Osservatore Romano* were clearly venting an upper-class contempt for the workers. Their sense of charity led them to declare that the strikers were acting against their own interests: after all, the workers had stepped outside the limits set by their tutors. The editorial writers were not above expelling the strikers from the human race—the "authentic people"—and presenting them as common criminals.

With its rejection of the workers' right to strike, the newspaper of the Vatican showed the church on the side of the capitalists in labor conflicts. This seriously jeopardized the church's efforts to counter Socialist propaganda and organizational gains among the Italian workers. It also gave the proletariat a clear idea of the limits of the "tutelage" that conservative Catholic social doctrine proclaimed as the duty of the superior classes: it obviously excluded any encroachment on the material interests of the upper classes.

In accusing Prime Minister Giovanni Giolitti of "encouraging" labor unrest by refusing to suppress waves of strikes in 1906 and 1907, for instance, the editorial writers of *L'Osservatore Romano* found themselves in very strange company, that of their traditional opponents, the conservative liberals, who also urged Giolitti to break up the strikes by force—if necessary, by the use of arms. Like Giolitti's conservative opponents in Parliament, *L'Osservatore Romano* argued that it was the duty of public authorities to repress strikes and dissolve the workers' organizations, especially the local Camere di Lavoro, which coordinated strikes and gave aid and comfort to striking workers. *L'Osservatore Romano* issued a call to the "ruling classes" to defend the principle of "authority" by suppressing the strikes, and darkly hinted about the possibility of a civil war if the strikes continued. "The patience of authentic people, of those who are not hooligans, has a limit and a measure beyond which it is not prudent to go," the paper stated.[42]

Where did all this leave the hapless Catholic labor activists and the priests for whose mediation *Azione Sociale* cried out? Incidentally, Pius X went on encouraging the priests to "become apostles of social action and the pope will always be with you," as he told a group of priests, graduates of the Scuola Sociale, in 1910. During the same year, *L'Osservatore Romano* approvingly reported Bishop Cazzani's proposition that clergymen should "promote" Catholic labor unions but "without taking a leading role" in them.[43] But what was the point of "promoting" labor unions without allowing for strikes? In trying to unravel what must have appeared a contradiction to at least some of the priests, one may point out that the strikes *L'Osservatore Romano* so resoundingly condemned were led by Socialists and other assorted envoys of the devil. Yet Catholic activists too called for, and conducted, strikes. But by and large, they must have tried to avoid them if they could help it. This, of course, did not endear them to the working classes, who, fortunately for the Catholic labor organizers, had not spent much time reading *L'Osservatore Romano*. Some of the local Catholic papers, such as the one in Turin, also took a view of the striking workers that coincided, point by point, with that of the local employers' association.[44]

It became *de rigeur* for Catholics, even the activists, to urge the *padroni* to parallel the simple unions by establishing their own organizations.[45] Molteni, for instance, concluded his treatise about strikes with a ringing call to the employers to do that. Catholic mediation, that of the priests and of the activists of the Economic Social Union, was conceived to evolve by building a bridge between two classes—or better put, two camps, one of which, as the employers in the Parma region had shown, was indeed heavily armed and whose terror tactics had to do with the collapse of the strikes. The Catholic activists' success as mediators was to be ensured by neutrality, which the Unione Economico Sociale proclaimed in tones reminiscent of Pius X's remarks about priests standing "above all social classes."

But the Catholic stance, at least as manifest in the pages of *L'Osservatore Romano,* could not be described as neutral any more than Bishop Radini's acts at the time of the Ranica strike could. Then there was the issue of "right to work," which Catholics proclaimed as inviolable. Bishop Giovanni Battista Scalabrini put it thus in 1899: "The right to strike is a corollary of freedom, but it ceases to be a right and becomes a crime when to the right to strike, limiting the freedom of others, [the right to] impose a strike, even through violence, is added." This "right to work" policy, an attempt to show evenhandedness and neutrality in class conflict, was solidly maintained even by Catholics of such overwhelmingly "liberal" reputation as Bishop Bonomelli.[46]

This stance, which was assumed by Catholics of both conservative and activist orientation, coincided with the policy of the liberal bourgeoisie represented by Prime Minister Giolitti. Historical experience from Italy and elsewhere suggests very strongly that the insistence upon the "open shop" and the "right to work" was a sign of intentions to limit the social importance of the labor movement. During the Giolittian era, it may have made sense for the government, intent on maintaining a balance of social forces, to use troops and police to get strikebreakers across picket lines. But given the fact that those were the very acts that led to the explosion of violence, even this can be questioned and Giolitti's policy declared a folly, especially by anyone with the workers' interests in mind even to a minimal extent. As for the Catholics, the preaching of the "right to work" in Italy, ravaged by unemployment and underemployment, in practice meant strikebreaking and defeats for strikers. This was asking for trouble by would-be labor organizers, as the Catholics fancied themselves to be. Their intention to take the workers' interest to heart appeared double-talk, and the Catholics were exposed to the accusation of *crumiraggio,* strikebreaking on principle.

The Catholics vehemently denied that they ever committed an act of strikebreaking. The responses returned to Mario Chiri in 1910 when he compiled his classic statistical work on the development of Catholic social organizations[47] were emphatic about that. As for the strikes themselves, Chiri listed a large number that were called by Catholic unions, but his tabulations as well as the descriptions he provided do not allow for a comparison between the frequency of the Catholic unions' use of the strike weapon and that of other organizations of labor. Chiri mentioned that Catholic unions on several occasions supported strikes called by non-Catholic unions. But he distinguished the strikes called by other unions from those initiated by Catholics by saying that the latter were characterized by the "lack of the principle of class struggle," adding that in a large number of cases, but not in all, this led to an "amicable solution" of the confrontation between the *padroni* and the workers.

Here we have a key to the interpretation of the Catholic attitude toward strikes: they were seen as class struggle only if their Socialist opponents called them. In those cases the Catholics' obsession with the need to differ from the Socialists predisposed them toward a neutral attitude, which in turn reinforced the Socialists' suspicion

that the Catholic unions were the "long hand of the *padroni.*" The
Catholic inclination to neutrality, which really amounted to opportunism[48] in labor conflicts, thus added to the weight of the old anticlerical argument that religion was an opiate for the people, an
argument that the Catholic emphasis on the workers' needs for spiritual rather than material gains helped to sustain. Seeing the Catholic activists criticized for "materializing" Catholic Action by insisting on material gains for the workers even at the cost of bringing
down the strike weapon on the *padroni,* the Socialists were not the
only ones to talk of the church siding with the *padroni.*

Pius X countered the argument in *Notre charge apostolique,* a
letter issued in 1910, by saying that the church "never betrayed the
goodness of the people by compromising alliances." Yet in the same
document, he condemned the activists' attempt to "escape the direction of ecclesiastic authorities" in connection with economic, social
and political issues. The pope judged this a "subterfuge." Social action, he argued, inevitably carried moral consequences; hence, it was
the subject of the vigilance of ecclesiastic authorities.[49]

Pius X clearly was not inclined to recognize any limit to his authority[50] and demanded absolute and unconditional obedience in
connection with not only religious doctrine and practices but social
matters as well. Thus, the principle of *confessionalità,* the religious
orientation of Italian Catholic organizations, including those of labor, was maintained during his papacy. The principle acquired a
special dimension when Pius X gave it a concrete meaning:

> . . . In these days hostile to Christ, it has become more difficult to
> apply the powerful remedies which the Redeemer has put into the
> hands of the Church in order to keep peoples within the lines of duty.
> . . . It is still more necessary to inculcate properly in the minds of all
> the moral maxim taught by Jesus Christ, so that everybody may learn
> to conquer himself, to curb the passions of his mind, to stifle pride, to
> live in obedience to authority, to love justice, to show charity towards
> all, to temper with Christian love the bitterness of social inequalities, to
> detach the heart from the goods of the world, to live contented with the
> state in which Providence has placed us, while striving to better it by
> the fulfillment of our duties, to thirst after the future life in the hope of
> eternal reward.[51]

The arguments presented by *Papa* Sarto in *Iucunda sane,* a 1904 encyclical, represented the continuation of his earlier views. As cardinal he stated in 1895 that "only in faith can we find tranquility and peace: through faith comes resignation to tribulations and succour for social inequalities."[52] And again in 1896: "an open confession of Christianity . . . will always be the most insurmountable obstacle to disorder, the most determined opponent of all excess, of all errors, the incorruptible guardian of all truth, divine and human."[53]

The consistency of Sarto the cardinal and Sarto the pope was consistency in a peculiar Catholic tradition. Pointing out that religion kept "peoples within the lines of duty," that it contained the social and political restlessness of the working classes, was the traditional method of selling religion to the upper classes, inclined toward an areligious if not antireligious stand since the eighteenth century. Toniolo's 1888 letter to the industrialist Alessandro Rossi extended the offer of an "alliance" between the clergy and the "superior" classes. In his 1901–2 articles, he offered the services of religion in preventing a "social conflagration" in return for the bourgeoisie's acceptance of the guidance of the church.[54]

The Alliance between Wealth and the Altar

What Toniolo talked about was becoming reality during the papacy of Pius X as an alliance against the working people was being forged. Leone Caetani, a contemporary observer, not unsympathetic to the church, remarked that it seems to have "forgotten its ancient popular traditions. . . . The church does not exist any more, as once it did, to defend the poor and humble against the rich and powerful of earth; it has become worldly, rich and powerful, attempts only to preserve unchanged the state of things, abhors every innovation and to the poor, to the humble preaches resignation to their destiny."[55]

Whether the inclination of Catholic leadership was due to power or to weakness and the threat represented by socialism is arguable. But what Caetani suggested was so strongly evident in historical data and the opinions of contemporary observers that it has become one of the major theses of the historiography of the era of Pius X.[56]

The historian Arturo Jemolo, whose study was not, like Caeta-ni's, focused on the issues of modernism but remained general and pathfinding because of its broad spectrum, spoke nevertheless with a degree of regret of the church's alliance with the "rich classes" and the modernists' drive to free it from this and "to make it the advocate of the poor against the rich in a vindication of rights and not the petrification of charity." The modernists were condemned because what they suggested ran against the "long tradition of teaching the necessity that the poor exist, that poverty was an indispensable ele-ment of a Christian society."[57]

The personal tragedies of people who, like Murri and Ravaglia, fell under the suspicion of social modernism because they spoke out against an obvious alliance between wealth and the altar lend them-selves to high drama. But they are a small part of the historical evi-dence dealing with the alignment of church policy and Catholic Ac-tion that shows Catholics on the side of the rich. The limited range of this study dictates caution about trying to settle the debate about the Catholics' "insertion" into the liberal-capitalistic system that, histo-rians of Marxist orientation are especially adamant, occurred dur-ing the papacy of Pius X.[58] Nevertheless, one does not hesitate to say that Catholic labor theory and the practice of Catholic social organi-zations point strongly in that direction, at least as far as intentions were concerned. A recapitulation of evidence previously presented shows the leadership of the church insistent on the mixed union, the purpose of which was to prevent the working classes from gaining social autonomy. When this organizational form failed to material-ize because of the refusal not only of the working classes but espe-cially of the *padroni* to join, when utopia did not materialize, the Catholics moved to organize the capitalists and landowners. A sug-gestion thrown in for good measure by an editorial in *L'Osservatore Romano* in 1906 advocated that local "civil guards" be created and armed to defend peace and property.[59] Furthermore, the leadership of the church was talking of neutrality in class conflict, but *L'Osser-vatore Romano* clearly stood behind the propertied classes when their power was thought to be challenged by a wave of strikes. How much evidence does one accumulate before coming to the conclusion that there was a policy alignment on the part of the pope—or rather, a realignment—during the papacy of Pius X?

As socialism transformed itself from the ominous foreboding it was during the times of Pope Leo XIII into a real threat, the old hostility toward the liberal bourgeoisie was abandoned in order to pave the way for an alliance with the propertied classes, an alliance against the industrial and agricultural proletariat. The have-nots, the proletariat, were closely associated in the minds of the church leadership with socialism and thus were the social component of the threat socialism was conceived to represent. The alliance between wealth and the altar was not something that sprang up on the spur of the moment, but was in the making for some time, not only through the church's defense of the principle of private property as manifest in Thomistic theology but also through a growing obsession with the "Socialist menace," which was but a corollary of a perception of socialism as a wave of the future. Thus De Mun, the apostle of the corporativist revival, said in 1878: "Socialism is the revolution and we are the counterrevolution. There is nothing in common between us. Between these two *termini* there is no place for liberalism."[60] It was not only the conservatives who took to prophesying about socialism becoming the main target for the Catholics' fire. Filippo Meda, too, predicted somewhat cryptically in 1898 that the appearance of socialism on the scene "will very much simplify the struggle for Catholics."[61] Sturzo also argued in 1902 that the choices for Italy's citizens were being narrowed down to two—socialism and Catholicism.[62] By 1907 this must have become a commonly accepted position, since a circular of the Unione Elettorale stated that "many predict that in the future there will be only two parties: a Socialist and a Catholic."[63]

By 1907 it became "safe and doctrinally sound," as the saying went during the papacy of Pius X, to venture such an opinion. Antonio Pavissich, one of the Jesuits of *Civiltà Cattolica,* who was known to be in close touch with the pope, suggested the very same thing in an article published by the *Civiltà* in 1904.[64] That Pius X perceived socialism to be the main opponent is an assumption very likely to be borne out by archival evidence. His very first experience as bishop exposed him to the threat of socialism as early as the 1880s in Mantova, a town that according to one of the pope's more reliable biographers "was then becoming a citadel of socialism, the progress of which desolated the churches."[65] The word *desolation* is an interesting reminder of the *religio depopulata,* "the desolation of religion," that was to haunt Pius X toward the end of his life.[66]

He sought relief from this nightmare by making a monumental change in policy, a change that could not be much less overwhelming for him than the threat of socialism was, for he chose not to announce it publicly. *Il papa tacera,* "the pope will remain silent," was the way he announced, and to private ears at that, the decision to lift the Non Expedit, the ban on Catholic participation in national elections in localities where the victory of a Socialist or radical candidate could be prevented by Catholic votes.[67] Since Pius X did not allow for a Catholic party, or even for Catholics to run as Catholic candidates, the lifting of the ban meant voting for candidates who rarely if ever identified themselves as antiliberal and often styled themselves as liberals. Thus, for all practical purposes, the war on liberalism ceased after Catholic fire aimed at the bourgeoisie stopped.

Once as cardinal, Sarto showed himself staunchly anti-liberal in the best tradition of Catholic conservativism by saying: "Priests should be on guard against accepting any of the ideas of liberalism that, a wolf in sheep's clothing, pretends to reconcile justice with inequity."[68] In later allowing what often became in practice a liberal-Catholic alliance in election times, he may have thought that political cooperation did not carry the acceptance of the ideas and values of one's allies. More likely what happened was that the hostility he once felt toward liberalism gave way as concern with the peril of socialism, and the need for all the forces to unite against the threat of revolution, grew in the Pope's mind.

When in 1898 the regime that preceded Giolitti's suppressed as "subversive" both the Socialist and the Catholic organizations, with mindless impartiality, Leo XIII indignantly declared that the Catholic organizations, by their very existence, constituted a "valid guarantee" of the "respect for social order." The ruling class "will never find among Catholics conspirators, inciters of disorder, rebels against law and authority," orators at the 1899 congress of the Opera intoned, following up on the pope's statement.[69] As for Leo's successor on the throne of Peter, his authorized biography speaks of Cardinal Sarto as "prudent, conciliatory and deferential, one who always advised the priests and the faithful he led to be also respectful of constituted authorities. He did all this not for the sake of appearance, but because he shared the real conviction of those who know that all power comes from God."[70]

Sarto's position was not without contradiction. When rejecting the principle of democracy as pope, he would make use of the Neo-Thomistic argument according to which "all power comes from God." The logic of this argument dictated that if indeed God was the source of all power and authority, then democracy and the principle of the sovereignty of the people represented a form of intellectual perversion. Nevertheless, Sarto was not only willing to accept "constituted authorities" whose power was based on popular vote, but eventually allowed Catholic forces to descend into the political arena and become part of the political system of an "Italian democracy in the making." In the very first encyclical he was to issue as Pope, Sarto used the terms *party of God* and *party of order* interchangeably in connection with Catholic Action.[71]

The perception of the need to respect the established order was rapidly growing in Catholic minds during the first decade of the twentieth century. It grew together with, and in proportion to, the concern about the "Socialist menace," which became evident again and again in waves of strikes and attempted general strikes. This was so much the case that one is surprised to read in Monetti's 1912 lectures that socialism and liberalism were "Siamese twins."[72] This represented a step forward from the old parable that attributed to liberalism a paternal relationship toward socialism. Toniolo used the "socialism, daughter of liberalism" metaphor, often tied to the description of socialism as "the latest form and degeneration of liberalism." But by the turn of the century, even he talked of socialism as representing the "pathology of society."[73]

The argument about "socialism, daughter of liberalism" showed up in a propaganda pamphlet published by the Unione Popolare as late as 1909. This identified both liberalism and socialism as enemies on page sixty-four, but somewhat confusingly, after having cried out

on page fifty-five, "*socialismo, ecco il nemico.*"[74] "Socialism, that is
the enemy!" neatly turned around Gambetta's cry "Le cléricalisme,
voilà l'ennemi!" It increasingly became the slogan as liberal-
Catholic alliances became the order of the day at election times. By
1907 the Catholics' enemies' list left out the liberals even in the pages
of the *Civiltà Cattolica*[75] and *L'Osservatore Romano,*[76] where socialism showed up in company other than liberal, such as that of the
Freemasons and the modernists.

    Tempora mutantur et nos mutamus in illis! The policy of the
church changed with the times, but how absurd the change must
have appeared to some. The Catholic veterans who fought for decades against the liberal bourgeoisie were now told to not only hold
their fire but to go out and vote for a once despised enemy. It may be
pointed out though that those old fighters often came from among
the wealthy, and the need for the defense of social peace and property was something they shared with those inclined to be less Catholic than they. In fact, Catholics had experimented with alliances in
local politics, where they had always been allowed to vote. Especially if the Socialists threatened to capture seats on municipal
councils, the Catholics in case after case threw their votes behind
conservative candidates and established tactical cooperation with
them after they were elected, even if they confessed liberal beliefs.
When he was the patriarch of Venice, Sarto allowed such an alliance
in local politics.[77]

    Still, what he ordered Catholics to do on an increasing scale
after he became pope—to make property safe for the bourgeoisie by
voting for candidates who more often than not came from among
the wealthy—must have appeared absurd to some of the parish
priests. Tragically enough, these were the least able to say what they
thought about the matter. But the priests knew that from among the
local worthies came the *mangiapreti,* the priest-baiting anticlericals
who did everything they could to make the life of the priests miserable and their ministry ineffective by turning their parishioners on
them. The religious indifference or, worse, the downright anticlericalism of the *padroni,* in part explains the failure of the Catholics to
lure them into the mixed union, with all its implied obligations of
religious origins. Such complaints are endemic in historical sources

from the turn of the century, suggesting that the old Catholic charges about the bourgeoisie were far from baseless.

Sturzo, a keen observer of things social not only in the south but also in the whole of Italy, remarked in 1901 that "the bourgeoisie for the most part is irreligious and greedy." His sense of charity allowed him to add, echoing the biblical tale of Lot, that "there are some good, honest, and Catholic capitalists and landowners." A year later Sturzo relayed the grievances of parish priests about the lack of respect among the wealthy Sicilians for religious customs, such as allowing for the observance of holidays by their workers.[78]

Sturzo was for once in agreement with Pope Leo XIII, who, in the aftermath of the 1901 strikes, blamed the landowners for a disinclination to practice religion, and for considering it only a tool useful "to defend the principles of authority, property, and order."[79] Evidence of the perceptions of Sturzo and the pope turned up en masse sixty-some years later, as the historian Angelo Gambasin sifted through immense archival evidence from the Venetian region at the turn of the century. Gambasin found as a recurring complaint of the parish priests the accusation of the "perversion of the minds and hearts of the ownership classes [*ceti padronali*]." The ruthless exploitation of the poor parishioners was tied in these complaints to irreligious, and even antireligious, attitudes on the part of the wealthy. "What God! What Providence! For you I am god, I am providence!"[80] The explanation by a local worthy to his workers of his own position in the universe, quoted at one of the congresses of the old Opera in a diatribe against "bourgeois speculators," seemed to have retained validity well into the twentieth century. Thus the alliance between wealth and the altar, as far as the interests of the church were concerned, bordered on the absurd, since this marriage of convenience was a convenience mostly for those who represented wealth.

7

Aversion to the Higher Classes Is Contrary to the True Spirit of Christian Charity

Catholics Confront Socialism

Their unwavering defense of the principle of private property set Catholics on a collision course with the socialists and drove them toward the alliance between wealth and the altar that was the denouement of the Catholics' war on socialism. In spite of this hostility, many Catholics retained a basic sympathy toward the Socialists' struggle to improve the lot of the working people.[1] Even Toniolo opined in 1897 that Catholics and socialists should "march separately" but "fight united."[2] The suggestion, which provoked a howl of protest by Catholic conservatives, for once was not off the mark. In 1897 the Socialists sat together with the Catholics at an international conference in Zurich. The theme of the conference was the legislative protection of the interests of the working classes.[3] This experience, which constituted the backdrop to Toniolo's remark, led to arguments in favor of cooperation with the Socialists on their minimal program, which, stressing social legislation, coincided with the traditional Catholic demand for social injustice.[4]

In 1898, a year after the Zurich conference, Italian Catholics shared with the Socialists something else: persecution at the hands of a government bent on destroying opposition; but the experience affected the two groups differently. The persecution made the Socialists more defiant. For the Catholic camp, it marked a significant advance in the direction of the Programma di Milano, the move toward an antisocialist alliance between Catholics and the bourgeoisie. Thus instead of talking of similarities between themselves and the Socialists, the Catholics emphasized the differences by contrasting the revolutionary threat represented by the Socialists with the conservative orientation of their own organizations. They styled themselves the "party of order," manning the bastions against socialism, "the modern Attila."[5]

Provincial Catholic papers issued rousing calls for a new crusade as the pope too raised his voice to stop the advance of Attila on Rome. Considering that he used to refer to Socialists as "barbarians" who carried a "deadly pestilence," Leo XIII's statements about them in *Graves de communi,* the encyclical issued in 1901, were surprisingly moderate in tone. The pope mentioned them in connection with the practice of charity and almsgiving, which the Socialists objected to but which the pope defended as absolutely necessary for maintaining a Christian community. This and other remarks defining the meaning of Christian Democracy as not political but social in nature, a social "action in favor of the people," firmly placed Catholic Action within the forces of order, giving them an essentially reformist orientation.

With *Graves de communi* the Leonine expansion of Catholic social theory ceased and the experimentation Leo had encouraged stopped. As for cooperation with the Socialists, Leo reminded the faithful that whatever the meaning and aims of the Socialists' minimal program, their ultimate goals represented a threat to the church.[6] Accordingly, the *incontro-scontro,*[7] the Catholics' encounter with socialism, tended to become an increasingly angry conflict; the love-hate relationship that a historian detected between them[8] was not developing very strongly in favor of love. In spite of a basic sympathy many Catholics felt for the moral concern involved in the Socialists' drive for social justice, the earlier cooperation between Catholics and Socialists in municipal politics became rarer and cooperation with liberals more frequent.[9] Suggestions for coordinating actions between their respective organizations of labor, as these were built up, ran into strong resistance on the part of the leadership on both sides.[10] A war on socialism (*guerra al socialismo*) was on for good.

The Catholics for the most part joined the war with a remarkable lack of knowlege about the enemy. Medolago had bitter words more than once about the Catholics' lack of concrete information when they discussed economic and social issues, but he was no less culpable than the others when it came to knowing about socialism.

His library, which apparently included virtually nothing written by those who represented the idea-world of socialism, was amply supplied with works by Catholics critical of socialism.[11]

In their secondhand knowledge of socialism, the Italians were not unlike the Catholics in other countries.[12] What was surprising, however, was that their abysmal ignorance, which often led to caricaturistic presentations of socialism, persisted for so long. Furthermore, these presentations tended to degenerate as time passed. Ugo Boncompagni Ludovisi's early 1880s statement suggested that the world made by socialism "will not have the family, will not have property, will not have genius because [socialism] will kill that off with equality; it will not have affection, generosity, and self-denial or gratitude because these qualities appear absurd and even crazy in the light of their principles."[13]

This was mild in comparison with the 1908 argument by Chiesa: "Do you want to know what the Socialists would like to do to priests? If they could, they would cut them up into pieces, every one of them. The only thing that would bother them would be that we don't have, all of us [priests] together, one single head so that they could chop it off with a single blow."[14]

Then there was the 1910 masterpiece by Burroni, complete with a mock Socialist catechism, including a prayer to "Father Ferri," the Socialist leader, who lives in the heaven of wealth. It presented the Socialist as one who enriches himself at the expense of the workers, and the Socialist union as an organization that "entraps the worker and forces him to pay [dues] and strike."[15] Showing that Chiesa and Burroni represented something like a style of talking about socialism, *Azione Sociale,* the official publication of the Economic Social Union, reporting in 1911 on the latest Socialist congress, referred to the participants as *condeliquenti camorristi,* linking them to mafia-like organizations, and talked of insolence and vulgarity as the characteristics of the meeting.[16]

These rather vulgar accusations matched the anticlericalism of the Socialists, their mock catechism, the caricature of fat and grabby priests and, what was a worse "blasphemy" for Catholics, the figure of "Christ the Socialist."[17] The Socialists, increasingly considered as the enemy, have been tarred and feathered for acts of puerile anticlericalism that others such as Freemasons committed, but their

own stance was uncompromisingly anticlerical as well. They introduced customs such as Socialist funerals and advocated civil marriage; they posted flags in front of churches announcing "neither
God, nor *padroni*"; they loudly proclaimed the conviction that religion served as opiate for the people, keeping them in the exploitative
grip of the owners of wealth.

As Italian Catholics became deadlocked into a confrontation
with socialism, it in turn largely defined the thematics of Italian Catholic Action. Thus it was in response to the challenge of socialism that
the program eventually known as Christian Democracy emerged.
Characteristically, the term first appeared in the antisocialist mani-
festo, the Programma di Milano.[18] And Toniolo, who was the father
of Italian Christian democracy, worked out the details of the concept in connection with his studies of that social "pathology," socialism. Others were driven into the concerns and hopes that Christian
Democratic activism represented by events such as the *fasci* episode
in Sicily.[19] Since the Socialists, claiming to represent the aspirations
of the working people, were active in organizing labor, they established this as a major concern of Christian Democracy. Probably no
other conflict within Italian Catholic Action matched the intensity
of the clash between the conservative leadership, insistent upon the
mixed union as the organizational framework of Catholic labor, and
the activists, who saw that as the epitome of impracticality.

Since *Rerum novarum* clearly did not charge Catholic Action
with the defense of the privileges of the upper classes but rather with
the saving of the proletariat, the activists represented the spirit of
Leo's "labor encyclical" better than the conservative leadership. Toniolo, who always attempted to strike a balance between opposing
tendencies,[20] was increasingly left behind as the activists took more
and more radical positions and felt that those held by the founding
father of Christian Democracy were turning into hindrances.

The more important socialism became in Italian life, the more
radical the Christian Democrats sounded and acted. How tiresome
Toniolo's approach of tracing problems back to the distant past appeared when compared with the directness of the activists. Murri's
response to the *fasci* was immediate, the point being that the Catholics would have to meet the Socialists head-on: "Socialism advances threateningly. Hundreds of thousands of workers joined the

fasci, and these men and women desert the churches en masse to go
to the meeting halls of the *fasci.* Let us take the lead in this movement and convince the people that the church is its salvation: we will
thus prevent [them] from falling into the jaws of socialism and anar-
chism."[21] Eventually a leader who was increasingly led, or better put,
dragged along, Toniolo too would arrive at a similar conclusion and
understand Christian Democracy as Murri and the other young activists did, as a means through which to take on socialism and "conquer the proletariat" for the Church.[22]

It took time and the trauma of witnessing the Socialists' success
in reaching the working masses for the conservative leaders of Catholic Action to come around to Murri's point. But eventually they
did: a 1907 circular of the Unione Elettorale was even more blunt
than Murri in stating that "it was convenient to imitate Socialist
propaganda." The desire to "imitate" the Socialists' propaganda methods became so intense that some appear to have worried about the
differences between Catholics and Socialists disappearing. Thus the
first competition announced in 1908 by the newly organized League
of Italian Catholic Propagandists involved essays defining the "dif-
ferential criteria between Catholic and Socialist propagandists."[23]

The need for defining the differences between themselves and
the Socialists became rather acute by the middle of the first decade
of the twentieth century because their attempts to match the Socialists' efforts item by item often led to failure. Yet because the obsession with the need to beat the Socialists in their own game persisted,[24] Catholic organizational and propaganda initiatives tended
to be hasty reactions rather than carefully planned and tactically
prepared actions. This is suggested by statistical information about
Catholic labor organizations. The number of Catholic locals was
374 in 1910. This shows a nearly threefold increase since 1907, demonstrating a remarkable recovery from the decline during 1903–7.
The average membership, however, which was 378 in 1906, went
down to 280 per unit by 1910.[25] The Catholic organizers appear to
have scattered their efforts by trying to take up the challenge of the
Socialists in every possible location. This argument can, of course,
be turned around by saying that an organization, however small,
was a proverbial foot in the door, a crack in a local Socialist monopoly in organizing labor, which was the driving motivation in the

Catholics' uphill battle against socialism.[26] Yet, without doubt, the numerical weakness of Catholic organizations reduced their effectiveness not only with regard to the Socialist unions but also insofar as gains for their own members were concerned. Often very small in membership, Catholic unions more than once played the role of fence-sitters, especially when strikes were called against enterprises that involved both Catholic and non-Catholic organizations of labor.[27] "Wait and see" was an attitude that betrayed weakness, and it also gave away something beyond the tactical situation. It bespoke the hesitation of the activists about involvement in "class struggle," which was, to say the least, frowned upon by the Vatican. But neutrality in a labor conflict, however benevolent toward the workers, risked the appearance of benevolence toward the *padroni*.

If its tactics indeed betrayed the weakness of the Catholic labor movement, so did membership statistics. In 1906 the combined enrollment of Catholic locals, reported at approximately 70,000, was only about 12.3 percent of the 570,000 inscribed in the organizations of the General Confederation of Labor (CGL) and the Chambers of Labor, both Socialist in orientation. By 1910 the Catholics' enlistment went up to 104,000, but this was still only about half of the CGL membership, which in turn represented less than 50 percent of the total number of workers in Socialist unions. When compared with the Italian national total of the organized labor force (exclusive of the Catholics but inclusive of all the other organizations), which was 817,000 in 1910, the Catholic unions, after an impressive growth during the years 1908–10, still showed no more than 12.7 percent.

Catholic Labor in the Industrial Sector

Statistical data suggest that during those years of growth Catholics exerted a greater organizational effort and succeeded in gathering larger numbers in industry than in agriculture. There was an especially heavy concentration of Catholic unionism in the textile industry, which provided wages far below the average because it employed women and youth in large numbers: 33,402 (41.5 percent) of the membership of Catholic industrial unions, came from the textile industry, with 22,397 (67 percent) of these women and 6,168 (18.5 percent) youths below 18 years of age. If one were to ascribe the large number of females in Catholic unions to the fact that women generally went to church more frequently than men and thus were more easily influenced by Catholic organizers, one would make a mistake. The Catholics might have gone the way of least resistance in organizing women, but they also committed themselves to gain improvement for a segment of the industrial working class that in Italy was both rapidly growing in numbers and outrageously poorly paid when compared with males employed in both industry and agriculture.[28] Of the 99,969 members of all the Catholic unions whose age and sex Chiri could identify, 35,841 (35.8 percent) were women and 10,268 (10.3 percent) were youths. These groups were in special need of improvements in both pay and working conditions.

As the Catholic effort to organize the industrial working class began in earnest, Medolago seems to have been somewhat hesitant because he felt the Socialists had already beaten him and his troop of organizers to it. At least, such was the impression he gave to Caissotti in 1898.[29] This initial hesitation, however, did not prevent a rather creditable performance, although the credit might be due more to the activists than to Medolago, depending on whether one is inclined to attribute a victory to the general or to the foot soldiers, or both. Nevertheless, during the nine-year period from 1901 through 1909, no less than 180 Catholic industrial unions were founded, and this represented 58.1 percent of the total of 310 established by Catholics. In 1910, 67,466 (64.5 percent) of the total membership of 104,614 came from industry. With 37,148 members (35.5 percent of the total) and 140 organizations (as opposed to 234 in industry), Catholic organizational effort among the peasantry remained below that of the Socialists. At the end of 1909, the CGL alone enlisted 130,000 rural people, 43.3 percent of a total membership of about 300,000. Data that excludes the Catholic organizations indicate that, in 1910, 48 percent of the organized Italian labor force of 920,000 came from agriculture and 52 percent from industry, far above the Catholics' 35.5 percent.

One obvious explanation of the Catholics' focus on the industrial sector in their organizational efforts is the rising concern with which they observed an increase in the numbers in the ranks of the industrial working class. Toniolo, who was then still acknowledged as the leader and chief ideologue of Christian Democracy, registered this alarm when in 1901 he declared that the very existence of the industrial working class, which was profoundly "antisocial" in nature, represented an evil that carried the threat of "an attempt at hand of overthrowing the whole social order."[30] The shrillness of the statement reflected a massive growth of urbanization and industrialization in Italy at the turn of the nineteenth century.

Those who lived in towns with populations of 20,000 or more represented 10.6% of the population of Italy in 1870, 15 percent in 1890, and 27.5 percent in 1910.[31] It might be argued that such statistics do not give a true picture of urbanization, since, especially in the southern part of the country, population centers with 20,000 or more inhabitants were nothing but overgrown villages, with the vast majority of the inhabitants deriving their livelihood from agriculture. Yet in these population centers, urban aspects of life often coexisted for centuries with elements of a rural life-style. Besides, the population living in urban centers of over 50,000, which undoubtedly represented an urban way of life, nearly doubled in Italy between 1871 and 1901: it rose from 2,820,446 to 4,669,909,[32] and went on growing as a result of increasing industrialization.

Industrialization was on the upswing to such an extent that economic historians talk of an "industrial revolution" at the turn of the nineteenth century. If we take 1938 as the base, the production of Italian manufacturing industries during 1891–95 represented 28 percent of 1938 output, and 59 percent during the years 1911–15.[33] The period between 1896 and 1908 registered an especially marked increase in industrial output, with an annual average growth of 6.7 percent.[34] The development of industrial production coincided with a European-wide economic upswing, but the growth in Italy was especially dramatic: per capita industrial production increased in that country by two-thirds during the 1901–13 period alone, and total production grew 87 percent. Italy's share of the world's industrial production rose from 2.7 percent during the last five years of the nineteenth century to 3.1 percent during the period 1906–10.[35] The Catholics' anxiety about the growth of the industrial working class was apparently built on the social reality of Italy. In 1861 there were only 9,000 industrial concerns in the kingdom. In 1903 there were

117,000, and by 1914, 244,000. The number of those employed by them was 188,000 in 1861, rose to 1,275,100 in 1903, and nearly doubled again to 2,304,500 by 1914.[36]

Rural to Urban Migration

A consequence of growing industrialization was a large-scale rural to urban migration. Because this involved social dislocation, it alarmed Catholics, especially those of conservative persuasion, many of whom seemed to have been convinced that the good life could be had only in the country. They saw the peasants who left the villages for jobs in the urban centers as committing an act of folly. They also labeled them "deserters." How widespread and lasting this perception was is shown by the fact that the term was applied to peasant migrants by *Azione Sociale* as late as in 1913, making the folly of the "deserters" fully clear:

> Leaving their villages, the migrants [to urban centers] often abandon religious practices and sometimes even the morality that these include. It becomes increasingly difficult to provide them with religious services; the family, the cell of social organism, disintegrates; the village of birth, with its old church tower, the house and land of the ancestors, its memories and traditions, are lost, and little by little even the idea of patriotism disappears. . . . The moral consequences of the urban agglomeration are disastrous. Certain theaters, cinemas, a variety of attractions, the bad newspapers with large circulation, and other forms of dishonest propaganda, all contribute to the ruin of people. Not only their morals but almost always their health too are wrecked as licentiousness and illness in most cases bring overwhelming, frightful misery.[37]

The *Azione Sociale* was voicing the constant conservative concern about "keeping them down on the farm" and away from the evil that awaited the peasant migrants in urban centers. This was a recurring theme at Catholic congresses and also the subject of circulars sent out by Medolago. The famous 1879 speech by Sassoli, which set up the landlords as little "kings," also displayed concern about them remaining without "subjects" because "the agricultural population deserts work in the fields." This was a sideline only, with the marquis's attention unselfishly concentrated on the damage the "deserters" did to themselves.[38] That concern was apparently shared by most village priests at the turn of the century. The priests, usually of peasant origins, saw in the urban center everything that was wrong with modern life—the seat of error and corruption, the kingdom of Satan, as their bishops perceived it as well. After moving to the towns, the peasant migrants, the clergy argued, ceased to keep their religious practices; they worked on Sundays and ate meat on Fridays. The *centro urbano* was seen by the clergy, as it was by Catholic conservatives in general, as the hotbed of religious indifference and even of downright hostility to religion, where Protestant missionaries, liberal ideologues, Freemasons, and Socialist agitators threatened the unsuspecting and innocent souls of the peasant migrants.[39] A priest reported from Turin that those coming from small rural communities carried the "Christian traditions of their villages"; but in the urban environment, they "come into contact with other people who are perverted and corrupted and who lead them into the ranks of the Socialists."[40]

Pastoral Work among the Migrants

The "dechristianization" of rural folk in an urban setting remained the dominant theme of the Catholics' discussion of the rural-urban migration. Their missionary zeal, attempting to save souls from the devil's grip, certainly had to do with all those agents of Satan who were out to ensnare souls, but it was also rooted in rapid industrialization and the attendant fast growth of urban centers. As cities like Turin burst at their seams and expanded outward, the new quarters of the towns were without religious structures. The priests who attempted to minister to the religious needs of the populace in these new *quartieri,* almost always inhabited by the working classes, were missionaries wandering among strange people. Such was not the condition to which the clergymen, often of rural origins, were accustomed. Their life-style demanded that they know their flock intimately, and their parishioners who were former peasants expected this. But because of the extreme stringency of the finances of the post-Risorgimento church, stripped of most of its economic assets, there was no money for the construction even of vestries, let alone of churches.

For lack of places to worship, those people in the new industrial suburbs who wanted to go to church had to travel to the central city, where large and splendid structures raised in the church's earlier and more prosperous times bespoke the glory of God but were largely empty during services. The peasants-turned-workers, used to the intimacy of small churches filled with folks they knew, must have found these houses of God strange and intimidating, especially since the upper-class people who worshiped there, ladies in fancy hats among them, looked down on them.

New parishes were gradually established in the working-class periphery of cities. Turin, for instance, registered four of these during the period 1897–1906, and seven during the ten years that followed. But the expansion of the church organizations and structures was not fast enough. Besides, it came in an ad hoc and haphazard manner because a strategy for dealing with the pastoral problems related to the growth of the industrial working class was lacking. That was the price paid for the wishfulness involved in the Catholics' hostility toward capitalistic development and their tendency to hide their heads in the sands of the past, hoping that industrialization, perceived as utterly unfitting for human nature, would somehow just go away.

The lack of financial resources and the weight of a negative view of social reality were not the only problems that held back the church's penetration into the ranks of the industrial working class. As the oldest bureaucracy in existence, the church was also burdened with the mentality that emphasized the interests and rights of those leading the bureaucratic structure, often at the expense of those the bureaucracy was called into being to serve. Thus the archdiocese of Turin, instead of providing leadership for an aggressive expansion of the church's presence in the new quarters of the city, was constantly bogged down with jurisdictional issues involving alleged violations of the territorial rights of the leaders of existing parishes as the newly established ones had to reach into areas under the control of old ones. These disputes demonstrated over and over that, aside from a bureaucratic mentality focused on defending bailiwicks, the clergy also had a tendency to alienate the faithful because of its inclination toward a relationship with parishioners based on power and authority. The immense respect awarded to the village priest who "reigned" over the peasants[41] was ill-fitting to urban situations, if not for other reasons, because it required time to be established among the newly arrived inhabitants of the urban peripheries.

The *contadini in città* ("peasants in the city") apparently were unwilling to accept violations of their rights and interests even if this was done by men in clerical garb. The Jesuits, especially insistent upon their property rights and the legalistic assertion of their authority, were embroiled in controversies in Turin for a long time. The fathers claimed that ecclesiastic laws gave "the faithful no rights whatsoever to interfere in the reorganization of parishes," but some of the parishioners wanted to break away and establish a new parish for themselves, eventually threatening to "invade" and "occupy" the church and throw out the Jesuits if they went on with their practice of "wanting to save only the souls of the rich." "They want the poor children to play on the street during the service"; they refuse "to hear the confession of [these] children; they send them away . . . ; they are busy with the confessions of all those *signori* and *marchesi,* the nobility of Turin."[42]

As these statements culled from petitions signed by working-class parishioners show, there was more to the decline of religion among the working classes than the influence of assorted agitators sent by the devil to corrupt the souls of those goodhearted but naïve peasant immigrants. The disinclination of the Turin Jesuits to take an interest in working people was not an isolated phenomenon. Some priests became frustrated because they failed to reach the urban working class, through no fault of their own but rather because of a lack of financial resources, and apparently turned to blaming the victim, as we often do in situations involving failures in human relationships.

"How will we ever reach the world of the industrial worker who runs away from us, considering us his enemies, while we are his best friends." This cry of a Catholic pamphlet issued in 1911[43] was ironic in light of the fact that workers in Turin still had to threaten to occupy a church in 1917 in order to secure for themselves and their children a place at services. Maybe it was because they were in earnest—they occupied factories a few years later—that they aroused the hostility of the clergy, trapped in their wishful thinking about the presumed docility of the "inferior classes."

The Aversion to the Industrial Working Class

The working classes' unwillingness to relate to the clergy and the upper classes as children to fathers came as a shock to conservatively inclined Catholics. If this unwillingness went as far as standing up to the father figures, the shock tended to turn to hysteria. The very existence of organizations of workers, independent of the *padroni* and of the supervision of the clergy, was conceived as a threat "to the moral order."[44] The challenge these represented was decried as a sign of selfishness on the part of the workers. The conservative understanding of the industrial working class was clearly and unequivocally laid on the line by a Catholic paper published in Turin. If it had to be said, it was best said in Turin, a major center of industrial development, and said in the pages of a publication called the *Voce dell'Operaio,* the *Voice of the Worker.* No doubt trying to reach out to the industrial working class, the paper spoke in 1908 of the workers' inclination to "work as little as possible and take the highest possible pay; and if they cannot get what they want, [they resort] to strikes, boycott, and now they are beginning to turn to sabotage. The less they work, the more they want to get paid, because they conceive work as suffering and pay as the most important coefficient of enjoyment."[45]

Those workers who wanted a clearer understanding of themselves could turn to another Catholic paper that detailed the problem with a neat summary at the end:

> The industrial worker believes he is a victim of destiny; he sees in his superiors tyrants and in the capitalists greedy exploiters. [The workers] submit to work out of necessity, but they hate it because they are persuaded that it benefits the hated *padroni.*

1. [The worker] is insatiable as far as pay goes and always discontented with his status.
2. His heart is full of bile and class hatred because he is convinced that the diversity of social classes is an injustice.
3. [He] does not like to work.
4. [He] has little patience and inclination to tolerate the miseries of life.[46]

An upper-class fear of the industrial working class, which was becoming increasingly rebellious and disinclined to accept "tutelage," merged with the hostility toward socialism in a Catholic publication's description of workers who "are leaving the plants with an insolence, a provocative smile on their faces, swear words on their lips, contempt for religion [in their hearts], and hatred for the rich. [They are] vulgar, arrogant, domineering, insulting; the dregs of society who disseminate disturbances among the masses; cowards who knife in betrayal; who break the display windows of stores and prevent people from really working."[47] The historian Daniele Menozzi, who discovered these pieces of wisdom, also uncovered evidence that these characterizations of the industrial working class coincided word for word with statements made by Bonnefon Craponne, the president of the Association of Industrialists.

One might assign little importance to statements by Catholic publications in one Italian city, even if this was the heartland of industrialization, but there were numerous other manifestations of hostility toward the industrial working class in Catholic publications. A pamphlet released in 1909 by the Unione Popolare, the propaganda organization of Catholic Action, depicted the *operaio*, the industrial worker, as a "vicious, nasty revolutionary in society, unfaithful to his employer because he had forgotten or rejected God, lost the idea of his proper dignity, lost his conscience."[48]

We might also recall the extremely hostile presentation of striking workers in *L'Osservatore Romano*, quoted earlier. Toniolo, who asserted that the very existence of the industrial working class represented a threat to society, expressed a view common among Catholic leaders. Furthermore, the hostility toward the industrial working class manifest in statements like these did not cease as time went by and very likely was a factor in the reorientation of Catholic labor organizing efforts toward the peasantry. The decline of industrial unionism and relative increase in the agricultural membership in Catholic unions that began in 1911 was not announced as an official policy. In fact, nothing was said about it at the most important Catholic congress in a decade, the meeting held in 1910 in Modena. But because it came in the immediate aftermath of that congress, the explanation of what appears to have been a change in the orientation of Catholic labor organizing has to be sought in what happened in Modena.

8

He Who Is a Saint Cannot Disagree with the Pope

The Vatican Attempts to Reintroduce the Mixed Union

The congresses of the Opera were once held annually, but it was not until seven years after the one held in Bologna in 1903 that another national Catholic congress was called. Pius X, like a monarch who decided it was quite possible—in fact, advantageous—to govern without a parliament, did not allow one to be called even years after the reorganization of Catholic Action he had ordered was complete and the new *unioni* were functioning, which had happened by 1907. If he was afraid the divisive fight between the conservative leadership and the activists would resume at a national congress, his fears were justified.

The activists' anger exploded when it became obvious that the delegates to the 1910 congress faced yet another attempt to reintroduce the mixed union, which they thought had been laid to rest seven years earlier. The perception of the demise of the *misto* in Bologna was so widespread that it found its way into historical works written decades after the events.[1] Francesco Magri was almost alone among the historians of Italian Catholic Action to notice that after the 1903 Bologna congress a systematic attempt was made to revive the mixed union. He connected this with some unnamed "conservatives" within Catholic Action.[2] The evidence that has accumulated since 1956, when Magri published his *From Christian Syndicalist Movement to Democratic Syndicalism,* strongly suggests that the return of the mixed was not just a quixotic attempt on the part of the conservatives within the Catholic leadership but an integral part of the pattern that Pius X prescribed for the reorganized Catholic Action.

While preparations were under way for the 1910 Modena congress, including the reintroduction of the *misto* as a basic organizational form, Mario Chiri, a functionary of the Economic Social Union, was hard at work gathering statistical data. Soon after the congress, Chiri provided some astonishing information when he reported that only 4 of the 374 organizations of Catholic labor could be classified as *misto*. As it turned out, even these four were not really mixed. Although they did not bother to replace old statutes that called for a mixed membership, these four organizations, in Chiri's words, "did not, in fact, include *padroni*" as members.[3]

The obvious question is whether anybody knew before 1911, when Chiri's findings were published, that in spite of decades of talk about it and efforts to create it, the mixed union remained a figment of the conservatives' imagination. When in 1905 Bishop Radini was about to occupy his episcopal seat in Bergamo, he was handed confidential memorandums detailing the difficulties he was about to face in "Italy's first diocese," as Pius X called the area where the central offices of the Economic Social Union were located. Monsignor Carlo Castelletti, who served for over twenty years as *Assistente Ecclesiastico,* informed the bishop with the memorandums that the mixed union was an utter failure in "Italy's first diocese."[4]

Nevertheless, in 1906, three years after the Bologna congress, which presumably concluded the debate over the usefulness of the *misto,* an article appeared in *Azione Sociale* entitled "The Past and Future of Economic Action among Italian Catholics." It clearly indicated that the mixed union was included in the marching orders given by the pope to the reorganized Italian Catholic Action. The article's critical importance was also highlighted by the fact that it was signed by Toniolo, the chief theoretician of Catholic social action. That he was in touch with Pius X as the pope personally oversaw the reorganization of Catholic Action became obvious later from Toniolo's published correspondence. Toniolo's message in the 1906 article was that, in spite of the decision reached in Bologna, the mixed union had to remain on the agenda. The *semplice* was to be restricted to "the great industrial enterprises and large landed estates where day labor is predominant and, because of the conflict of interests, any other combination would be impossible and complex." The *misto* was to be organized in "small-size industries, collective rentals [*colonia parziaria*], and among small landholders, where the intimacy of life and of interests favors solidarity."[5]

An editorial in *L'Osservatore Romano* in May, 1910, shortly before the Modena congress convened, forcefully reminded readers that the mixed unions were an indispensable means of "social regeneration" and that they "represent, and must represent, the true ideal for Catholic social action."[6] The double affirmative of the official paper of the Vatican was reaffirmed by the leaders of Catholic Action when they finalized the plans for the congress, which included the organization of labor as a major topic of discussion. Beginning in June the General Directorate of Catholic Action held a series of meetings, and by the third one, on September 25, the program of the congress was decided. The General Directorate sent a telegram announcing the agenda to the pope, speaking of "filial attachment" "to the Apostolic See, infallible Teacher of the truth." The format of the pass to be used at the congress was also made public: it carried the picture of Pius X framed in lombard-gothic motifs, the pope's favored style in art. The tenseness in Catholic leadership, submerged in the terse reports about the meetings on the pages of *L'Osservatore Romano*,[7] came to the surface in a circular released by the General Directorate on September 12.[8] It issued a stern warning against "vain and sterile discussions, useless and untimely complaints," and urged a "concord of intentions and of zeal for doing good."

The meetings of the General Directorate were called to coordinate the proposals of the various *unioni,* which were prepared at the assemblies of their own governing bodies. The Economic Social Union held its first meeting in April. Medolago's presidential address displayed a studied opaqueness, a tendency to deal only with generalities. He spoke of internal conflict between "diverse tendencies" that "paralyzed" Catholic Action in previous years. He also criticized the prevalent tendency in the Catholic labor movement "to be concerned almost exclusively with gaining limited goals and immediate economic advantages" instead of following "the light of the immutable principles of sciences, Catholic doctrine, and the instructions of the Holy See."[9]

Aside from this veiled reference, he did not mention the labor movement. His avoidance of the topic might have given hope to some of the activists, but it bothered Toniolo's professorial inclination toward orderliness. "We are in trouble if we don't bring forth our ideas in neat and positive [forms]," he wrote in a letter to Caissotti in August.[10] But the professor did not need to worry. Further careful considerations and, one may add without hesitation— although it cannot be documented with extant evidence—consultation with the Vatican eventually produced a document of great clarity. The theses that the Unione Economico Sociale proposed for acceptance in Modena twenty days before the congress advocated "mixed professional unions in situations where the economic and moral interests of the *padroni* are closely tied to those of the workers (rentals in agriculture [*agricoltura a colonia*] small-sized industries, and small commercial enterprises) . . . [and] simple professional unions in situations where such sharing of interests does not exist."[11]

To what extent this was a case of *Roma locuta* will remain a subject of debate until the background materials become available, but ten days before the congress, the editors of *L'Osservatore Romano,* anxious to make things clear and unequivocal, printed the proposals that were to be presented by Niccolo Rezzara on behalf of the Economic Social Union.

There are some intriguing questions for Vaticanologists in connection with Rezzara's report. For instance, how "official" was the official paper of the Vatican? Pius X, who was more than once quick to react to what he did not like on the pages of provincial Catholic papers,[12] cannot have disagreed with the assertion of *L'Osservatore Romano* in May that the mixed unions "represent and must represent the true ideal for Catholic Action." This was the opening shot in the battle about the mixed union in Modena. If it was not a direct expression of the pope's wish, was it a trial balloon testing the possibility of something Pius X thought would be nice to have if it could be had?

This suggestion appears to be a sacrilege in connection with a pope whose virtues gained him sainthood and who was very forcefully consistent when it came to principles. Yet though he represented eternal truth, as the head of an organization he could not always remain above practical and tactical considerations. His office demanded that he stress what society should have been and eventually ought to be, but at least on some occasions he also had to come to terms with reality by finding out what could and could not be done. That he used the pages of the *Civiltà Cattolica* for testing public reaction to ideas is documented irrefutably.[13] If indeed the *Civiltà,* to quote Pius's secretary, Monsignor Bressan, always said "what the pope desired," how did the editorials in *L'Osservatore Romano* relate to the directing will of the pope?

Aside from issues of interpretation of sources, the battle over the mixed union in Modena and Rezzara's report open questions of a personal nature. Why was the report not delivered by Medolago? Was this connected with the fact that the count's presidential address in April deliberately avoided the theme of the organizational forms of labor? Questions might be raised about Toniolo as well. He was the *rapporteur* on the subject of labor at previous congresses, and was asked as late as 1906 to write a programmatic article for the Economic Social Union. In Modena he did deliver an address, but this was to the plenary session of the congress and not to the meeting of the Unione Economico Sociale, which held separate sessions like all the other *unioni.*

Toniolo's Modena address was general in nature but did touch upon the organization of labor. The reference, somewhat veiled, seems to have been to the simple union alone,[14] giving the impression of a contrast with Toniolo's 1906 article, which clearly presented both the mixed and the simple unions as the forms Catholic labor organizations would take. If indeed this was the case, and Toniolo's Modena speech represented a change in position, was it an expression of disapproval of Rezzara's report? In view of the fact that in every situation he accepted the will of the pope as the will of God, [15] it is unthinkable that Toniolo joined the ranks of the activists in a rebellion against the pope. Thus Toniolo's advocacy of the *semplice,* if indeed his speech can be called that, weakens arguments that suggest determination on the part of Pius X to bring back the mixed at whatever cost. Toniolo always seemed to be aware of inclinations "up there," in the Vatican, and by 1910 he became extremely wary of saying or doing anything contrary to the pope's wishes. Hence an advocacy of the simple union as the sole organizational form of Catholic labor on Toniolo's part can be taken as an almost certain sign that Pius X may not have been firmly committed to the mixed union as a viable form for the present. He is likely to have thought that it was something that should have been, or even could have been, in existence, and hence the drive to reinstate it. But in the end, it was likely to be rejected at the congress as impractical, since this view was so widely held that it could not have been hidden from the pope. In fact, one is inclined to posit the rather cynical hypothesis that both Medolago and Toniolo avoided delivering the report, which represented an attempt to reinstate the mixed union, because they found this suggestion unrealistic. For whatever reason Rezzara got stuck with it, and one is inclined to pity him because the insistence upon the mixed must have represented an even greater violation of his perception of reality than it did for Medolago and Toniolo.

Rezzara was an activist who came to Modena as the hero of the 1909 Ranica strike, which he led, amid national publicity, to victory over the *padroni.* "Which one is the real Rezzara?" asks the historian Dino Secco Suardo.[16] Is it the Rezzara of the Ranica strike, or the Rezzara of the Modena congress who a few months after Ranica drew the ire of the activists and eventual historical ignominy for attempting to revive the mixed union. Secco Suardo leaves the question unanswered, but there is no need to posit a paradox in connection with this case. Secco Suardo gives the key to the explanation when elsewhere in his volume he notes that the affairs of Italian Catholic Action during the papacy of Pius X reminded him of Napoleon's dictum according to which the "best soldier was not the most courageous, but the most obedient one." Rezzara, to his merit, was apparently willing to take on a battle in which he was sacrificed in an attempt to regain a position, for no better reason than to prove that the position could not be regained.

That this was the case is strongly suggested by Rezzara's behavior in Modena. He showed no resentment for getting stuck with an unpleasant task that Medolago probably imposed on him in a manner typical of bureaucratic organizations, in which the bosses inevitably dump such tasks on subordinates and reserve for themselves chores that promise to prove them clearsighted, wise, and successful as leaders. Rezzara backed up the proposals of the Unione Economico Sociale in his report[17] by arguing that

> every apostle of this beneficial action has to try to arrive, little by little and through a methodical and rational process, at the organization of professional corporations either mixed, where these are possible, or simple unions where the first cannot be constituted. Since capital and labor within branches of activities share common interests to develop, protect, and defend, their harmonious coordination is indispensable. This can best be achieved in the mixed unions, with the natural and permanent organisms of these. [But such a task] is more difficult in the simple unions, which have distinct and separate organisms, even if these do not suffer from convulsions.

Rezzara then pronounced something that must have sounded like a call for retreat: "No one among us has any illusion about the possibility of constituting mixed unions. A little bit because it is believed or feared that there is conflict among classes, something that clouds even the brightest minds, a bit because of the ignorance of certain working classes, too abandoned and depressed, a distance between the two factors [classes] is maintained, and these accuse each other of distrust."

The Activists' Refusal

In trying to please everybody, Rezzara managed to say the right thing in the wrong way as far as the more radical activists were concerned. His attempt to blame the failure of the mixed union somewhat one-sidedly on the "ignorance" of working people, when everybody high and low knew that the *padroni* too avoided joining the workers in common organizations, could hardly be pleasing to the activists' ears. But that was only a side issue in the attempt to discard the conclusions reached and duly approved by a majority vote at the previous Catholic congress in Bologna. In view of an apparent contradiction in the keynote address, which insisted upon the mixed union but acknowledged its impracticality, the activists could not be blamed if they wanted clarification as to exactly what direction their efforts were to take in the future.

The activists were charitable enough not to personally attack the hero of the Ranica strike, who, in the language of bureaucracy, was just doing his job. They vented their anger and frustration on the institution Rezzara represented. What followed his report, which closed with the suggestion to accept the proposals for the mixed union, was, in the words of the reporter for *L'Osservatore Romano,* a "violent indictment of the Unione Economico Sociale."[18]

Rezzara can hardly be said to have fought over the mixed union. Apparently he went to the congress instructed to concede this point if necessary, and he conceded rather quickly, admitting that the "mixed professional unions are by now a utopian dream of the past." He had a position, prepared by Toniolo years before, to retreat to, a position that was a marvel of compromise between ideals and reality: "The mixed organizations," Rezzara said, "must remain abandoned for now, but they must not be forgotten, like a torch that must never be extinguished." The hope for the eventual victory of truth, charity, and the mixed union was apparently enough to placate worries "up there."

The modification of the resolution proposed by the Economic Social Union, involving the deletion of the mixed union from the final version accepted by the congress, was a clear victory for the activists. But letting this initiative die was apparently as far as Pius X was willing to retreat in the face of the rebellion of the activists. As for strikes and class struggle, another issue that concerned the activists very much, Rezzara remained firm in the face of a flood of criticism: "It cannot be our program, because it is not Christian, it is not civil, it is not social to organize the professions in order to line them up, one against the other, as if the transitory fact of seeing some in conflict with others would be considered permanent and would have to be accepted as the principle and basis for professional organizations."

But activists like Restito Cecconelli, a priest from Padua, persisted. Criticizing the resolutions proposed by the Economic Social Union, he said:

Look at the verbs that fill this document: orders, wants, deliberates, advises. . . . Now this preoccupation induces fear in me. . . . We had better stay home if we cannot say what's in our hearts. In the report presented by Rezzara, there is no mentioning of strikes, yet we had to organize and sustain several of them, but from the Economic Social Union never came advice, never instructions in spite of the fact that it was indispensible that we make these strikes. . . . As far as the mixed unions are concerned we declare to be absolutely against them. Those who know about organizing from practical experience know about the difficulties of propagandizing. The peasants watch us carefully, us Catholics and priests, to see if we are sincere, if, after delivering our propaganda, we end up riding with Count A and Baron B. . . . They will respect us only if we return home on our own poor wagons.

Because the clamor of the activists would not cease, Filippo Crispolti, the president of the congress, interrupted the debate to warn that "congresses can be useful, but they are not indispens-able."[19] Crispolti's remarks clearly reflected the position of Pius X better than Cecconelli's. Approval of strikes as legitimate means employed by Catholic labor unions was not forthcoming from the pope's lips or pen. He did not even say a word that would have indicated his acceptance of a temporary abandonment of the mixed union. If he indeed "accepted" it, his acceptance was announced by silence. "The Pope will remain silent," he remarked when he con-sented to a change of momentous importance, the lifting of the *Non Expedit* on a case-by-case basis. But in one of his last public pro-nouncements, in May, 1914, Pius X referred to those who misinter-preted him "by attributing a meaning entirely contrary to the one wanted by the pope, and consequently taking for agreement some-thing that was but a prudent silence." He thus warned those who would interpret his silence as agreement.

What he said was not new. One of the basic principles of church history is that changes in the position of the church often become manifest by the silence of pontiffs about subjects that might have been dear to the hearts of one or more of their predecessors. Given the fact that, as Toniolo observed, one pope "does not all of a sudden deny the direction given by another,"[20] changes in the life of the church come through the gradual abandonment of positions previously taken. Change comes in the church by drawing a veil of silence over subjects.

Later events strongly suggest that the silence of Pius X immediately following the Modena congress was not an act of approval. Yet the historian has to deal with evidence from the aftermath of Modena that is unequivocal in indicating some degree of hesitation on the part of the Vatican. Right after the meeting closed, in an approving review of the decisions of the Modena congress *L'Osservatore Romano* did not mention the mixed union, and emphasized the participants' "desire to spend Catholic social efforts especially in favor of the proletariat."

Four days later, on November 18, the editors returned to the proceedings of the congress in a more critical mood, warning Italian Catholics of their duty to submit to the Holy See:

> Obedience to pontifical leadership means [for Catholic Action] that it must not only resolutely escape every suspicion of class struggle, the suspicion of which in itself was nobly avoided by the congress, but it also means acquiring the marked characteristics of an action that, without weaknesses and unbecoming servility, is an element and a precious coefficient of harmony and concord between capital and labor, and of the pacification of various social classes by disciplining, coordinating them, and harmonizing their interests, rights, and reciprocal obligations. Obedience to pontifical leadership means to imprint our professional organizations with a markedly Catholic characteristic, flying freely in the light of the day the flag of our sacred principles as the voice of our supreme Teacher reminded and ordered us to do.[21]

If we read this statement, and we must, as a rejection of class struggle, what are we to do with an editorial in *L'Osservatore Romano* that, seventeen months later in April, 1912, seemed to express resignation to the "peaceful struggle of competition [*pacifiche lotte della concorrenza*]" carried on by the "professional" organizations? Whatever the exact meaning of the sentence, with it the editors of the Vatican's official paper came as close as they ever would to presenting as legitimate the economic conflict among classes. In this they concurred with Biederlack's updated and especially German Catholic understanding of conflict and strikes.[22]

How much of what *L'Osservatore Romano* wrote was on instructions from above and how much was due to the principle of objective reporting, which the editors presumably accepted, is an interesting if frustrating subject for those scholars who attempt to unravel the history of Italian Catholic journalism. The Vatican's paper did report the activists' argument that the Catholics should organize "the working classes alone, since the superior classes possess a natural inclination [*cemento naturale*] toward organization that is lacking in [working-class] people." But these arguments did not prevail in the end; the accepted resolution spoke of the importance of "giving attention and care to the professional organization of the middle class [*ceto medio*], which constitutes a great moral force and exercises a balancing socioeconomic function, an influence that sometimes is more prevalent than any others."

Then, to be sure that nobody would be deprived of the beneficial activities of the Unione Economico Sociale, there was the effort to organize the *padroni* too. The resolutions of the Modena congress did not specifically mention this, but year after year Medolago sent out circulars about the *organizzazioni padronali*. The one mailed out on November 23, 1912, quoted a *motu proprio* of Pius X stating that "the concept of Christian Democracy has to be cleansed [*bisogna rimuovere*] from the inconvenience that concentrates all the effort in favor of the lowest classes and seems to neglect the superior classes, which are no less important in the conservation and perfecting of society."

Self-accusingly, the signatories of the circular—Medolago, Rezzara, and Monsignor Luigi Daelli—"confessed" that "until now" "Catholic social action was almost exclusively focused on the needy classes, while the *classi padronali* were almost forgotten."[23] The fact that a circular during the next year was still asking for suggestions as to how to organize the *padroni* indicates that Medolago, who did not manage to perform the magic of pulling one mixed union after another from his hat, was failing his taskmaster in the Vatican once more when the pope demanded that he organize the *padroni* in order to parallel the organizations of the workers.

It was not that the worthies of industry and agriculture did not see the need for organizing. For the landowners there was the Associazione Agraria, which gave such an excellent account of itself with armed terror squads during the Parma strike in 1908. For industry, associations representing particular lines of production were rapidly being consolidated into organizations gathering the employers of more than one industry. An example of such organizations was the Piedmont Industrial League, which was established shortly before the General Confederation of Labor was called into being in 1906. Then the regional confederations of employers were in turn consolidated into a single national unit. When in 1911 the Associazione fra le società per azioni, a national body, held its first congress, the delegates represented more than half of the corporate capital of all Italy.[24]

9

Religion, the Best Custodian of Justice

The Landless Peasants and the Catholic Labor Movement

The *padroni* organized, but apparently refused to submit their organizations to Catholic control because they did not want to assume the paternalistic obligations that Thomistic theology assigned to them. Admitting that the age of paternalism was over meant abandoning the intellectual baggage of Neo-Thomism, and that did not come easily while Pius X sat on the papal throne. The weight of this intellectual tradition, which demanded the avoidance of class conflict and strikes, is at least a partial explanation of an apparent turn away from the industrial working class. The conservative leadership felt fear and aversion toward this class because they considered it hostile toward the "superior classes," and thus bound to bring conflict to society.

A reorientation of Catholic labor organizing efforts away from the industrial working class and toward the peasantry seems to have picked up momentum soon after the Modena congress, in which the leadership of Catholic Action insisted upon the avoidance of class struggle. As early as 1911, the proportion of agricultural as opposed to industrial members in Catholic unions began to change in favor of the agricultural category, which was 35.5 percent in 1910. In 1911 it was 39.2 percent, 42,392 of a total of 108,021. By 1914 the number of those who derived a livelihood from agriculture was 63,317, 61.3 percent of a total of 103,326.[1]

If these statistics reflect a conscious turn away from the industrial sector and toward the peasantry,[2] this might be explained by the fact that the hold of religion was thought to be greater among peasants than among industrial workers. Thus more compliance with the demands of Thomistic theology was expected in rural society and consequently an easing of the conflict between the Catholic leaders and the activists.

If indeed such expectations motivated the leadership of Catholic Action, a number of activists must have known this to be an illusion, as many activists found out by 1910, the priests among them in an especially dramatic way. Although during the previous five years a fairly widespread movement among the rural clergy toward taking the side of the peasantry in conflicts was suppressed by the Vatican, the activities of those priests became a part of the dialectic of the development in the countryside of an ideology based on class consciousness. The men of cloth advocating and sustaining strikes[3] did more than any Socialist propagandist could to free the rural population from the old-style paternalistic perception of the social order.

Even though class consciousness and the willingness of the peasantry to take on the *padroni* was on the rise, the Catholics were probably right in expecting that class conflict, at least as far as their organizations were concerned, could be kept to a minimum in the countryside. This was in part because they declared it their major task to defuse conflict, and they did their best to avoid strikes. Their hope of being able to minimize them was likely sustained by the characteristics of the membership of their rural unions.

When organizing among the peasantry, the Socialists concentrated their efforts on the *braccianti,* the landless peasants, and had trouble even considering the membership of smallholders and *mezzadri,* peasants who sharecropped land on a permanent basis. With the Catholics it was the other way around. They considered the day laborers the rural equivalent of the urban proletariat and were not exactly enthusiastic about organizing them. They were certainly more disposed to turn to the smallholders and the sharecroppers.

Exactly how this prejudice affected the membership of Catholic unions is a subject of further research, which should be forthcoming even before materials in central archives become available because sampling techniques and the use of computers will allow for reasonably accurate understanding on the basis of limited data. But even before the results are in, one can posit a tentative hypothesis on the basis of expressed intentions and ideological motivations. This hypothesis would be that the number of the *braccianti* in Catholic unions will eventually be proved to be insignificant in comparison with the other two categories, the smallholders and the *mezzadri,* the sharecroppers.

If such was the case, the Catholics were failing to reach a large part of the rural population when they ignored the *braccianti* in their organizational efforts: the 1911 national census showed just about half of the peasants to be in that category. Of the 10 million or so active in agricultural occupations, less than 2 million were land-owners, about 1 million rented the land they worked, with another 2 million sharecropping; 5.1 million, over half of the total, were *braccianti,* landless laborers.[4]

For them, given the high and increasing population densities in rural areas, unemployment was always a threat and underemployment a permanent condition of life. In some areas like the communities near Ferrara, they usually worked no more than 90 days a year. Almost everywhere, if they had 150 days of work, it was a good year for them.[5] As for their living conditions, data suggest they had not improved much since 1886 when Bishop Bonomelli, who had a high concentration of *braccianti* in his diocese, observed them:

> The duties of our ministry often led us into the homes of peasants, . . . and we found ourselves not in dwellings intended for men but in what appeared to be stalls, or better put, dens. And we cannot fail to mention that we saw really luxurious stalls as well as peasant dwellings that were tumbledown and dilapidated! We saw stalls with glass windows to give light to the animals and rooms of peasants, from the windows of which the glass was missing, with paper, often rotten, providing protection for the inhabitants. During the cruel winter one could see through the ill-fitted ceiling the blue of the sky! *Padroni,* do not excuse yourselves by saying: "the peasants looked it over and accepted them at free will, in fact we did them a favor by letting them live there."[6]

The landless laborers had to accept whatever employment they could find, and the miserable housing conditions that went with it. The alternative to local employment was seasonal migrant labor, and although this was to be found within Italy, it separated the laborers from their families and was likely to offer housing, nutrition, and salary conditions even worse than those on the local estates. Moreover up to 10 percent of the money earned by the migrant workers went to the *incettatore*, the man who located and contracted the work.

Historians describing the seasonal migration of labor in Italy at the turn of the century often compare it to conditions in the United States during the depression of the 1930s. The similarities were indeed remarkable, not only in the miserable conditions of life, which were without the minimal requirements of nutrition and hygiene, but also in the high degree of exploitation, which produced an incredible variety of conditions in the salaries of the seasonal migrant workers, who numbered nearly a million in 1905. They had to take any available jobs and wages. Hence the migrant workers were the despair of labor organizers, for they turned up, trainload after trainload, as strikebreakers. Only by organizing the migrant workers, a group as impossible to unionize as any ever will be, could labor hope to make headway in confronting the *padroni*. The drive and despair of organized labor are reflected in the fact that the first years of the twentieth century saw an increasing number of migrant workers appearing in unions.[7]

But these would rarely if ever be Catholic unions. Day laborers, migrant or not, were not the Catholics' favored people: the landless peasants reminded them too much of the industrial working class. By ignoring them, the Catholics wished them away. But the Catholics' neglect of the *braccianti* left them the tempting targets of the Socialist agitators, who were attracted to the rural proletariat for the very reason that repulsed the Catholics: their proletarian nature. Not having a share in the system of private property, the *braccianti* were considered by Catholics to be unstable as a social class. They could just as easily be swayed by revolutionary propaganda as the industrial proletariat; hence, their very existence, like that of the industrial working class, represented for Catholics a threat to the social order.

This made the *braccianti* a group favored by the Socialists, some of whom were anxious to gain a foothold among the peasantry. But others looked upon the countryside as a minefield to be avoided. Italian socialism might have indeed had its roots among peasants, as some of its historians were to argue.[8] But within the peasantry was a dialectical unity of opposites that attracted not only love but hostility as well on the part of Socialists. This was connected with the existence among the peasantry of the *piccola proprietà,* smallholdings, that positioned a part of the rural population on the side of the capitalistic order. At least such was the view of doctrinally oriented Socialists. But even those who were not inclined to make doctrinal propositions into dogmas had trouble deciding whether the smallholders were on the side of socialism or capitalism, or, as a Socialist with some religion in his background put it, "the devil's or God's."

The debate, which exploded at one Socialist congress after another, resembled the famous *disputatio* on the number of angels on the head of the pin. The stenographic records detailing it are also reminiscent of the debates of Catholic congresses. Groups of idealistically motivated intellectuals in both cases focused not on what the world was but on what it should have been, and what did not fit into the preconceived ideas of those intellectuals was simply ignored as if it did not exist.[9]

There were those who played a role at the Socialist congresses that was the functional equivalent of the activists' at Catholic meetings. They would point out that smallholdings were often nothing but "tiny pieces of land" amounting sometimes to less than an acre, leaving the owners for all practical purposes *braccianti* who had to hire themselves out almost year around to earn a living. Those who represented the reality principle in the debates would also argue that the unionization of the day laborers was in jeopardy if the smallholders were left out because they were available for hire almost year round, and thus were potential strikebreakers. Moreover, the Socialists needed the votes of the smallholders to establish pluralities in rural locations.[10]

Some suggested the cooperative movement as the way to "socialize" and "collectivize" the smallholders and build a "rural democracy." Others, like Gaetano Salvemini, created something of a scandal among fellow Socialists by talking of land reform, the "expropriation" and breakup of the large landed estates into smallholdings as a way to make a rural democracy a reality. But views such as his remained dissenting voices at Socialist congresses, which one after another reasserted the doctrinal position that smallholdings, like all private property, would eventually have to disappear as part of the collectivization of all means of production, including land. The Socialists' efforts on behalf of the smallholders masked a latent hostility that surfaced as talk about "neutralizing" the peasantry as a class.[11]

Such remained the position of the Italian Socialist party until after World War I, when the extreme left began to heed Lenin's advice and work, too late, toward an alliance with the peasantry. Given the lateness of this change in theoretical position, the Socialists' earlier success among the Italian peasantry seems to have come not because of, but somehow in spite of, their intentions. Their success came about in part because the smallholders, whom they tended to antagonize, were relatively small in numbers and almost nonexistent in some parts of Italy. Thus to a larger extent than in other countries, the impact of the international crisis of agriculture in Italy involved landless peasants who consituted over half of the active rural population. Largely neglected by the Catholics, the landless peasants became increasingly radicalized at the turn of the century and turned to socialism for a "new faith," to use the words of a speaker at the founding congress of the Federterra, the National Federation of Landworkers, which was heavily under Socialist influence.[12]

In embracing socialism with a fervor that resembled a religion, the *braccianti* gave away the intensity of their despair about the conditions of their lives. When it was established in 1901, Federterra represented over 700 labor leagues and rural unions with more than 150,000 members. Within a year, membership went up to 240,000, which was then just about the number of industrial workers in Socialist-inspired unions.

The Socialists managed to maintain a significant edge over the Catholics in organizing the peasantry. In 1913, for instance, the number of "red" Socialist-led rural labor leagues was 2,151, with 286,181 members. The number of "white" Catholic locals was 315, with a total membership of 52,220. In 1914 the membership of rural Catholic organizations went up to 63,312, a 21.2 percent increase, but that of the Socialists' showed a slight decline to 282,731. The

Catholics' concentration of their organizational efforts on the peasantry was paying off: at least in some areas, Catholic unions evidently began to succeed in competing with the Socialists. Even a comparison of the incomes of members shows the "white" leagues slightly ahead of the "red" ones in the Cremona area, Bonomelli's diocese.[13] These locals, which were often criticized by conservative church leaders for "classist excesses," probably included a large, if not overwhelming, majority of *braccianti:* their leader, Guido Miglioli (1879–1954), who was a layman, could afford to take the side of the working classes clearly and unequivocally. His followers idolized him; after a remarkably successful career as a Catholic labor organizer, he ended up as a deputy in the Parliament and a spokesman for the peasants, eventually gaining an international reputation.[14]

No doubt the leaders of Catholic Action thought that "classist excess," which was a code name for confrontation with the *padroni* and strikes, was less likely in union locals that primarily enrolled smallholders rather than *braccianti.* In defending private property and aiding those who were connected with it, however marginally, conservative Catholic leaders, who were themselves men of means, found themselves in the company of their onetime opponents, the liberals, who considered private property a "natural right," as did Thomistic Catholics. The Catholics were consistent in arguing that smallholders were respectful of law and order, whereas the landless peasants were destined to become prey of Socialist propaganda. Typical of the arguments that sustained the preference for organizing the peasant strata was Julien Fontaine's, a fighter against sociological modernism who was considered by Pius X to be of "profound theological and societal knowledge." In 1909 Fontaine indicated the aim of Christian Democracy to be the "gradual elevation" of the masses "to private property" and, with that, to "Christian virtue."[15]

If there was a conjunction between Catholic and liberal social doctrines on the question of the beneficial effects of property, there was also a basic agreement between the church leadership and the activists about the desirability of the survival of small landholdings. But when the activists carried the logic of the Neo-Thomistic argument one step further and talked of land reform, the breaking up of the *latifondi,* the large landed estates, into smallholdings, the limits of agreement between the activists and the conservative church leaders became clearly marked.

The Activists Press for Land Reform

The demand for land reform and the establishment of a system of smallholdings turned up both in Italy and abroad in Catholic debates about the European-wide "rural crisis."[16] Sometimes the argument in favor of distributing the *latifundia* emerged as a threat to the absentee aristocracy, who were reluctant to mend their sinful ways and reside at least a part of the year in the countryside. Their absence showed a failure by the upper classes to perform the paternalistic charitable functions; hence the threat, not illogical from the point of view of Neo-Thomistic theology, of the loss of their wealth.

Everywhere in Europe the Catholic invective against absentee landlords often degenerated into anti-Semitism through attacks on capitalism. This masked the anxiety of the rural aristocracy, which increasingly lost land to bourgeois entrepreneurs interested in investing their money in land. But to suggest that these were "mostly Jews" in Italy, as Medolago did at the 1891 congress of the Opera, was absurd. The count, in a mood of self-flagellation that sometimes overtook him, issued, in the words of the historian Giovanni Spadolini, "a violent invective against the *latifondi,* and latifundistic property," which Medolago said "were created by the big capitalists, mostly Jews."[17]

The activists, cognizant of the needs of rural people, developed the often misdirected Catholic criticism into a systematic attack on the *latifondi.* Perhaps because the stranglehold of the big estates was the strongest in the south, Sturzo's home ground, his relevant arguments were the most articulate, and incidentally often in agreement with those of Gaetano Salvemini, an unorthodox but persistent Socialist.

Sturzo considered the survival of medieval forms of land tenure one of the most important aspects of the economic problems of the south, especially Sicily. The system of *latifondi* implied agriculture of low labor intensity and did not provide enough jobs for the rapidly growing population. It also maintained an extreme contrast between the enormous wealth held by a few families and the poverty of landless peasants.[18]

One of Sturzo's complaints against the southern *latifondisti* was their absenteeism. Many of them lived in towns away from their property, which was left in the hands of caretakers whose prime concern was to enrich themselves at the expense of the peasants who worked the land. *Latifondi,* or parts of them, were often left uncultivated, depriving the landless peasants of their only possible employment. The accusing tone of Sturzo's analysis of the situation could easily be seen as expressing "an aversion for the higher classes," which according to Pius X was "contrary to the true spirit of Christian charity." But the aversion became a threat as Sturzo went on to demand land reform, the breakup of the *latifondi* into smallholdings.[19]

The activists searched for a historical precedent that would convince the church leadership of the validity of their suggestion of land reform. Thus Avolio praised the initiative of some Renaissance popes who "authorized the poor to cultivate to their advantage a third of the land left uncultivated, even against the will of the owners."[20] But the Renaissance popes, maybe because they studied Aquinas less closely, were apparently more inclined toward radicalism in the resolution of the Social Question than their modern successors. Both Leo XIII and Pius X apparently saw in the suggestion of land reform an assault on the principle of private property, rather than an extension of the benefits of property to large numbers of people, as the activists would have it.

The subject of land reform did not appear in *Rerum novarum* in spite of the fact that such a high-ranking churchman as Cardinal Manning suggested its inclusion.[21] Apparently Leo's mind was too enveloped by the Neo-Thomistic arguments in defense of private property to consider Manning's proposal. As for his successor, it is very unlikely that a study of his papers will modify the considered judgment of the historian Arturo Jemolo. In describing the willingness of Pius X to "accommodate" those who fought the Socialists in the defense of private property by lifting the Non Expedit, Jemolo characterized the pope's attitude by stating that "the poor could aspire to the charity of the rich, but were not entitled in the name of justice to any part of the goods of the rich."[22]

During the papacy of Pius X, the church leadership remained silent on the subject of land reform, which would have involved the expropriation by public authorities of large landed estates and their distribution as smallholdings. Such a move remained unthinkable for high churchmen not only because it would have violated the sacrosanct right of the *padroni* but also because of their mistrust of the state, in this case certainly not unjustified. A much publicized land reform immediately after Unification that involved the large holdings of the church, which the government confiscated, left these lands in the hands of either capitalistic entrepreneurs or local aristocrats, in both cases in the form of large estates.[23]

Mistrust of the state's involvement in land reform was a realistic position, but in view of the massive decline in the number of smallholdings, the continued Catholic insistence upon the importance and indispensability of the *piccola proprietà*[24] appeared anything but a manifestation of social realism.[25] As for the cultivation of the large estates, the Catholics advocated the consolidation of the old institution of the *mezzadria,* sharecropping, and of other somewhat similar forms, such as collective rental.[26] They considered these useful for eliminating the socioeconomic category of the *bracciante* by securing more stable situations through contractual obligations, either individual or collective. The Catholics' attempts to create long-range and eventually permanent relationships between the rural working class and the *padroni* represented a compromise. It left the owners' right to property intact, but at the same time stabilized the conditions of a large segment of the rural population, thus relieving the Catholics' great concern about the depopulation of the countryside, not to mention the aristocratic landowners' worry about becoming "heads" that possessed no "arms" to do the work for them. Yet another compromise was manifest in the arrangement: a resignation to the absenteeism of the landlords, who could secure themselves income for years to come and lounge in their urban *palazzi* knowing that what could be eked out of the land would be produced by peasants who also gained in a sharecropping arrangement if they produced more. The *mezzadria* came into being as an institution during the late Middle Ages when the feudal nobles drifted into towns for the first time and the nascent bourgeoisie, insecure about the future, turned to land, the ultimately secure investment. From its beginning, the *mezzadria* was tailored to absenteeism and suited perfectly the needs of a *dolce vita* in urban centers.[27]

Nonunion Economic Institutions

The significance of organizing activities, such as collective rentals as well as other "economic" institutions like cooperatives and credit unions, is not fully reflected in the historiography of Italian Catholic Action. This probably originates in the fact that Chiri's statistical volume, the most important source of information, tabulated only about half of the nonunion economic institutions. Even so, they added up to 2,891, almost eight times the number of labor unions. With a combined membership of 308,919, they had about three times as many members as the Catholic organizations of labor.[28] Most of them clearly came into being in response to the real needs of medium and small landholders, and those among the landless peasants who rented and sharecropped. To quote the historian Angelo Gambasin, these organizations saved some

> from misery and hunger, from usury and distress. In a way they slowed down the migration to urban centers and abroad, introduced better agricultural techniques, contributed to the construction of hygienic houses to replace primitive cottages. Those institutions were safety planks to peasants who owned the farms with the lowest incomes, which were always in danger of failing if animals got sick, if a hailstorm or drought came, not to speak of the fact that they were oppressed by excessive taxes and persecuted by the tax authorities.[29]

The recognition of the social usefulness of Catholic economic institutions does not, of course, negate the fact that the Catholics pushed these organizations because they reflected their ideal, a socially mixed membership. Two types of organizations came especially close to the mixed union and were initially considered as the first stages from which the *misto* would eventually be developed. One of these, the *unione rurale,*[30] having become a notorious failure, was not even among the categories Chiri surveyed in 1909–10. Not mentioned by name, it was probably hidden under the term *cooperatives,* which represented only 2 percent of the economic institutions in Chiri's tabulations, and about 1 percent of their total membership. During the last years of the nineteenth century, it was propagandized as a means to help smallholders and touted as an institution that brought "together the day laborers and smallholders with the *padroni* of vast possessions." As such, it was to be the precursor of the rural version of the mixed union. But as its demise showed, institutions that promised to be all things to all men were out of season even in the countryside.

The mutual aid societies, another type of Catholic economic institution, were more successful, very likely because they enrolled people from a single social stratum, the urban and rural working classes, and thus fit better into a social atmosphere charged with class consciousness. But from the beginning, their membership tended to be open to all; and when during the 1880s a search was on for a model for implementing the corporativist labor theory, the mutual aid societies were designated as the initial stage toward the mixed union. As late as 1906, Toniolo referred to these institutions, "numerous amongst us," as the "nuclei" of mixed unions coming into being as they "enlarge themselves and grow toward the inexhaustible sources of personal and spiritual charity."[31] How many, if any, of them eventually turned into labor unions is impossible to tell from the extant data, which suggest that their numbers and membership grew rather rapidly. In 1883 there had been 90 mutual aid societies under Catholic leadership; by 1891, 274; in 1902, 550; in 1905, 763. Chiri's 1911 survey listed 799, with a membership of 88,508, but according to information released by Medolago, Chiri took into account less than half of the existing mutual aid societies.[32]

10

The Pope Will Remain Silent

The Religious Nature of Catholic Organizations and the Issues of Lay Autonomy

Statistical data indicate that Italian Catholics were more successful in organizing "economic" institutions, such as mutual aid societies, than they were in recruiting people into labor unions.[1] To a large extent, this was a manifestation of conflict avoidance on more than one level. Unlike the simple unions, which carried by their very existence the potential of strikes and confrontations with the *padroni*, "economic" institutions would rarely, if ever, be caught in a class struggle. Thus they freed the activists who organized them from the potential of conflict that developed in Catholic Action between a conservative leadership, which conceived class struggle as contrary to the basic tenets of Christianity, and Catholic activists, who saw manifestations of class struggle in strikes as inevitable.

Those who were charged with organizing "economic" institutions, such as credit unions, insurance and consumer cooperatives, and mutual aid societies, could justifiably hope to avoid confrontations between the rich and the not-so-rich. The commonality of interests and mutual charity that Thomistic theologians insisted should exist between the *padrone* and those who worked for him were certainly easier to find among the members of "economic" institutions. Their membership was more homogeneous in outlook, expectations, and interests than that of the mixed unions would have been if they ever were organized.

Homogeneity was a crucial requirement imposed on Catholic Action by the principle of *confessionalità*, which prescribed that the institutions under the leadership of the Economic Social Union be guided by the principles of religion, and that their members be practicing Catholics. Insistence upon this rule is also a likely explanation of the Catholics' apparent concentration of labor-organizing efforts among the peasantry during the last years of the papacy of Pius X. Rural people were seen as devoutly religious, whereas industrial workers were often described by Catholic publications as in danger of losing their faith, if they had not already lost it. The presence of someone who was not a practicing Catholic was perceived as a threat to those who lived by the tenets of their faith. Hence the principle of *confessionalità.*

Because this principle applied to organizations of labor, the activists, especially those working in urban situations, found themselves caught in yet another conflict between the demands of an idealistically motivated leadership and the realities of life. There was a need for class solidarity. Workers, regardless of religious beliefs, had to close ranks in order to wrest concessions from the *padroni.* Furthermore, activists often ran into enormous difficulties in trying to find workers who could be said to meet the doctrinal soundness that the principle of *confessionalità* imposed.[2]

It was the pressure of reality that led to the easing of the strict religious requirements for membership in Catholic unions at the Bologna congress in 1903. The resolution adopted there allowed, at the discretion of local leaders, the acceptance of members who were doctrinally "not quite secure." One is inclined to suggest that the dissolution of the Opera that followed the Bologna congress was in part caused by this drift away from the principle of *confessionalità* toward the religious "neutrality" of the labor movement. Pius X, who ordered the dissolution, fought the notion of "neutrality" with increasing vigor. Canon Ravaglia's troubles were rooted in the fact that his name came to be associated with that notion. The rejection of "neutrality," of freedom from church authorities in the economic and political activities of Catholics, was the central issue of the pope's objection to the Lega Democratica Nazionale and to Murri, who dared to question the proposition that the pope enjoyed "special light from the Lord" in connection with social and political matters.[3]

Pius X was not inclined to limit his own authority to strictly religious concerns. He made that clear. "If you love the Pope, [he said,] you do not debate his dispositions, . . . you do not set limits as to the areas in which he can, and has to, exercise his authority."[4] The pope stated this to a group of clergymen, but his claim to unrestricted authority certainly was intended to cover laymen as well. A drive to stamp out "neutrality" and its implied independence from church authorities came to be one of the major characteristics of his papacy. His stress on *confessionalità,* in fact, brought a change in the role played in Catholic Action by laymen, substantially reducing the freedom they had enjoyed under his predecessor.

During the papacy of Leo XIII, laymen began to play a new role in Italian Catholic Action. Perhaps the Vatican did not fully realize where this new development would lead. Whatever the reason, there came about a degree of independence on the part of Catholic activists. Old-style conservatives like Medolago were hesitant to make a move without checking with church authorities. Typically, he submitted for the pope's inspection not only major policy statements but apparently all the circulars he was to issue as the president of the Unione Economico Sociale.[5] Just as typically, Guido Miglioli, representing the new lay activists, proceeded to do what he thought had to be done even after some high-ranking churchmen strongly criticized it. The young generation of activists were more courageous in the sense that they were willing to risk censure by acting on their own.

This willingness was in part the consequence of the generally conservative attitude of the church hierarchy. The activists knew their bishops often sought to prevent them from performing tasks that, from the point of view of those who were attuned to reality, were long overdue. This explains why the activists pressed for independence from church authorities, which implied "neutrality" in the Catholic labor movement.

But the activists were also motivated by new trends in Catholic theology, trends that were not to be taken into full consideration by the leadership of the church until Vatican II. Theological arguments according to which laypersons, by virtue of their baptism, gained a right to act on their own in certain fields of human endeavor certainly were not to the liking of Pius X. In refusing to consider such suggestions, the pope disregarded the experiences of German Catholics, whom he always held up as an example to his Italian followers. The formidable success of the Germans in organizing the Catholic masses was due to a very large extent to the fact that laymen, whom the circumstances of the *Kulturkampf* thrust to the fore of Catholic Action, remained active and relatively independent from direct and everyday control by the church hierarchy, at least as far as their political activities were concerned.[6]

The issue touches upon something perennial in the life of the church. As James O'Gara was to observe a half-century later, if the hierarchy insisted on breathing down the necks of laymen, it immobilized Catholic Action: "Clericalism and lay apathy go hand in hand. The combination does more than alter the basic spirit of the liturgy; it reduces the role of the layman to that of passive bystander in almost every area. While clericalism seems to guard the strength of the Church in the face of attack, it in fact weakens it and reduces the area of the Church's influence."[7]

O'Gara talks of generalized conditions, but his description certainly fits the papacy of Pius X, under whose leadership the "clericalization" of Italian Catholic Action reached its modern apogee. In a 1906 encyclical entitled *Vehementer nos,* Pius X reminded the faithful that the "Church is essentially an unequal society, that is, a society comprising two categories of persons, the Pastors and the flock, those who occupy a rank in the different degrees of the hierarchy and the multitude of the faithful."[8] The statement was a denial of the arguments of those who, in the words of the historian Roger Aubert, were inclined to understand the church not as an organization centered on a hierarchy but as "a communion of the faithful." For Pius X such an understanding was an aspect of the modernist heresy.

Very few even among the most extreme modernists questioned the authority of the pope or that of the bishops and the clergy to act as "pastors" for their flocks. The issue was how far clerical authority, and especially that of the pope, went in directing the lives of laypersons. As for Pius X, he clearly recognized no limit to his authority, which he conceived as covering not only the religious but the social and political aspects of life as well. This was thought to flow from the wisdom of Aquinas. When the successor of Pius X decided to relinquish the church's direct control over Italian Catholics' political activities, the two leading Thomists left over from the era of Pius X vehemently protested. Both Monsignor Francesco Olgiati and Father Agostino Gemelli criticized as absurd the lay autonomy implied in the functioning of the Partito Popolare. Sturzo, the leader of the new party, defended autonomy for the layman as a way of "gaining a personality." Amid all the debate, the Vatican remained silent.[9]

Lay autonomy was one subject about which the Vatican certainly was not silent during the papacy of Pius X. During the last months of the papacy of Leo XIII, Toniolo addressed the problem in an open letter to Grosoli. As usual he attempted to strike a compromise, but once again he ended up trying to reconcile the irreconcilable. Catholic Action, he said, had to be firmly under church control, but at the same time its initiatives had to come from the laity, "originating in the womb of Christian people and not imposed from above by church teachings since that would be impractical."[10] Then came Pius X with his practice of telling the faithful not only what to believe but also what to do and how to go about it. Autonomy for Catholic Action quickly became a dirty word and eventually, after Murri insisted upon it and questioned the application of the dogma of papal infallibility to social and political action, an aspect of *murrismo*. Little word games were then played in Catholic publications, such as *murrismo è modernismo, e modernismo è murrismo.* Thus the idea of autonomy, independence from church authorities (that is, from the pope), was identified with "modernism," and as such was considered heretical. By 1909 *autonomia* and *laicismo,* autonomy for the laymen, was mentioned in association with socialism.[11] Laymen were reduced to silence during the papacy of Pius X, and even bishops were turned into "robots manipulated from Rome," to quote a contemporary observer.[12]

The "clericalization" of Italian Catholic Action took the form of an ever increasing emphasis on *confessionalità,* the reinforcement of the religious nature of labor organizations. Immediately after he dissolved the Opera, the pope reaffirmed not only the religious nature of all Catholic organizations but also their strict dependence on the ecclesiastic authorities.[13] The religious orientation of Catholic organizations returned as an issue when Toniolo, Medolago, and others so charged by the pope worked out the statutes for the new *unioni*. In a letter to Medolago, Pius X accused Toniolo of trying to "exempt the Unione Populare from the surveillance of church authorities." Poor Toniolo: it was a good thing he did not know about the pope's accusation, which was a response to Toniolo's attempt to accommodate with his draft statutes the suggestions of the Christian Democratic activists, ideas that Pius X referred to as "crazy" in his letter to Medolago.[14]

The details of what went on behind the scenes are impossible to fix on the basis of extant information; but it is beyond imagination that Toniolo deviated in this one instance, since throughout his life he insisted upon submitting Catholic Action to the directive will of religious authorities, and perceived the role of the pope in the strict medieval sense as the arbiter of the affairs of the world.

If he did deviate, this was corrected by the all-knowing father; for in the end, Medolago's and not Toniolo's draft appears to have carried the day, and Murri talked of "religious exaggerations" (*esagerazioni confessionali*) after reading the statutes of the Popular Union.[15] If the religious orientation of an organization charged with Catholic propaganda is not surprising, one does read with a degree of astonishment about the *confessionalità* of credit unions, the religious orientation of which seemed to have been a major concern of Pius X, a concern enveloping not only Italian but French institutions as well. Apparently only money saved by solid Catholics could be deposited at financial institutions, which also had to be staunchly Catholic.[16]

As for the organizations of labor, their religious orientation was reaffirmed in a letter by Pius X in January, 1907, that gives interesting insight into the pope's thinking. It states that if doctrinal soundness prevails within the organizations of labor, this will render "new aid to the clergy, making their sacred ministry among the people more efficient."[17] Then in 1909 came the reaffirmation of the reaffirmation in the papal letter to Medolago and in further forceful pontifical statements.[18] These clearly indicated that the issue remained very much on the pope's mind, in part because even people like Medolago began to doubt the practicality of maintaining the strictly religious character of labor unions. But the more he was pushed, the more Pius X resisted.

The issue leads, of course, to the very core of the aged pope's greatest concern, the maintenance of doctrinal purity, which, as shown by the antimodernist struggle, became a near-obsession for him. However, the impracticality of the strict religious character of organizations of labor came back to haunt Pius X. Chiri's statistical study shows that of the 198 statutes of Catholic union locals he examined, only 4 specifically excluded religious orientation. Thus from the point of view of formal compliance, the pope was obeyed. But Chiri drops more than one hint that in practice what happened was anything but strict adherence to the papal directives and the circulars of the head office.[19]

"Good moral conduct," to which the religious orientation prescribed by the statutes often came to be reduced in practice, was not sufficient for the pope, who was increasingly concerned about "infections" of heretical ideas and enemy "infiltrations" into Catholic organizations. Consequently the statutes of the Economic Social Union were changed in 1911. The new *statuto* is seen by historians as a step forward in Catholic labor theory. Massimo Salvadori goes so far as to suggest that it was "inspired" by the Modena congress, and that with it the "Catholic labor movement was freed from the residues of corporativism and assumed a modern character in the form of the simple organization that included the workers only. This represented a defeat for the conservatives."[20]

All this might have been true; yet in one way the 1911 statutes represented a step backward, a step of such great importance that it threatened to undo all the gains of modernization brought about by the Modena congress. What occurred was a dramatic change in the supervision of the social and economic activities of Italian Catholics, hitherto left out of the direct control of the church hierarchy. When Pius X dissolved the old Opera, he made it clear that whatever new forms Italian Catholic Action took, they would be under the leadership of the bishops or they simply would not be allowed to exist. Yet he specifically exempted the Second Session of the Opera, which later developed into the Unione Economico Sociale. This clearly had to do with the fact that the Second Session was under the leadership of Medolago, the most docile of very docile leaders, who not only always did exactly what the pope told him to do but had an almost uncanny sense for anticipating the way the thinking "up there" was turning. Furthermore, he never made a move without ascertaining that it was the "right" move, and unfailingly submitted all the acts of his leadership to papal inspection before they became public. According to the Jesuit Father Alfonso Casoli, Medolago's biographer, the count "submitted to the Pope the proofs of every circular, of all the statutes he planned to send out. The pope reviewed these point by point, adding, making changes and corrections if they were needed, but he never touched substantive matters: those he always agreed with."[21]

The fact that Pius X personally went through the motions of that inspection shows that the exemption of the socioeconomic activities of Italian Catholics was due not so much to any doubt as to limits of his own and the bishops' authority but because through Medolago, on whose leadership Pius X insisted throughout his papacy, the pontiff found a convenient way to assert his own control. Whether this showed a degree of mistrust toward the Italian bishops is a question that is unlikely ever to be answered. Another issue, somewhat more likely to be resolved on the basis of archival evidence, is why in 1911 Pius X decided to place the activities of the Economic Social Union under the direct control of the bishops. One is even inclined to venture a tentative explanation based on currently available information: the pope relinquished his personal control because, for a variety of reasons, including his declining health and advancing age, he simply could not find the time to carry on the control down to the minutiae, such as "correcting" Medolago's circulars.

Yet another suggestion offers itself for consideration: the pope may have concluded that the previous system was not working, as shown by the successful revolt of the activists in Modena that eliminated the mixed union from the picture. So the activists would have the *semplice* they wanted, but with it went tight control by the local church hierarchy, who in turn owed unquestionable and unquestioning loyalty to the pope. That something like this was the case, that the 1911 statutes represented a tightening rather than a loosening of the reins, is strongly suggested, not by the new *statuto* itself, but by the instructions Medolago sent out with the document to the Diocesan Directorates. The instructions,[22] so far ignored by historical research, demand attention because in a highly condensed form they reflect the conditions of the Catholic labor movement in the aftermath of Modena. Moreover, given the strict orthodoxy of the signatories, Medolago and Rezzara, they provide reliable information as to the thinking "up there" in the Vatican.

The Reinforcement of Clerical Control
over Catholic Action

What the instructions made very clear was that from then on the Unione Economico Sociale, like all the other Catholic organizations whatever their scope and nature, had to be under the control of the Diocesan Directorates, outside of which there was not, and could not be, "in Italy neither real organization nor legitimate Catholic Action." Thus the circle of the clericalization of Italian Catholic Action closed, for the Diocesan Directorates were under the direct control of the bishops. In fact, in the vast majority of the dioceses the bishops *were* the Diocesan Directorates, since these institutions simply did not exist. Medolago characteristically mailed the new statutes to the bishops, requesting that they provide him with the names and addresses of the heads of the Diocesan Directorates, and "where these do not exist, we beseech Your Excellence provide us with the names and addresses of two or three persons . . . so that this office can be in a position to nominate them, according to art. 11, as correspondents." Information in *Azione Sociale* indicates that in only seventy-seven of Italy's more than two hundred dioceses were Diocesan Directorates in existence, and even these were often headed by clergymen. Thus in 1911 Italian Catholic action was, in effect, as far as leadership and even initiatives were concerned, action by the episcopate.

In view of this, one is baffled as to why "surveillance" had to be the recurring theme of the instructions sent out by Medolago. Furthermore, the bishops, and through them the activists, were informed that there was not a chance for the kind of "untimely" criticism that exploded in Modena. In the future, the instructions announced, the General Assembly of the Economic Social Union was not going to be constituted "by delegates elected according to a complicated method . . . but simply, by the natural consequence of the logic of the general idea, constituted by the presidents of the economic-social sessions of the Diocesan Directorates."

As to the qualifications of these persons, they had to be not only doctrinally sound but also advanced in years in order to avoid what happened in the past, namely, that "persons not sufficiently mature brought to Catholic Action damaging divisions and disturbances." They were to have free time and also financial "independence": here we face a reference to the aristocracy. This was somewhat veiled in the instructions, but a little later an article in *Azione Sociale* explained that the rural aristocrats were the best leaders for Catholic Action for a number of reasons. They had time to spare ("independence"), unlike professionals and social types like the bankers and capitalists, who would limit the time they gave to sacred causes.

The instructions that went out with the new statutes indicated the "defense of the sacrosanct rights of the church and of the Roman pontificate" as the goal of Catholic Action, adding almost pathetically that "it must not be forgotten that Catholic Action includes another component as well, which absolutely must not be neglected, [and that is] social action." The humor of the statement coming from the leader of Catholic social action could not have been lost on some of those who read Medolago's instructions, which were thorough enough to indicate the intellectual framework for Catholic social action and the "reconstruction of human society on a Christian and Catholic basis," which the count predicted this would bring out:

> As for the unity of intents and criteria, it is easy to arrive at: it will suffice that the Diocesan Directorates keep eyes fixed on a single point: the teachings contained in the pontifical documents related to Catholic Action. . . . There will be some who demand that we adapt our doctrines to the present, and call us by the nickname [*nomignolo*] backward. But we can respond: what you ask us we can never do because our doctrine comes from the highest authority on earth, comes from the Holy See inspired by God, and God does not change.

If doctrine did not change, the rules governing Catholic organizations did change. Yet, in a way, the more they changed, the more they remained the same. The 1911 statutes accepting the simple union as the basic organizational form of Catholic labor reflected a change, but Medolago's instructions showed that the new *statuto* was also an attempt at a conservative consolidation. It called for building a bureaucratic structure, a fortress, manned by laymen but clearly under the command of the church hierarchy. It is somewhat superfluous to point out that the structure did not amount to even a facade, that it was nothing but a figment of the imagination of a man anxious to please a master whose mind, like God, apparently never changed.

The Encyclical *Singulari quadam* and the Last Battle of the Papacy of Pius X

The closest Pius X came to changing his mind was a year after he approved the 1911 statutes for the Unione Economico Sociale. Characteristically this was in relation to issues involving not Italian Catholic Action but the activities of Catholics abroad. For some time he had been called upon to settle a row between two wings of German Catholic Action. For a while he tried to be cryptic, but this just aggravated the situation in Germany. Thus in 1912 he faced the issue squarely and announced to his astonished followers in an encyclical[23] that he did not consider the principle of *confessionalità* valid in the absolute sense and that in order to "improve the workers' living conditions," Catholic unions could "collaborate" with non-Catholic organizations of labor. This concession on the principle of the religious orientation of the Catholic labor movement was followed in the encyclical *Singulari quadam* by a still more astonishing change: Pius X also allowed for organizations of labor that included both Catholic and non-Catholic workers.

In a way, *Singulari quadam* represented a somewhat delayed acceptance of the decision of the German episcopate. German bishops decided as early as 1869 to let Protestant workers join Catholic organizations of labor. But during Pius's repeated and firm assertion of the principle of *confessionalità,* German conservatives too battled for the purity of Catholic organizations. With *Singulari quadam* Pius X took the side of those German Catholics who wanted to allow for religiously mixed membership in Catholic organizations of labor.

The pope made it clear in the encyclical that the concessions were made specifically for Germany, a religiously mixed society in which Catholics constituted a numerical minority; hence they were not inconsistent with his previous statements, such as the one in the papal letter *Notre charge apostolique,* which condemned interconfessional action by Catholics. The response to *Singulari quadam* was nevertheless immediate and strong enough in Italy to be characterized as a firestorm.

As leaders of the world's largest international organization, the hierarchy of the church could not fail to be affected by the international experience of Catholics. It was natural that the misfortunes of Catholics in one country were projected by Catholic publications as object lessons for the faithful in another, and the successes of Catholic communities were carefully scrutinized by the Vatican and presented as positive examples to be followed elsewhere. Teaching by example was the church's traditional way of teaching. Pius X followed this tradition with his cry *Germania doceat!,* and from the very beginning of his papacy set the Germans as examples for the Italian faithful to follow.[24] In spite of the fact that the pope made it clear that it was anything but *comme il faut* in this case, it was inevitable that the issues connected with the concessions granted to the Germans in *Singulari quadam* would be discussed in Italy.

What followed—"the last battle of the papacy of Pius X," as the historian Emile Poulat called it—centered on the *Civiltà Cattolica.* During the initial phase, the battle took a bizarre turn when the Florentine conservative Catholic paper *L'Unità Cattolica,* clearly more Catholic than the pope, attacked the *Civiltà* for taking the side of those German Catholics who felt vindicated by the papal encyclical. *Civiltà Cattolica* responded with self-righteous indignation: "Frankly, we deplore, and only for reasons of conscience, that there are even in Italy Catholics who, not understanding that it only helps the enemies of the church, especially the modernists, if the press, whose task is to combat for the cause of Jesus Christ, His church, and His vicar on earth is shown in a bad light."[25]

As often happens in wars too, there was some confusion during the initial skirmishes. But this was rectified and the battlelines clearly drawn by the beginning of 1914, although some rather unexpected developments followed. The situation in Germany constituted the subject of the first phase of the debate in Italy, giving the discussion a degree of unreality since, by talking about the Germans, both sides were obviously saying what ought and ought not to happen in Italy. But in 1914 the *Civiltà Cattolica* changed the focus of the debate by discussing the problems not within the specific German context but in broad general terms.

In February, 1914, the periodical ran an article entitled *"Sindacalismo cristiano,"* "Christian Labor Movement." At first it was thought that the unsigned essay was the work of Father Chiaudano, the director of the *Civiltà*. Later, to their horror, Toniolo and the others, already upset by the article, found out that it was in fact written by Father Monetti, the pope's favored "sociologist." Monetti's stock stood so high in the Vatican that, according to a sarcasm rare in Toniolo's correspondence, he was thought "up there" to be "a modern Artistotle upon whose words one could swear without fear of committing an error." Monetti, whom Secco Suardo, a historian of charitable inclinations, was to describe as "hung up on ideas thirty or forty years old," carried out a devastating attack on the principles of the Catholic labor movement as these were accepted in the aftermath of the Modena congress and reflected in the 1911 statutes of the Economic Social Union.[26] If carried to a logical conclusion, Monetti's arguments implied undoing the decisions of the Modena congress. The "modern Aristotle" began by expressing his aversion to the word *sindacalismo,* which was distasteful to him because of its revolutionary origins. But Monetti's objections went beyond etymological issues, which in themselves gave away his backwardness. By 1914 the word *syndicalist* ceased to imply revolutionary aims in Latin-language areas and simply denoted organizations of labor, as it does today. Perhaps that was the point of it all, for Monetti's arguments called into question the reasons for the existence of the labor movement as such.

According to Monetti the idea of an organization of labor implied a "bellicose alliance through which the members of a social class unite in a compact army to confront another class, [thus] consecrating the idea of class struggle." The trouble with the unions was not only that they were dedicated to the use of "brutal force" but also that, when it came to their activities, "nobody wanted to assume responsibility." Monetti remarked that it was just as La Tour wanted it: the corporations "becoming states within the state." The critical attitude he assumed toward La Tour, the venerated founding father of Catholic corporativism, gave an indication of the scope of Monetti's undertaking: clearly he was determined to wipe clean the slate of labor theory. But that was not all. The sacred cow of Neo-Thomistic social philosphy—the principle of the social function of property—also came under devastating attack. Monetti declared it a "socialistic prejudice" that "property should not be conceived any-more as an absolute right of the owner to use and validly dispose as he saw fit what he possesses, but that he has to take into considera-tion a social function."[27]

Refuting the notions advanced by "modern" sociology that the poor had claims on the rich and their possessions, the learned Jesuit led his readers back into the idea world of the Manchester school of economics. He saw in the organizations of labor a violation of the owner's absolute right to property because the existence of unions, especially if their right to strike was recognized, raised questions as to "who commanded in the factory." The "modern Aristotle" had no illusions left about professional-occupational solidarity, which was so loudly proclaimed by the corporativists. Whatever existed of soli-darity in modern times, according to Monetti, was not "virtue" "but a heap of aberrations, because in more than one way it stood against the natural order."

The solution was very simple. Charity had to be "brought back" and restored to its proper place in the life of society: "Much better than the exotic social justice that some try to make credible for us, . . . [charity] will provide a quiet life and prosperity for our workers by leading them onto the path of docility." According to Monetti, charity would also transform the *padroni* into "venerated fathers of their workers and servants." He concluded the essay with the hope that the "Catholics of good will manage to open their eyes in time to see how much evil is hidden in the bosom of such organiza-tion of labor [*quanto male covi in seno tal sindacalismo*]."[28]

By the time the second installment of Father Monetti's wisdom appeared in the pages of the *Civiltà Cattolica,* the activists and their supporters in the church hierarchy were in an upheaval that was tinged with despair. Modena was hard enough for them to take. Sturzo, who at first hesitated to speak in Modena, eventually decided to participate in the discussion and went home reassuring himself by saying that voices like his represented reality:

> There were two forces [*anime*] that brought information to the congress, one open and the other hidden [*sottintesa*]. . . . On the one hand, there were the young propagandists and organizers who work and suffer while in touch with reality, which they represent; on the other hand, there were the scholastics who follow our social thought from high up, inventing formulas that are derived from ideas and not from facts and who worked behind the scene at the congress.[29]

What he suspected was at work behind the scene in 1914 sent the Turinese activist Luigi Caissotti di Chiusano into depression. He was already in despair in the aftermath of the Modena congress, concluding in a letter to Toniolo that "for a few years now the church seems to be opposing efforts by good men toward the establishment of the Kingdom of God," and began to question the limitless claim to papal authority and the direction this imposed. "But it is almost always better to remain silent about this subject than it is to speak up," he wrote, to which Toniolo replied: "Let us remain silent about that argument, or rather let us say: who would dare to define the limits of the authority of a father concerned about the salvation of his children." In spite of the fact that both men suspected the 1914 articles in *Civiltà* were "inspired from high up," they were indignant enough about the attack on the *raison d'être* of the labor movement to do something.

At first their attention was focussed on Medolago. Toniolo had a tale to tell, typically Catholic, showing the moral failure of upper-class people and intemperate hell-raising by workers as the causes of troubles:

> I admit that I knew about the secret development of the drama since last fall, and in part I predicted what happened. Last year there oc-

curred an unrest [*agitazione*] among the members of the Catholic
league of land workers in northern Trivigiano, agitation against landlords who denied the peasants the right to organize a union to oppose
the *padroni,* among whom was the Count Passi . . . a relative of Medolago. The few intemperances shown by the peasants were exagger-
ated and in any case, condemned by all. . . . But at the same time
denunciations and sinister information about the most popular among
the [local] Catholics went to the Vatican.

Presumably an aversion toward labor unions followed on Medolago's part and "up there" as well.

One's first reaction is to take Toniolo's letter for a manifestation
of the old rivalry between Medolago and himself. Also obvious in it
was an attempt to make the count a scapegoat in order to avoid
placing the blame on the "highest authority on earth." One ventures
to suggest, subject to later confirmation, that Medolago was better
informed than Toniolo, and, in supporting Monetti's position, he
was taking the side on which the pope was positioned; furthermore,
this was not a change in Medolago's attitude.

Throughout the years that followed the Modena congress, in
one circular after another, Medolago pushed the *organizzazione
padronale,* upon which Pius X insisted in spite of the fact that the
Catholics appear to have made little headway, if any, in taking control of the employers' associations that were being established all
over the country. The pope stressed the need for these in order to
counterweight the gains in importance and power the working
classes were expected to make through being organized in simple
unions. The bilateral organizations of the workers and the *padroni,*
linked through mixed commissions with powers of arbitration, were
to maintain a balance of power and social harmony that the mixed
union, kept as a long-range goal, was to eventually establish.

But the mixed union, abandoned for all practical purposes since
Modena, crept back into the picture as an immediate goal in May,
1914, in a way that was associated with Medolago. A circular signed
by him called a meeting of the presidents and ecclesiastic assistants
of the northern Italian Diocesan Directorates. The resolutions
adopted by this assembly presented the simple and mixed unions the

way they were talked about before Modena, as either/or propositions, setting as the goal of Catholic Action "the organization of the *padroni* [*classi padronali*] and workers [*classi operaie*] either in a single organization [*in un unico sodalizio*] or in parallel associations, connected through a permanent mixed commission."[30]

Whether the waving of the torch, which Rezzara said in Modena "must never be extinguished," occurred on instructions from the pope, or the reintroduction of the mixed union came in anticipation of the changes in Catholic social doctrine that Monetti's articles heralded, cannot be decided on the basis of available information. One does not hesitate to suggest, however, that at the time of the May meeting Medolago was likely to be aware of what soon became widely believed: that the articles in *Civiltà Cattolica,* the first of which appeared two months before the meeting Medolago called, were trial balloons for the ideas of an encyclical Pius X intended to issue.

Toniolo became aware of this relatively early and advised extreme caution, suggesting that if "laymen criticized the *Civiltà Cattolica,* this easily could be denounced as a manifestation of modernism." During the last year of the papacy of Pius X, things had degenerated to the point that opinions could only be conveyed to the Vatican through churchmen of the highest rank. What Toniolo organized, in fact, was a letter-writing campaign by cardinals, both Italian and foreign. The effort to prevent the promulgation of an encyclical that would have called into question the existence of the Catholic labor movement as it was established all around the world was not without strange twists and turns. Toniolo encouraged Caissotti to write a rebuttal of Monetti's articles, promising to publish it in the periodical that was pretty much under his control. But by the time Caissotti's essay was finished, Toniolo changed his mind: "The *Rivista internazionale* [*di scienze sociali*] cannot publish materials of a controversial nature, no matter how well balanced, without running the risk of losing the little trust it retains." In fact, he advised Caissotti, it was better

not to publish your beautiful essay [*bel memoriale*] in any Italian review. It should be made into a monograph and sent as printer's proofs [*bozze*] to secure and authoritative Catholic reviews published abroad, beseeching them to take into account the arguments presented in the essay as expressions of the feelings aroused by the unfortunate publication of the well-known articles, and [insisting] that, without mentioning that the request came from Italy, these foreign reviews make private observations which are to be sent confidentially [*riservata-mente*] but directly to the editorial office of the *Civiltà Cattolica* and also to the holy father.[31]

Toniolo added that the information sent abroad could be signed, but that his cardinal archbishop, Pietro Maffi, thought it might be better to send it anonymously so as "not to compromise" Cardinal Agostino Richelmy, the archbishop of Turin, Caissotti's hometown.

Caissotti expressed in his reply the "most certain" conviction that "no Roman pontiff as such would proclaim *ex cathedra* the errors" manifest in Monetti's articles, but he also noted that no disapproval of these came from the Vatican. Thus he proceeded with the printing of the essay at his own expense. Showing a courage that *noblesse oblige* and despair dictate, he refused Cardinal Maffi's advice and not only signed the essay but also mailed out prepublication copies to virtually everybody whose name counted in Catholic Action in Italy and abroad.

Caissotti's essay, entitled *Il sindacalismo cristiano in un articolo della "Civiltà Cattolica,"*[32] carried a dedication "to those who, obedient to the appeals of two Roman pontiffs flew in Italy and abroad the flag of the professional unions [and] hope to be able to prove that, today, as before, the reward of Christian obedience is the sacred liberty of the spirit." The essay drew on several dozen sources, ranging from the Aquinas to modern French, German, Belgian, and Italian sociologists, ironically enough one by the name of Monetti. (Caissotti pretended not to know who the author of the *Civiltà* articles was and created confrontations between the Monetti of the *Problemi varii* and the Monetti in *Civiltà Cattolica*). At the very beginning, Caissotti expressed the astonishment of "social Catholics" at the fact that the official publication of the Economic Social Union reprinted the articles of the *Civiltà* with the sole comment pointing to their importance. It should have been the duty of the

Unione to refute the articles, since they represented an attack on the principles that sustained Catholic social action. In the disguise of a "war on syndicalism," Caissotti argued, the articles carried out a "radical revision of Catholic social doctrine." Declaring the owners' right to property absolute and denying the validity of the Thomistic principle of the social functions of property, the *Civiltà Cattolica* led its readers straight into an "economic liberalism" of a very old-fashioned kind.

The attack on syndicalism and the workers' right to associate in the defense of their interests was also presented by Caissotti as an attempt to realign Catholic social doctrine with the outlook of those representing classical liberalism, who were in the habit of granting in principle the workers' right to associations of their own, but did everything they could in practice to deny this right. In the concluding part of his essay, Caissotti quoted the Programma di Milano: "We aim to reconstruct that social order which only the Church can give us. . . . This ideal carries the marks of the most splendid period in history, [a period] called the centuries of the people. If against our intentions it will be necessary, we will not hesitate for a second to align ourselves with the people." Then he continued:

> This sounds today as the language of an excited cad because it is really not fitting for the present situation, but twenty years ago . . . these words appeared to be most natural, and they were because they reflected reality then perfectly, so much so that the Count Medolago Albani, currently the president of the Economic Social Union, made them his own by signing . . . the Milan Program. We live in different times today. Society is not neatly divided anymore into "weak and suffering on the one side and strong and merry on the other." Not surprisingly, our judgment changed too, and with it our language. Thus we should not be astonished if in the encyclicals of Pius X we do not find the fiery expressions of *Rerum novarum* that stigmatized monopoly in production and trade. . . . [But does] admitting all this mean that the changes that came legitimize not only changing our judgment and our language but also imply a really substantive change, a change of flag? Confronting a persistent and ever more aggravating class struggle do we have to abandon the proletarian camp and go over to the capitalists? . . . Twenty years ago the people we faced were

dispersed and nameless. We were to have a roll call for them and gather them in Catholic corporations. For a large number of reasons, and this is not the place to list and explain them, we did not measure up to the task: those people did not receive a Christian baptism but went to join the Socialist organizations. A battle was lost, but there is still time to win another.

Toniolo, who was somewhat tardy in acknowledging receipt of the copy of Caissotti's essay, excused himself by saying that he had waited to see the "first impressions" the little work made "among the public." But it turned out that he was waiting for a letter from "Cardinal M."—Desiré Mercier, the Belgian cardinal and Thomistic scholar—who was among the high-ranking churchmen Toniolo tried to reach while organizing his letter-writing campaign. Mercier, it turned out, disapproved of Monetti's articles. So did the prime minister of Belgium, who felt the future of the Catholic party he headed was placed in jeopardy by the action of the *Civiltà*. A host of other important personalities, both lay and clerical, also spoke up against the articles, some in public and others in private, in letters and through audiences with the pope. Those who acted behind the scenes included the secretary to the head of the Jesuit order, who found what Monetti wrote "deplorable," and Toniolo, who not only sent a long letter to Pius X but requested and received an audience with him. When he wrote to Caissotti, Toniolo was in a mood of high optimism: "Victory is yours," he said.

But Caissotti, who concluded his essay by confidently declaring that "the *Civiltà Cattolica* is not the Church," was becoming rather wary: "It is too early to sing victory," he told Toniolo, and his caution, as it turned out, was justified. Toniolo was in fact forewarned about the futility of trying to persuade Pius X: during March, through his private secretary, the pope sent Toniolo a message that deemed what appeared in the *Civiltà Cattolica* "worthy of approval" and the objections to it "unjustified." What Toniolo did not know, though, was that on the previous day Pius X had been even more unequivocal to Father Chiaudano, the director of the *Civiltà,* as a letter writen by Chiaudano to Monetti shows: "I do not want to delay a minute conveying to you very consoling news. This morning

I went to see the holy father. As soon as he caught sight of me, he told me smiling: Well, they are waging a war on you, are they not? Remain firm. Advance, fight against Catholic syndicalism. Many of them cry because you put your finger on the evil. The Count Medolago is right. Tell Father Monetti that I am satisfied." "War," "advance": the last battle Commander in Chief Sarto was to fight! After a pause while he listened to all those arguments against it, and in spite of them (or was it because of them?), the battle resumed. At the end of May, while Toniolo deluded himself about having convinced the pope, the *Civiltà Cattolica* was preparing a new series of articles; and who would suggest on the basis of extant evidence that this did not happen at the pope's insistence? The new articles, the first of which was published on May 28, reviewed and rejected the criticism raised against Monetti. Caissotti's essay rated one footnote, which summarily dismissed it. Knowing that he was saying what was right, Chiaudano, the author of the new articles, then moved on to a systematic review of all the papal documents relevant to the issues raised by Monetti, showing, of course, that what the *Civiltà* said was right on the dot. Since the review of previous papal pronouncements traditionally constituted the first part of papal encyclicals, what was happening came to be seen low and high as the preparation of an "anti-syndicalist syllabus," a "definitive attack on syndicalism" in the form of an encyclical. Even the date of the promulgation was bandied around: a clergyman close to Cardinal Mercier suggested it was December, 1914. But as befits a tale involving Catholics, an act of Providence intervened. Pius X died on August 20, 1914, "reknown for saintliness," according to one of his biographers, and of a "broken heart," finding himself in face of the horrors of the Great War, according to another. The most human of historical accidents, death, prevented *Papa* Sarto from carrying his last battle to a victorious conclusion. It is proper for a story in which this enigmatic figure is a central character to end with question marks. Was it that Pius X, persuaded by the critics of the articles in *Civiltà Cattolica,* abandoned plans to issue an anti-syndicalist encyclical?[33] Or did death prevent the release of a document that would have moved Catholic labor theory and practice back by four decades, exactly to the beginning of this story?

Conclusions

In 1984 the international press reported a statement by Pope John Paul II. It was a condemnation of class struggle as a "social evil" contrary to the spirit of Christianity. The statement, which rejected one of the basic tenets of "liberation theology," was a very old wine in a new bottle. It reflected a contradiction that ran in an uninterrupted line through the history of modern Catholic social thought, which recognizes distinct social classes but denies the reality of conflict among them.

That age-old contradiction touches upon a concept that is at the very core of Catholic and, indeed, all Christian theologies, the idea of *caritas,* Christian love. In applying this theological concept to modern society at the turn of the nineteenth century, Catholic sociology drew heavily on the writings of Aquinas, whose works represented the most sophisticated elaboration of the concept of *caritas.* Becoming an official philosophy of the church, Neo-Thomism provided important elements in Italian Catholic social doctrine in general and labor theory in particular. One of these was the concept of the *misto,* the mixed union, an organizational form that was the source of a great deal of discussion, frustration, and conflict in the Italian Catholic labor movement during its formative years.

The mixed union was to include among its members both the workers and the capitalists, thus establishing a symbiotic relationship between various social strata, a relationship based on shared love. The *misto,* which subjected the workers, the "inferior classes" in the parlance of Catholic sociology, to the charitable care and "tutelage" of the "superior classes," was a manifestation of paternalism, a system of labor relations that was rapidly becoming obsolete at the turn of the nineteenth century. Nevertheless the church leadership, wary of a social climate increasingly charged with conflict, supported the concept of the mixed union because it promised to avert class struggle.

Preventing the working classes from gaining autonomy and becoming a viable social and political force that would confront the upper classes was the aim of corporativism, an international ideological current that inspired the speakers at the congresses of Italian Catholic Action as they formulated the concept of the mixed union in the 1870s and 1880s. But during the last decade of the century, it became increasingly obvious that the *misto,* which was modeled on an idealized version of the medieval guilds, was an idea whose time had passed long ago.

Though it may have been a portent of hope and love for Italian Catholics, the mixed union became the source of a conflict between ideals and reality, between church leaders—the custodians of Catholic ideals—and Catholic activists, who were called upon to put these ideals into practice. The activists, daily facing reality, learned that the Italian workers were less and less inclined to submit to the permanent social inferiority implied in the "tutelage" of their interests within the mixed union.

It was a sign of realism on the part of Pope Leo XIII that in 1891 he decided to allow Catholic activists to organize simple unions, which were to enroll workers only. The pope stressed the importance of the mixed union as the ultimate aim, and his acceptance of the *semplice,* the simple union, was somewhat tentative, a part of the experimentation with new ideas and practices that characterized the Leonine period of church history. For instance, he encouraged the participation of priests in social action. The massive growth of the Italian Catholic labor movement during the last years of Leo's papacy was in part the result of the work of activist clergymen who, side by side with their lay brothers, brought one Catholic local after another into being.

However, those years also saw internal strife increasing in Italian Catholic Action, with the conservatives giving battle to the activists. Among those involved with organizing labor, the conflict centered on the simple union and was an unforeseen consequence of

Leo's acceptance of the *semplice*. As those who confronted the activists pointed out, this organizational form carried within it the potential of class struggle and of strikes, which Catholics of conservative persuasion considered manifestations of class struggle. The activists who organized simple unions were issuing an invitation to class struggle. Those who took the side of the workers in strikes—and what else could union leaders do?—were seen as violating the principle of *caritas*. The sight of priests on the picket lines was especially horrifying to Catholic conservatives, who argued that by taking sides in a social conflict these clergymen put the universality of their ministry in jeopardy.

Since the activists did not cease and desist, the conservatives' pressure for restoring the harmony between Catholic ideals and practices mounted. By 1903, when Pius X succeeded Leo XIII, the conflict between the two factions became so intense that it threatened Italian Catholic Action with paralysis. *Instaurare omnia in Christo*, "to restore all things in Christ," the motto Pius X announced for his papacy, implied the need for change. The new pope turned out to be a reformer who introduced an unprecedented number of changes during his relatively short papacy, but these changes involved the internal life of the church, such as improvements in religious practices, liturgy, church music, and administration. As far as social, political, and economic theories and practices were concerned, Pius X was not innovative but profoundly conservative, and considered the tenets of Thomistic philosophy working propositions for modern society. With the election of Pius X, the Leonine expansion of Catholic social theory ceased and experiments such as priests' participation in the Catholic labor movement were called off. For Pius X, who ordered a thorough reorganization of Italian Catholic Action, *instaurare omnia in Christo* meant making *caritas* the governing principle of social life. In *E supremi apostolatus*, his first encyclical, published in 1903, the announcement of the program of "restoring all things in Christ" was preceded by a stern condemnation of class struggle. And as late as 1910, Pius X insisted upon the mixed union as the basic organizational form of Italian Catholic labor.

During the years between 1903 and 1910, Italy experienced massive labor unrest in the form of wave after wave of strikes. Instead of waning, class consciousness was on the rise not only among the workers, who avoided the mixed union, but also among the *padroni,* the owners of industrial and agricultural enterprises. The *padroni,* of course, supported the idea of the mixed union because they recognized it for what it was, a means to keep the workers under paternalistic control. But their support was manifest more in words than in deeds. In practice the *padroni* were no less reluctant than the workers to join the mixed union. Unwilling to extend the effort and resources required by "angelic charity," which the theologians proclaimed the guiding principle of the mixed union, they organized employers' and property owners' associations instead.

The pope's insistence upon the mixed union and the avoidance of social conflict and strikes put Catholic labor organizers at a disadvantage in a time of labor unrest. The Catholic labor movement declined, and this was probably just as well as far as Pius X was concerned. The 1910 congress of Catholic Action refused to accept the mixed union and opted for the *semplice,* amidst an angry confrontation between the activists and the leaders, who echoed the pope in demanding the *misto.* Furthermore, a year later a statistical study appeared that showed the lack of realism in the pope's stance: the study revealed that among the hundreds of Catholic locals not one was a mixed union.

The situation clearly called for a doctrinal adjustment, which, dramatic as it sounds when mentioned in connection with religious doctrine, is not unknown in the history of the church. Catholic theology, like all religious doctrines, changes by shifting emphasis from one doctrinal element to another, focusing upon one part rather than another in the inexhaustible riches of the church's traditions. But how could a pontiff do anything but emphasize the need for Christian love; how could he not demand that *caritas,* the very essence of Christianity as it was the essence of God, guide the activities of the faithful? That which was contrary to Christian love had to disappear. Just before he died, Pius X was apparently preparing to issue an encyclical that would have called into question the very existence of Catholic labor movements and the simple union.

Some extant evidence suggests that during the last weeks of his life the pope may have decided against this move. His reconsideration might have been a response to the consternation of, and protest by, leading churchmen and lay activists that flooded the Vatican from all over the world. The protest and the influence it may have exerted point to an anomaly in church history. Pontiffs always tended to lavish special attention on the Catholics of Italy, not only because until 1870 popes were the heads of an Italian state, but also because they were of Italian origin. This attention meant closer supervision. Thus the shadow of the Vatican fell heavily on Italian Catholic Action, whereas Catholics abroad had somewhat greater freedom.

This was especially true at the turn of the nineteenth century, when the Italian faithful constituted an indispensable force for pontiffs in their struggle with the Italian state. This was shown by the Non Expedit, the ban on the participation of Catholic citizens in national elections, which, applying to Italy alone, gave Italian Catholic Action a distinctiveness that placed it outside the mainstream of the universal church, a uniqueness that brought with it the very close scrutiny of the Vatican.

Yet the pontiffs, leaders of a worldwide organization, daily observed and pondered the experience of the universal church, and this influenced their attitude toward Italy. More than once they looked abroad for examples for Italian Catholics to follow. Teaching by example was the church's traditional way of teaching. Thus, *Germania doceat!*—"teach us, Germany"—became the password Pius X handed down to his Italian followers.

However, this way of teaching by example implied that the experience of Catholics abroad had validity for Italian Catholics, and this meant a break with the uniqueness of Italian Catholic Action, which the pope wanted to maintain. The activists arguing against the Non Expedit would typically point abroad, especially to Germany and the success of German Catholics, not only in propaganda but in politics as well. By pointing to the need for a Catholic political party, Germany was teaching a lesson Pius X did not want Italian Catholics to learn. It was also teaching them the need for greater freedom, the need to get out of the shadow of the Vatican, to break out of the iron cage of conservativism that prevailed in the Vatican during the papacy of Pius X.

What Germany taught became a source of yet another conflict during the last year of the papacy of Pius X. The conflict had been smoldering for some time, but it exploded then in a very dramatic way. It was centered on the principle of *confessionalità,* the pope's insistence that Italian Catholic labor unions remain strictly religious in nature. The Catholic activists pointed out that this principle was damaging to the prospects of Catholic labor, for members who were practicing Catholics and doctrinally sound were hard to find, especially among the industrial workers. Nevertheless the relaxation of the principle of *confessionalità* in Italian Catholic social action did not come during the papacy of Pius X; it was to be one of the first acts of his successor. Pius X remained adamant about it as far as the Italian Catholic labor movement was concerned.

In 1912 he decided to grant a request that German Catholics had put forth for decades, and allowed German Catholic unions to enroll non-Catholics as members. *Singulari quadam,* the encyclical that announced the concession, was addressed to the German situation. Thus the Vatican maintained that since Italy, unlike Germany, was a religiously homogeneous society, *confessionalità* would remain valid for Italian Catholic labor. Pius X might have made a concession to this rule a few weeks before he died. If that indeed happened, this concession coincided with other signs indicating that the pope might have decided against issuing the antilabor encyclical, which would have placed the Catholic labor movement all over the world in jeopardy from a doctrinal point of view.

If indeed Pius X did make such a decision, this represented a change in position. Did Pius X, a headstrong man, change his mind? The acts of his life speak against such an interpretation. The hallmark of his style was consistency, both in doctrine and in the application of doctrine to life. His consistency in social doctrine was that of Neo-Thomistic social philosophy. The failure of the mixed union, indicating the ultimate failure of Neo-Thomism as a social philosophy, is the most important marker on the road of the development of the Italian Catholic labor movement during the papacy of Pius X, an era that resounded with conflict between ideas and reality, with a battle between an idealistically motivated leader and social activists who represented reality. Ideas eventually had to give way to reality.

If everything could have been restored in Christ and all men subjected to His laws, as Pius X hoped, there would have been no class conflict. Equilibrium among classes would have prevailed, and cooperation among classes and productive social peace would have been possible. If only everything could have been restored in Christ and everyone subjected to His laws! For above all the laws of Christ demanded *caritas,* love and consideration for one's fellow man. The laws of Christ prescribed concise and abiding duties to individuals as well as to classes.

But the laws of Christ did not govern society. They never did except in the medieval utopia of Neo-Thomists like Pius X. Hence the expectations of Pius X appear highly idealistic. But do all social programs not appear idealistic, especially as seen through the looking glass of time? Nonetheless, it is also true that all social reformers have to confront reality: they must come to terms with it in order to transform it.

"Even though we aspire to the infinite, to act we need concrete, limited, finite goals, a practical ideal, a specific program," said Luigi Sturzo.[1] The Catholics' confrontation with reality came as they attempted to work out such concrete programs. In the crucible of life, the ideal of the mixed union melted away into a heap of ashes. When faced with reality, the ideal world of Neo-Thomism proved itself to be a utopia. Thomism had the potential to become a tool of realistic social analysis, and to some extent it became one in northern Europe, especially in Germany and Belgium. But in Italy, Neo-Thomism degenerated into something to which the label "philosophy" might justifiably be denied, since Italian Neo-Thomists seem to have forgotten too often that philosophy means asking questions.

The promise represented by the works of early Italian Thomists like Matteo Liberatore proved to be false in the long run. The dialectical method, intrinsic to the works of Aquinas, was put to masterly use for analyzing the ideas of mid-century Catholics in Liberatore's 1846 dialogue.[2] But one searches in vain for the dialectic in the social analyses of Neo-Thomists at the turn of the century, who allowed the dialectic to become the exclusive property of Marxists. It is rare to see in their works a creative application of Thomistic ideas to the modern world. Instead, they attempted to fit modern society into a rigid, dogmatic framework of Thomistic principles. And if these principles turned out to be straitjackets, neither philosophy nor Aquinas but only the Neo-Thomists are to blame. For Aquinas's philosophy, as Etienne Gilson and Ralph M. McInerny have recently pointed out,[3] was an extremely creative adaptation of Aristotle's thought to medieval intellectual, social, and political conditions, as well as to the principles of Christianity. But Aquinas's method of continuous questioning stood in contrast to the dogmatism of most of his self-proclaimed disciples at the turn of the century, whose work more often than not was an exercise in what Gilson described as interpreting "a universe that has long ceased to exist."

It is, however, unfair to fault only scholars for the shortcomings of modern Thomism and to lavish praise, as Gilson did, on the Neo-Thomistic initiatives of the leaders of the Catholic church. In so doing Gilson seems to have overlooked the fact that it was the church that made the thought of Aquinas a philosophy *ex decreto.* Monsignor Amato Masnovo, a historian of Italian Neo-Thomism who cannot be accused of either antichurch or anti-Thomistic bias, observed that soon after the publication of *Aeterni Patris,* the encyclical that turned Thomism into an official philosophy of the church, the Neo-Thomistic current that "gained in extension" began to "lose in profundity." Its newly gained popularity amounted to vulgarization and led to superficiality.[4] One is tempted to ask if this is not the fate of every official doctrine.

The Neo-Thomistic scholars who attempted to force the modern world into a straitjacket of dogmatic Thomistic principles were following the lead of papal doctrinal statements. Because these papal teachings often took the form of an encyclical, a weighty form of expression for Catholics, the burden of an inflexible Thomism came to rest on the consciences and intellectual outlooks of Catholics all over the world, but especially in Italy. The ossification of Thomism, already at work under Leo, reached its height during the papacy of Pius X. A study of the directives and practices of this pontiff leaves one with doubts about the positive contributions Gilson and McInerny claimed for papal Thomism and leads one to suspect that the ossification and sterile orthodoxy of Neo-Thomism did not come in spite of the intentions of the church leaders, as Gilson and McInerny suggested, but because of them.

Throughout his career as a churchman, Giuseppe Sarto insisted that the Thomistic doctrine had modern validity.[5] One of the last documents released in his name was the *motu proprio* "Doctoris

Angelici," which ordered Italian seminaries to make scholastic philosophy the basis of "sacred studies." "Doctoris Angelici" was followed by a decree of the Sacred Congregation of Studies that summed up Thomistic philosophy in twenty-four "theses." The publication of the "theses" was the culmination of the development of Neo-Thomism during the papacy of Pius X. With its method of confining Thomistic doctrine to dogmatic "theses," the decree was symbolic of the quality of philosophical research involved in the church-sponsored Thomism. This very method leads one to question the praise James A. Weisheipl directed at the "ardent" Neo-Thomistic efforts of Pius X. Ironically, the same writer pointed out that Thomism became "closed, safe, and sterile," "imposed by legislative authority. Legislation did not stimulate a return to the true thought and spirit of St. Thomas relevant to our day."[6] The reduction of the thought of Aquinas into dogmatic "theses" whose unquestioned acceptance was expected of all Catholics shows that Pius X did not believe, to paraphrase McInerny, that Thomism had to meet the same demands in the intellectual marketplace as any other philosophical position. In a 1911 editorial comment, the *Rivista di filosofia neoscolastica,* a church-sponsored publication, reflected the "stupor" of many of the pope's contemporaries who renewed the old objection to making Thomism a philosophy *ex decreto;* but the editors denied, of course, that something like that was happening.[7]

Although both the *motu proprio* and the decree of the Sacred Congregation dealt with theological problems, it would be a mistake to conclude that for Pius X the doctrinal validity of Thomism never extended into the realms of social and political life. He condemned the modernists precisely because they argued that theology and religion could be separated from social and political problems, and that the pope's authority should be limited to theological and strictly religious matters. Murri expressed this position when he declared that he doubted the pope enjoyed "special light from the Lord" in connection with social and political problems.[8]

The pope's insistence that he spoke with an authority binding on all the faithful in social matters implied a serious restriction for Catholic social doctrine. It tied the solutions of modern social problems to a program of "restoration" based on the Thomistic utopia of medieval society. One of the "errors" of the modernists mentioned in *Pascendi,* the encyclical Pius X addressed to the problems of modernism, was their desire to see the church's attitude towards social questions changed. That was, for Pius, an aspect of the modernists' "reforming mania." "Social modernism," associated by orthodox theologians with ideas such as those expressed by Romolo Murri and the Lega Democratica Nazionale, came to be connected with a rejection of the applicability of Thomistic principles to modern society. In this Pius X gave the lead in *Pascendi.* The modernists, the pope stated, wanted to abandon the old ways of the Thomistic synthesis and to "relegate" scholastic philosophy to the realm of the history of philosophy because they considered it irrelevant to modern realities.[9]

But the pope silenced those who, like Giovanni Ravaglia, attempted to relate the principles of Thomism to modern social conditions, and in so doing implied that social justice went beyond charity to include the right of the workers to demand what was their due. The *forma mentis* that prevailed in the Vatican during the papacy of Pius X was mirrored in a papal letter to the archbishop of Los Angeles.[10] Dated January 27, 1910, this letter tied together in a single Latin sentence the suggestion that Aquinas is "leader and teacher" with the demand for submission *omnio et in omnibus* to the Apostolic See. This obedience entailed the final degeneration of Thomism from a tool of social analysis into a dogmatic rehashing of selected sayings of the Angelic Doctor. This was shown by the fact that in 1914, according to Toniolo's carefully considered judgment, the *Rivista internazionale di scienze sociali*—established by Pope Leo to foster Thomistic research—could not publish "materials of a controversial nature," such as Caissotti's essay that questioned the social philosophical wisdom emanating from the Vatican through the *Civiltà Cattolica.*

The degeneration and ultimate decline of Thomism was the eclipse of Toniolo, whose *oeuvre* in Italy, if not worldwide, was the most significant attempt to create a social science and an understanding of modern society based on Thomistic notions. Toniolo was the revered master of a generation of Catholic intellectuals and a teacher who broadcast from the speaker's platforms of Catholic congresses that social science had to be an "apology for charity" and that charity was "a scientific category." Today he is almost completely forgotten. During the 1950s someone in a position of importance must have thought that Toniolo was a great thinker, for the Vatican published his *Opera Omnia* during the same decade that Pius X was elevated to sainthood. But the glory reflected by the figure of the pontiff, the first pope to become a saint in several centuries, was not enough to revive the fortunes of his faithful servant and adviser. The publication of Toniolo's collected works just proved that he was hopelessly obsolete as a social scientist. More than that, he became nearly incomprehensible even to the very small group of experts who use his works as documents of an age. His writings are monuments to the failure of the Neo-Thomistic revival.

One might say that whatever existed in the past, by virtue of its existence, is safe from being called a failure. It is true that, when it first appeared, Neo-Thomism acquired historical significance by providing key elements for an ideology that served, as all ideologies do, to justify as well as to cover up particular social interests. Like the veils painted over the naked figures of Michelangelo's frescos in the Sistine Chapel, Neo-Thomistic ideas were used to cover up the naked class interests of the rural aristocracy. The beginning of the Neo-Thomistic revival coincided with the halcyon days of the Restoration: the ideas of the Angelic Doctor were recalled to combat the ideology of the Revolution of 1789. Not unexpectedly, Thomism went into decline as the alliance between the aristocracy and church lost its actuality, and as a new social force—the bourgeoisie— replaced the landed aristocrats in social and political importance. A sign of the waning of Thomism was that the Thomistic review *Divus Thomas,* published in Rome since 1880, folded in 1905, apparently because the dwindling number of subscribers did not provide sufficient support for its survival. It was to be "revived" in 1909 under the personal guidance of Pius X in the form of the *Rivista di filosofia neo-scolastica.*[11] But the new review, at least during the era of Pius X, was characterized by an almost total lack of interest in the application of Thomism to social and political problems.[12]

The last two decades of the nineteenth century witnessed the elaboration of a Thomistically-oriented Catholic social and political philosophy. During those years Italian Catholic Action evolved under the overbearing influence of Neo-Thomism. But the very fact that at that time Catholics stressed the need for a total transformation of society amounted to an admission of the inapplicability of the Thomistic vision of life to modern society. With their advocacy of a corporative "reconstruction" of society, the Catholics conceded that the Thomistic ideas were working propositions only for a society reconstructed along medieval lines. Thomism as a program for social and political action was a dead-end street. It led Catholics into the rejection of the social and political world in which they lived, into a program of action that was no less utopian than that of the revolutionary Socialists, whom the Catholics so bitterly opposed.

During the first two decades of the twentieth century, many Italian Catholics gradually abandoned the Neo-Thomistic utopia of medieval society, and with it the insistence upon the all-encompassing modern validity of notions like charity and alms that grew out of Thomism. The more they became involved in social action, the more insufficient the reliance on the individual conscience alone in dealing with the problem of the working classes appeared to Catholics. They had to realize that the fate of the "poor," the working classes, had to be a subject of legally guaranteed rights. What this implied, in turn, was that the Catholics, those self-proclaimed champions of the "poor," had to gain representation in the Parliament, where laws were made and modified.

Yet Pius X did not allow for the establishment of a Catholic political party. Lacking a party through which to channel their efforts toward social reforms, the Catholics increasingly drifted toward an alliance with the political forces under Giovanni Giolitti's direction, for they were attempting to see through Parliament some of the very same social legislation the Catholics were urging. This alliance, tentative at first, became increasingly important toward the end of the papacy of Pius X and was consummated on a very large scale with the Gentiloni Pact in 1913.

The pact, which represented the virtual abandonment of the principle of the Non Expedit and allowed Catholic voters to go to the polls in very large numbers, was shrouded in secrecy. Prime Minister Giolitti, a representative and leader of the liberal bourgeoisie, never admitted that he had anything to do with it nor that it involved some of his men. But V. O. Gentiloni, the president of the Unione Elettorale, one of the Catholic national organizations that appeared after Pius X remade Italian Catholic Action in his own image, claimed that hundreds of candidates signed individual agreements promising to uphold Catholic interests in the Chamber. It was also public knowledge that there were Giolittian liberals among the two hundred deputies, whom, Gentiloni asserted, were elected with Catholic votes in the 1913 elections.[13]

Pius X, who kept a tight rein on Italian Catholic Action, and whose confidant Gentiloni was, certainly knew about the pact. Indeed, it must have originated with him. It appears to have been the culmination of a policy initiated in 1904, when for the first time the pope lifted the Non Expedit in a few localities where Catholic votes were deemed necessary to prevent the election of radical and Socialist candidates. What was in 1904 a trickle of Catholic votes became a flood with the Gentiloni Pact. This retreat from the policy of Non Expedit, like the insistence upon the mixed union, was an integral part of a drive to prevent the industrial working class from becoming a viable social and political force, or, as the Socialists would have it, "the arbiter of the future." Behind it was an obsessive concern with the threat of socialism and an equally obsessive fear of the industrial working class, which in the minds of Catholic conservatives like Pius X, was associated with socialism.

In searching for a base from which to confront the "Socialist menace," something that he apparently considered a mortal threat to the church, the pope reached out toward the bourgeoisie. The outline of an alliance between wealth and the altar was slow to emerge, but it eventually became one of the defining characteristics of the papacy of Pius X. As this alliance was becoming a working proposition, Thomism was turning into a burden. Reminding men of means of the obligations the laws of *caritas* imposed on them became something of an anomaly. Thus a year after the alliance between wealth and the altar came to a denouement with the Gentiloni Pact, Pius X not only tolerated but apparently approved arguments that implied the abandonment of the Thomistic principle of the "social functions of property."

But with a conservative like Pius X as their taskmaster, Italian Catholics were condemned to run forever behind the spirit of the age. In 1914 the pope was apparently ready to abandon the old struggle against liberal social philosophy. Drawing conclusions from the alliance between wealth and the altar, he seems to have contemplated an alignment of Catholic social doctrine with the tenets of Manchesterian capitalism. However, by 1914 liberal bourgeois like Giolitti were giving up many of these tenets as obsolete, rejecting, for instance, the idea of the permanence of poverty on the social landscape. "New Liberalism," a liberalism with a social conscience, was on the rise.[14]

Notes

Introduction

1. See my "Giolitti's Reform Program: An Exercise in Equilibrium Politics"; "Christian Democracy and Social Modernism in Italy during the Papacy of Pius X"; "The Road of Charity Leads to the Picket Lines"; " 'Germania Doceat!' "

2. Salvatore Talamo, *La questione sociale e i cattolici.* Talamo, "one of those who inspired" *Aeterni Patris,* the Thomistic encyclical of Leo XIII, was the founder and director of the Neo-Thomistic *Rivista internazionale di scienze sociali e discipline ausiliarie* (Jean-Marie Mayeur, "Catholicisme intransigeant, catholicisme social, démocratie chrétienne," p. 489).

Chapter 1

1. Leo XIII, encyclical *Inscrutabili Dei consilio,* p. 8.

2. Leo XIII, encyclical *Aeterni Patris,* passim, especially p. 23; also Roger Aubert, "Aspects divers du Néo-thomisme sous le pontificat de Léon XIII," pp. 135ff., 211; Giovanni Bortolaso, "Il centenario dell enciclica " 'Aeterni Patris.' "

3. Aubert, "Aspects divers du néo-thomisme," pp. 159, 200, 214, 218. (Here and throughout this volume, translations of quotations from sources other than English, unless indicated otherwise, are my own.)

4. The importance of scholastic philosophers other than Aquinas, particularly of John Duns Scotus and Francisco Suarez, was such as to induce some historians to talk of a Neo-Scholastic intellectual current distinguishable from Neo-Thomism, with the latter apparently prevalent in Italy. (Oskar Köhler, in Roger Auber et al., *The Church in the Industrial Age,* p. 311ff.; also Giuseppe Rossini (ed.), *Romolo Murri nella storia politica e religiosa del suo tempo,* p. 387ff., especially the contributions of Paul Droulers, Emile Poulat, and Roger Aubert.

5. Aubert, "Aspects divers du néo-thomisme," pp. 150ff., 165ff., 238ff.; also remarks by Pietro Scoppola and Giacomo Martina in Rossini (ed.), *Romolo Murri nella storia,* pp. 387ff. and 428ff. The entries in the diary of a young cleric, Angelo Roncalli, the future Pope John XXIII, testify to the importance of Aquinas and Thomism in the intellectual and spiritual education of Catholic clergymen at the turn of the century. (See his *Journal of a Soul,* pp. 181, 221.) References to Aquinas recur in the biographies of Catholic laymen also. For an example see Alfonso Casoli, *Un campione della causa cattolica,* p. 14.

6. Aubert, "Aspects divers du néo-thomisme," pp. 136–37; and Pasquale Orlando, *Il tomismo a Napoli nel secolo XIX. La scuola del Sanseverino,* expecially p. 12.

7. Angelo Marchesan, *Papa Pio X nella sua vita e nella sua parola,* p. 87. This is the only biography of Pius X that may be considered "authorized," not only because it was written by a close associate of the pope but also because Pius X read and corrected the first draft.

Among the most useful of the other biographies of the pope are René Bazin, *Pie X,* especially pp. 19, 27; and Igino Giordani, *Pio X, un prete di campagna,* especially pp. 13–14. The "official" biography, instrumental in the canonization of Sarto, reports extensively on his involvement with Thomism. It tells, for instance, that Sarto enjoyed the years he spent as chaplain in a small village because he had then time to deepen his knowledge of the *Summa.* And later, as *vicario capitolare,* the temporary head of a diocese, he talked to his clergy about the need for studying St. Thomas, and the *Summa* in particular (Girolamo Dal-Gal, *Il Papa santo, Pio X,* especially pp. 16, 173ff.

8. The remark of De Maistre about Romantic philosophy applies to the Neo-Thomistic current as well: "Nous ne voulons pas la contre-révolution mais le contraire de la révolution" (quoted in Karl Mannheim, "Conservative Thought," p. 80).

9. Aubert, "Aspects divers du néo-thomisme," pp. 133 and 166; also remarks by Scoppola in Rossini (ed.), *Romolo Murri nella storia,* especially p. 393; Mayeur, "Catholicisme intransigeant," pp. 483–99, particularly p. 489. For a recent historiographical account about the Neo-Thomistic revival, see Marcia L. Colish, "St. Thomas Aquinas in Historical Perspective." For some of the most significant reflections on the Italian aspects of the revival, see Salvatore Talamo, *L'odierna scuola tomistica e i suoi avversari;* Giovanni Gentile, "Neotomisti"; Amato Masnovo, "Il prof. G. Gentile e il Thomismo italiano dal 1850 al 1900"; "Il neotomismo in Italia dopo il 1870"; "Il significato storico del neotomismo"; Benedetto Croce, "I 'neo' in filosofia."

10. Leo XIII, encyclical *Aeterni Patris,* especially p. 25; also Rogert Aubert, *The Church in a Secularized Society,* pp. 9, 171ff.; Oskar Köhler, in Aubert et al., *The Church in the Industrial Age,* p. 307ff.; and my "The Road of Charity Leads to the Picket Lines."

Chapter 2

1. The chapter title is from Leo XIII, encyclical *Quod apostolici muneris,* p. 11; Leo XIII, encyclical *Rerum novarum,* p. 257; Geremia Bonomelli, "Il clero e la società moderna," p. 268.

2. Aquinas, *Summa Theologica* (henceforth referred to as *Summa*), I-II, q. 66 and II-II, qq. 23–27; Leo XIII, encyclical *Graves de communi,* pp. 482–83; Pius X, encyclical *E supremi apostolatus,* p. 10; *motu proprio* "Fin dalla prima," pp. 5–6; *L'Osservatore Romano,* Sept. 13, 1905, and Sept. 17, 1905; Alfonso Capecelatro, *Amiamo il popolo,* pp. 5–6; Giacomo Radini Tedeschi, *Discorso tenuto nell'adunanza generale della Società di S. Vincenzo di Paoli,* pp. 3–4; Julien Fontaine, *Le modernisme sociologique,* p. 468. Arguments presented by Fontaine will frequently appear in this volume: Pius X praised the author for his "profound theological and social understanding" (*Acta Apostolicae Sedis,* 1 (1909): 719).

3. *Summa,* II-II, qq. 31–33; Raimondo Spiazzi, "Il trattato teologico della carità," in Spiazzi et al., *Teologia e storia della carità,* p. 178. Spiazzi's essay testifies to the overwhelming importance of Aquinas in Catholic theology even today: his treatise on the theological aspects of charity is built almost entirely on Thomistic ideas. His, as well as two other essays in the volume (Tullio Goffi, "La carità e l'elemosina," and Carlo Messori, "La carità e la pubblica assistenza"), were helpful for my initial understanding of the problems involved in the theological principles of charity.

4. Leo XIII, encyclical *Rerum novarum,* pp. 246–47; Pius X, encyclical *E supremi apostolatus; motu proprio* Fin dalla prima," p. 5; Simon Deploige, "La théorie thomiste de la propriété," p. 293; Radini Tedeschi, *Discorso tenuto,* p. 6; *L'Osservatore Romano,* April 18, 1912; Eugenio di Carlo, *La filosofia giuridica e politica di San Tommaso d'Aquino,* p. 105; Francesco Olgiati, "La politica di S. Pio X e il conservatorismo," p. 53lff.

5. *Summa*, II-II q. 66; John A. Ryan, "The Economic Philosophy of St. Thomas," pp. 245–46; Spiazzi (ed.), *Teologia e storia*, pp. 251, 264; Glauco Tozzi, *I fondamenti dell'economia in Tommaso d'Aquino*, p. 163ff.

6. Alfonso Capecelatro, *La quistione sociale e il cristianesimo*, pp. 12–13; also Geremia Bonomelli, "La questione sociale è questione morale" p. 125; *Summa*, I-II, q. 94.

7. Deploige, "La théorie thomiste de la propriété," pp. 166–67. As examples of the property debate, see Alfred O'Rahilly, "S. Thomas's Theory of Property"; J. B. McLaughlin, "S. Thomas and Property"; Januarius De Concilio, *The Doctrine of St. Thomas on the Right of Property and Its Use*, pp. 29–30; also William Edward Hogan, *The Development of Bishop Wilhelm Emmanuel von Ketteler's Interpretation of the Social Problem*, p. 240. A wide range of other interpretations are mentioned in Adolfo Vykopal, *La dottrina del superfluo in San Tommaso*.

8. *Summa*, II-II, q. 66. All passages quoted in English from the *Summa*, unless otherwise indicated, are from the translation published in London by Burns, Oates & Washbourne, 1920.

9. *Allarme!*, handbill of the Unione Popolare, No. 31 (1910); Andrea Cappellazzi, *Le moderne libertà esaminate secondo i principii della filosofia scolastica*, p. 201ff.; Giuseppe Toniolo, "L'Unione cattolica per gli studi sociali in Italia," pp. 96–97; Talamo, *La questione sociale*, p. 38; Geremia Bonomelli, "Proprietà e socialismo," p. 20ff.; Bonomelli, "La questione sociale," p. 125; Angelo Brucculeri, *La funzione sociale della proprietà*, pp. 105–6; Tozzi, *I fondamenti dell'economia*, p. 125ff.; Giulio Monetti, *Problemi varii di sociologia generale*, 1:47ff. Monetti's work is of special importance for the study of the social doctrine of the church: Pope Pius X, who appears to have read these volumes, felt compelled to tell the author in a widely publicized letter that he found Monetti's treatise "doctrinally sound and of indispensable utility" (*Azione Sociale* 7, Nov. 1913, pp. 197–98).

10. For examples see Ryan, "The Economic Philosophy of St. Thomas," pp. 242–43; O'Rahilly, "S. Thomas's Theory of Property," pp. 349–51. The relevant discussion is in *Summa*, II-II, qq. 57, 66.

11. Leo XIII, encyclical *Rerum novarum*, pp. 242, 246–47; Pius X, *moto proprio* "Fin dalla prima," p. 5; Fontaine, *Le modernisme sociologique*, pp. 162, 245, 322, 431ff.; Bernard Roland-Gosselin, *La doctrine politique de Saint Thomas d'Aquin*, p. 152ff.; Vykopal, *La dottrina del superfluo*, pp. 32ff., 42ff.; Richard L. Camp, *The Papal Ideology of Social Reform: A Study in Historical Development, 1878–1967*, pp. 14, 60.

12. Saint Augustine, quoted in O'Rahilly, "S. Thomas's Theory of Property," p. 344.

13. *Summa*, II-II, qq. 31–32; also Monetti, *Problemi varii*, 2:118; and Spiazzi et al., *Teologia e storia della carità* pp. 176–77, 260–64, 273.

14. Leo XIII, encyclical *Rerum novarum*, pp. 246–47; Pius X, letter to Count de Mun, Jan. 7, 1913, in *Azione Sociale* 7, Jan. 1913, pp. 1–2; also De Concilio, *The Doctrine of St. Thomas*, pp. 38–43; Deploige, "La théorie thomiste de la propriété," p. 290ff.; Capecelatro, *La quistione sociale*, pp. 12–15; handbill *Allarme!* No. 31, 1910; Vykopal, *La dottrina del superfluo*, pp. 12ff., 22ff.

15. Shepard B. Clough, *The Economic History of Modern Italy*, pp. 59–60.

16. Vykopal, *La dottrina del superfluo*, p. 66ff.; Francesco Vito, "Trasformazioni economiche e dottrina cattolica," p. 28ff.

17. Edoardo Briére, *Ai padroni: loro missione e doveri*, pp. 18–19. The productive social use of property is also emphasized, and Aquinas quoted in support of the argument, in Talamo, *La questione sociale*, p. 13.

18. O'Rahilly, "S. Thomas's Theory of Property," p. 345ff.; also Ryan, "The Economic Philosophy of St. Thomas," pp. 246–47; Vykopal, *La dottrina del superfluo*, p. 24; Tozzi, *I fondamenti dell'economia*, p. 118ff.

19. Aquinas, quoted in De Concilio, *The Doctrine of St. Thomas*, p. 41.

20. Bonomelli, "La questione sociale," p. 122.

21. Concerning Thomistic doctrine being "truncated," see Oskar Köhler, in Aubert et al., *The Church in the Industrial Age*, pp. 196–99. Luigi Taparelli d'Azeglio (1793–1862) was the teacher of Leo XIII and a leading Thomist. As the editor of *Civiltà Cattolica* and because of his publications, which were widely read, he became a major figure in Catholic intellectual life. Some of his short pieces about property were reprinted as appendixes to Angelo Perego's *Forma statale e politica finanziaria nel pensiero di Luigi Taparelli d' Azeglio*, especially p. 272ff. Aquinas is quoted in De Concilio, *The Doctrine of St. Thomas*, p. 38; see also Deploige, "La théorie thomiste de la propriété," p. 290; O'Rahilly, "S. Thomas's Theory of property," p. 352ff.

22. Achille Sassoli de' Bianchi, *La questione sociale nelle campagne*, pp. 15–18. It appears that the speech acted as a catalyst in forming the social ideas of the leaders of Italian Catholic Action. Their biographies mention that the marquis's arguments were decisive in forming the intellectual outlooks of Stanislao Medolago Albani and Nicolo Rezzara. (See Stanislao Medolago Albani, *Due campioni dell'azione cattolica bergamasca*, p. 8ff.; Casoli, *Un campione*, p. 10ff.) Sassoli's speech was reprinted in 1922 as the first in a series of Catholic propaganda pamphlets. The editor stated in the foreword that "the passing of time did not effect the eternal actuality of this speech." Here is a passage from it: "We have to become convinced that every landed estate is like a state, that within its confines the landowner is a little prince, who, in order to preserve the legitimacy of his power, has the duty to assure the well-being of his dependents." Elsewhere the marquis mentions the employees of the landowner as his "subjects." (See also Angelo Gambasin, "L'utopia sociale dei congressi cattolici in Italia prima dalla 'Rerum novarum,' " p. 40.)

23. Bonomelli, "Proprietà," pp. 5, 49–50; Stanislao Medolago Albani, *Le classi dirigenti nella società*, pp. 13–14.

24. For an example see Brière, *Ai padroni*, p. 12.

25. Old Roman traditions survived in this perception, as M. I. Finley, in *The Ancient Economy*, pp. 18–19, suggests: "The Latin familia had a wide spectrum of meanings: all the persons, free or unfree, under the authority of the *paterfamilias*, the head of the household; or all the descendants from a common ancestor; or all one's property; or simply all one's servants (hence the *familia Caesaris* comprised all the personal slaves and freedmen in the imperial service, but not the emperor's wife and children)." See also Medolago, *Le classi dirigenti*, p. 32; Alfonso Capecelatro, *La povertà, l'industria e il sapere in relazione al cristianesimo*, p. 22; Brière, *Ai padroni*, p. 45; Antonio Boggiano Pico, "Attualità del pensiero di Giuseppe Toniolo," p. 58; Vykopal, *La dottrina del superfluo*, p. 22ff.; Donald H. Bell, "Worker Culture and Worker Politics: The Experience of An Italian Town, 1880–1915," p. 5.

26. Alessandro Cantono, *Le Università popolari e la democrazia*, particularly pp. 13, 23, 42. For similar opinions see Murri's preface to Cantono's volume and Gennaro Avolio, *I cattolici di fronte a'mali sociali*, particularly p. 31; Lorenzo Bedeschi, (ed.), *I pioneri della D.C.*, which reprints writings by Christian Democrats; also Geremia Bonomelli, *La Chiesa e i tempi nuovi*, p. 28. Bonomelli's pastoral letter, which also appeared to have been in favor of a reconciliation between the church and the Italian state, met with the severe disapproval of Pius X.

27. For Leo's concept of Christian Democracy, see his encyclical *Graves de communi;* Pius X reiterates this position in his *motu proprio* "Fin dalla prima," p. 6.

28. Briére, *Ai padroni,* p. 12.

29. Marchesan, *Papa Pio X,* pp. 344, 409; Eugenio Bacchion, *Pio X, Giuseppe Sarto, Arciprete di Salzano,* particularly pp. 126, 139; Giordani, *Pio X;* Dal-Gal, *Il Papa santo,* particularly pp. 32, 123; Nello Vian, "Umanità e umorismo di Pio X." The testament of Pius X stating, "I was born poor, I lived poor, and I desire to die poor," is quoted in Hary Mitchell, *Pie X et la France,* p. 238.

30. For a review of nineteenth-century Italian writings about the Social Question, see Rodolfo De Mattei, "Le prime discussioni in Italia sull'esistenza e sull'essenza d'una 'Questione Sociale.' "

31. Unione cattolica per gli studi sociali in Italia, *Atti e documenti del secondo congresso italiano degli studiosi di scienze sociali tenutosi in Padova nel giorni 26, 27, 28 Agosto 1896,* pp. 111–12.

32. Talamo, *La questione sociale,* especially p. 39; Capecelatro, *La povertà,* p. 18, *La quistione sociale,* p. 20, and *Amiamo il popolo,* pp. 19–21.

33. Pius X, encyclical, *E supremi apostolatus,* p. 10, and the encyclical *Il fermo proposito,* pp. 37, 40; also Medolago Albani, *Le classi dirigenti,* particularly pp. 12–13. My presentation of this particular relationship as a symbiosis originated in a discussion not related to the era of Pius X in Carl E. Schorske, "The Idea of the City in European Thought."

Chapter 3

1. The chapter title is from Leo XIII, encyclical *Quod Apostolici muneris,* p. 13. Aquinas, *Summa,* I, q. 108; II-II, qq. 58, 61; also De Concilio, *The Doctrine of St. Thomas,* pp. 18–19; Achille Malagola, *Le teorie politiche di San Tommaso d'Aquino,* p. 98; Ryan, "The Economic Philosophy of St. Thomas," pp. 239–40; F. C. Coplestone, *Aquinas,* p 239ff.; also my "The Road to Charity Leads to the Picket Lines." As Ernst Troeltsch pointed out, social organicism in its medieval formulation was somewhat less emphatic on the biological analogy, yet it was just as pointed as its modern versions about the need for unity and harmony among the members of the organically ordered social body. See Troeltsch's *The Social Doctrine of the Churches and Christian Groups,* p. 284.

2. For a detailed discussion of the organic analogy in Leo's encyclicals, see Camp, *The Papal Ideology of Social Reform,* p. 29ff.; also Leo XIII, encyclical *Graves de communi,* pp. 481–82; Giacomo Radini Tedeschi, *San Giorgio M[artire]e la questione operaia,* p. 7; Fontaine, *Le modernisme sociologique,* p. 139ff.; I. Imberciadori, *L'Unione Popolare fra i cattolici d'Italia,* p. 19; Monetti, *Problemi varii,* 2:125ff.; Gianfranco Legitimo, *Sociologi cattolici italiani,* pp. 88–89.

3. Aquinas's treatment of "justice" in *Summa,* II-II, qq. 58, 61, may have given them the lead: for the Angelic Doctor stressed the social dependence of the parts on the whole. According to a reliable interpreter of Catholic social doctrine, Pope Pius XI later "added a new element to Catholic teaching." In opposition to the totalitarian annihilation of the individual, he emphasized the importance and indispensability of the individuals, of the parts in the life of the social whole (see Ryan, "The Economic Philosophy of St. Thomas," p. 239ff.).

4. Medolago Albani, *Le classi dirigenti,* p. 9ff.

5. Giuseppe Toniolo, *Lettere,* vol. 3, especially p. 220; Bonomelli, *Il clero e la società moderna,* p. 273ff.; F. F. Chiesa, *L'Unione popolare spiegata ai contadini,* p. 9; Capecelatro, *Amiamo il popolo,* p. 3; *Azione Sociale* 1, Jan. 1907, pp. 107–8, and 2, Aug. 1908, p. 482; *Allarme!* No. 31, 1910, p. 3ff. The perception that equated the working classes with the "poor"

was apparently not unique to Italian Catholics, or Catholics in general, but persisted throughout Christendom (see Adam Wandruszka, "Il cattolicesimo politico e sociale nell'Austria-Ungheria degli anni 1870–1914," p. 160).

6. Toniolo's importance is clear in that even the activists, who eventually parted company with him, considered Toniolo their master at first. Murri, for instance, in 1899 acknowledged Toniolo as the "captain" when it came to leadership in social philosophy, which according to Murri was "capitanato in questi ultimi anni da un uomo che dice solo tutto uno programma, il Prof. Toniolo" (quoted in Giuseppe Are, "Introduzione," p. 37).

7. Gabriele De Rosa, *Il movimento cattolico in Italia dalla Restaurazione all'età giolittiana*, p. 336ff.; P. Pratesi, "Luci e ombre nella sociologia di Toniolo," particularly p. 17; Paolo Emilio Taviani, "Il concetto di democrazia cristiana in Giuseppe Toniolo," particularly p. 11. For Cardinal Sarto's approval of Toniolo's arguments, see Pius X, *Lettere, raccolte da Nello Vian*, pp. 259–60.

8. Leo XIII, encyclical *Graves de communi*, p. 484; Pius X, encyclical *Il fermo proposito*, p. 39.

9. *L'Osservatore Romano*, April 6, 1910; *Allarme!* No. 31 (1910); *Azione Sociale* 3, June 1909, p. 145ff., and Briére, *Ai padroni*, p. 33. For a description of the "buon padrone," see Salvadori, *Il movimento cattolico a Torino*, pp. 103–4.

10. Giuseppe Biederlack, *Principi dell'ordinamento economico-sociale cristiano*, p. 141ff.; Medolago, *Le classi dirigenti*, pp. 23–24; Sassoli de'Bianchi, *La questione sociale*, p. 5.

11. Salvatore Talamo, *Il cristianesimo e il lavoro manuale*, p. 6ff.; Toniolo, *Lettere*, 3:61, 97, 147–48; also my " 'Germania Doceat.' "

12. Toniolo, as quoted in Taviani, "Il concetto di democrazia," p. 11.

13. Toniolo, as quoted in Are, "Introduzione," p. 24; also Toniolo, "L'Unione cattolica per gli studi sociali," p. 90. Often the term *hierarchical* was tied together with the word *organic* in Catholic writings. For an example see the unsigned article entitled "L'Unione Popolare Italiana: avvertenze," in *Civiltà Cattolica* 58 (1907), vol. 1, pp. 134–35.

14. Leo XIII, encyclical *Quod Apostolici muneris*, p. 13; Pius X, encyclical *Pascendi Dominici gregis*, pp. 80–81, 90; Pius X, letter *Notre charge apostolique*, pp. 621–22; "L'Unione Popolare Italiana: avertenze," especially p. 129ff.; Fontaine, *Le modernisme sociologique*, p. v; Monetti, *Problemi varri*, 2:97–98; Medolago, *Due campioni*, p. 10; Olgiati, "La politica di S. Pio X," p. 538.

15. Reflecting upon the overwhelming importance of a hierarchical understanding of society in medieval thought, Troeltsch was critical of Aquinas: "Even in a man of such deep ethical feeling as St. Thomas it is amazing to see how unquestioningly he accepts the Aristotelian point of view that aristocratic and ruling classes are the logical result of Nature" (*The Social Doctrine of Churches*, p. 298).

16. For examples see Toniolo's "L'Unione cattolica per gli studi sociali," p. 75ff., and his *Lettere*, especially vol. 3; also Franca Falcucci, "Lo stato nel pensiero di Giuseppe Toniolo," and Bonomelli, "Il clero e la società moderna," p. 283.

17. Toniolo, "L'Unione cattolica per gli studi sociali," p. 90; Monetti, *Problemi varii*, 2:121ff.; Raffaele Molinelli, *Il movimento cattolico nelle Marche*, p. 108ff.; Bruno Malinverni, *La Scuola Sociale Cattolica di Bergamo (1910–1932)*, p. 106ff. Sassoli too argued that "God delegated to some men a part of His authority to command others," but "according to the tenets of Christianity, the right to exercise this command was legitimate only in order to provide a tutelage to those commanded." The ownership of property, Sassoli pointed out, imposed "on those who held it, duties proportionate to their wealth." (Sassoli, *La questione*

sociale, p. 7; also Gambasin, "L'utopia sociale," pp. 39–40.) The influential French Catholic social philosopher and activist Le Play defined the concept of "superior classes" by pointing to their dedication to public service, including the "tutelage" of the "inferior" social strata, which in turn was characterized by Le Play by their lack of interest in public obligations and the pursuit of only individual and family interests (quoted in Luisa Riva Sanseverino, *Il movimento sindacale cristiano dal 1850 al 1939,* pp. 57–59).

18. For examples of the activists' attitudes, see Cantono, *Le Università popolari,* pp. 14–15, 19, and Avolio, *I cattolici di fronte a'mali sociali.* For Toniolo's perception see his "Lettera aperta al conte Grosoli," especially p. 389; and *L'Unione cattolica popolare italiana, ragioni, scopi, incitamenti,* especially p. 29ff.; also Falcucci, "Lo stato nel pensiero di Giuseppe Toniolo." There was an inherent moral and intellectual elitism in turn-of-the-century Neo-Thomism that grew out of Aquinas's high ethical expectations from the state: if the state had to become the framework of a *communitas perfecta,* as the Angelic Doctor demanded, leaders had the obligation to live as examples of virtue, acting out the dictates of a superior consciousness of God's laws, a consciousness clearly connected with education. (Alessandro Passerin d'Entreves, *La filosofia politica medioevale,* p. 129ff.; Ezio Flori, *Il trattato "De Regimine Principum" e le dottrine politiche di S. Tommaso,* p. 59ff.; Antonio Burri, *Le teorie politiche di San Tommaso e il moderno diritto pubblico,* p. 5ff.) Burri presented a curious mixture of the Neo-Thomistic elitism and the Comtean claim for the social scientists in the management of society as he argued that "since the beginning it was the intelligentsia (*classe della Intelligenza*) that directed and governed society." He praised the Neo-Thomistic initiatives of Pope Leo XIII for putting "science" on the right road and preparing the intelligentsia for their leading role. During the first years of the twentieth century, Neo-Thomistic arguments defending the hierarchical perception of society increasingly drifted off into an open elitism. In these arguments against the principle of equality as something contrary to nature, the word *elite* began to appear. (For an example see Fontaine, *Le modernisme sociologique,* pp. 65, 455ff. Fontaine argued that in every society there are "the talented ones, the geniuses, and the imbeciles, there are the brave ones and the rogues," as there is a "duality of those who rule and those who are ruled . . . the elite and the masses, the nobles and the people." One wonders at the judgment of Pius X, who praised Fontaine for his "profound theological and social understanding," especially as one reads Fontaine's quote of Gabriele d'Annunzio saying that "the world is a magnificent gift given by the elite to the masses.") The drift into an open elitism shows Neo-Thomism advancing toward a linkup with the elitist doctrines developed by Gaetano Mosca and Vilfredo Pareto. Elitism was very much in the air, and would come to fruition in the fascist corporative theory, which was to be supported by many conservative Catholics.

19. Medolago, *Le classi dirigenti,* p. 11ff.

20. Bonomelli, "Il clero e la società moderna," p. 28ff.; Monetti, *Problemi varri,* 2:5ff., 68–69, 97–98; Imberciadori, *L'Unione Popolare,* p. 61; R. Bettazzi, "Il compito sociale delle Società di S. Vincenzo de' Paoli"; Fontaine, *Le modernisme sociologique,* pp. 64, 244; Antonio Arena, *Il lavoro manuale e la chiesa cattolica;* Mathieu Robert, "Hiérarchie nécessaire des fonctions économique d'après Saint Thomas d'Aquin"; Walter Farrell, "The Fate of Representative Government," p. 416; Camp, *The Papal Ideology of Social Reform,* p. 30ff.

21. Bonomelli, "Proprietà," p. 7.

22. Capecelatro, *La quistione sociale,* p. 8.

23. Aquinas, *De Regimine,* book 4, chapter 9, as quoted in De Concilio, *The Doctrine of St. Thomas,* pp. 24–25. A twentieth-century scholar will sum up the theme of the hierarchical

understanding of society in Thomistic philosophy by suggesting that "the Universe is a harmonious ladder, the top of which is occupied by God. . . . On this ladder every being has a stable place and consequently an immutable relationship with superior and inferior beings" (Vykopal, *La dottrina del superfluo,* p. 10).

24. See Mathis's "Introduction" to *De Regimine Principum.* On the basis of stylistic and content analysis, he suggests that only the first book and the first four chapters of the second were written for certain by Aquinas; the rest of *De Regimine* was authored by somebody else, probably by Tolomeo da Lucca, one of Aquinas's disciples.

25. Aquinas, *Summa contra Gentiles,* 1. III. c. 81, as referred to in Passerin d'Entreves, *La filosofia politica medioevale,* p. 129; *Summa,* I-I, q. 96, and II-II, q. 104; also Farrell, "The Fate of Representative Government," p. 297; and Tozzi, *I fondamenti dell'economia,* p. 132ff.

26. For a somewhat extreme position in this debate, see Ernesto Pisoni, who quotes the theologian Jose Maria Gonzalez Ruiz in arguing that the principle of poverty is "valid only in the vertical sense, in relation of man to God, not in relationships among men." Pisoni concludes that "poverty imposed upon man by man is a sin that cries for the vengeance of God: it is a scandal that has to be combatted and eliminated, in the way the Catholic church, together with the [other] Christian churches and all men of good will attempt to do." ("La posta dell'anima," in *Amica,* an Italian weekly for women, June 25, 1968.) And for a still more dramatic sign of the change in Catholic social philosophy, a statement by Pope Paul VI serves admirably: he urged men "to seek Christ's help in overcoming inequality" (Christmas message referred to in the *Detroit Free Press,* Dec. 26, 1969).

27. Neo-Thomistic conservatives, rejecting the idea of democracy, combined Aquinas's notion concerning "natural" inequality with another long-standing Thomistic argument, according to which the source of political authority was God and not the people's will manifest in votes. Nonetheless, Aquinas's stance has been a subject of controversy among his interpreters, some of whom have pointed out that the *Summa* (which followed Aristotle's classification of political systems) represented an essentially neutral position because it presented both the advantages and disadvantages of monarchy, aristocracy, and democracy. According to other scholars, Aquinas displayed a marked preference for the monarchical system of government because this fitted best into his hierarchical perception of the social universe. Recently, however, other interpreters of his thought have argued that Aquinas considered democracy preferable over other forms of government. This last group of Thomistic scholars lined up substantial textual evidence suggesting something akin to a conviction on Aquinas's part that a democratic regime would assure a greater social and political coherence and peace. Thus it was destined to be more successful than other political systems in achieving the ultimate goal of human communities, the salvation of the citizens. Furthermore, Aquinas appears to have suggested that democracy would provide a better check against possible abuses of power. We are thus left bewildered in the presence of four different Aquinases clearly contradicting each other: will the real Saint Thomas Aquinas please stand up? (Here I follow the arguments of my "Christian Democracy and Social Modernism," especially p. 36.)

28. Bonomelli, "Proprietà," p. 60. Reading this magnificent compendium of Neo-Thomistic Italian Catholic social philosophy focused to project an image of paternalism, one cannot resist showing how universal the appeal of social paternalism was by quoting somebody eons away in time and space: "Who works with his mind rules; who works with his hand is ruled" so said Signor Confucius. (Quoted in Harriet C. Mills, "Thought Reform: Ideological Remolding in China," Eric and Mary Josephson [eds.], *Man Alone: Alienation in Modern Society,* p. 557.)

29. Bonomelli, "Proprietà," pp. 47–49.

30. See my "Giolitti's Reform Program."

31. The text of the letter is in Lorenzo Bedeschi, *La curia romana durante la crisi modernista; episodi e metodo di governo*, pp. 276–77. Agliardi and Rampolla were cardinals and, like Capecelatro, supporters in varying degrees of the Christian Democratic activists.

32. Gaetano Zocchi, *La questione sociale ossia onde il popolo possa sperare pane, lavoro e pace*, pp. 7–8. Zocchi was a very influential figure among the leaders of Italian Catholic Action. His voice, according to historian Camillo Brezzi, amounted on occasions to a veto in debates (Brezzi, *Cristiano sociali e intransigenti. L'opera di Medolago Albani fino alla "Rerum Novarum,"* pp. 313, 492–94).

33. Medolago, *Classi dirigenti*, pp. 8–12.

34. Pius X, *motu proprio* "Fin dalla prima," pp. 4–5.

35. Cardinal Sarto, in Unione Cattolica per gli studi sociali, *Atti e documenti del secondo congresso*, p. 112ff.

36. Pius X, allocution to the Sacred College on Dec. 23, 1903, quoted in Jean-Claude Poulain, *L'Église et la classe ouvrière*, p. 77; also Pius X, letter *Notre charge apostolique*, p. 611; Leo XIII, encyclical *Graves de communi*. Showing the stubborn persistence of the concept of inequality in the official doctrine of the church, Poulain refers to more than one of the successors of Pius X, with Pius XII as the last being quoted. The world apparently had to wait until the 1960s to hear a pope, Paul VI, laud the "beautiful ideas of democracy and equality" as this writer did on St. Peter's Square.

37. Pius X, encyclical *Pieni l'animo*, p. 60.

38. "Class struggle, whoever the person who leads it or on occasion seeks to give it a theoretical justification, is a social evil. Likewise, obstinate confrontation between blocs of nations, between one nation and another, between different groups within the same nation—all this, too, is a social evil:" Pope John Paul II, as quoted in the *London* [Ontario] *Free Press*, Dec. 22, 1984.

39. Pius X, speech to a group of pilgrims, quoted in *Azione Sociale* 7, May 1913, pp. 77–80; also Poulain, *L'Église et la classe ouvrière*, pp. 84–96; and Malinverni, *La Scuola Sociale*, p. 91ff. It is a measure of the change in the social doctrine of the church that Pope John Paul II said loud and clear that not only are unions "indispensable and irreplaceable," but also defended the workers' right to strike. That he did this in Katowice, Poland, where the Solidarity movement was banned by the government shortly before was as significant as the statement itself (*London* [Ontario] *Free Press*, May 23 and June 21, 1983).

40. Leo XIII, encyclical *Rerum novarum*, pp. 245–46, 251, 253; also Vito, "Trasformazioni economiche," p. 15ff.; and Oskar Köhler in Aubert et al., *The Church in the Industrial Age*, p. 224.

41. Antonio Fappani, "Le società operaie cattoliche nel Bresciano," pp. 42ff., 73–78.

42. Giovanni Spadolini, *L'opposizione cattolica da Porta Pia al '98*, p. 267; Legitimo, *Sociologi cattolici*, p. 53ff.

43. Rubbiani as quoted in De Rosa, *Il movimento cattolico*, pp. 78–79, 105–7; also Gambasin, "L'utopia sociale," pp. 12–13; Mario G. Rossi, "Il movimento cattolico nelle campagne fino al primo dopo querra"; and Silvio Tramontin, (ed.), *Il movimento cattolico e la società italiana in cento anni di storia*, pp. 29–30, 48, 71–72.

44. Giuseppe Mezzetti, as quoted in Gambasin, "L'utopia sociale," pp. 36–37.

45. Troeltsch, *The Social Doctrine of Churches*, p. 318; see also Pietro Scoppola, remarks in Rossini (ed.), *Romolo Murri nella storia*, p. 389.

46. Medolago, *Le classi dirigenti*, p. 8.

Chapter 4

1. Mannheim, "Conservative Thought," p. 94ff. The chapter title is from the resolution of the first congress of the Opera, quoted in Mario Chiri, *Le organizzazioni operaie cattoliche in Italia*, p. xv.

2. For examples see Gambasin, "L'utopia sociale."

3. Poulain, *L'Église et la classe ouvrière*, p. 97ff.

4. As quoted in Riva Sanseverino, *Il movimento sindacale cristiano*, pp. 211–12; also Giacomo Corna Pellegrini, "L'evoluzione del concetto di classe: dal pensiero di Toniolo, al pensiero cattolico contemporaneo," especially p. 448; and Clough, *The Economic History of Modern Italy*, p. 150ff.

5. Toniolo, "L'ordinamento della classe operaia nelle corporazioni," especially pp. 499, 503–5; also Are, "Introduzione," p. 24.

6. Corna Pellegrini, "L'evoluzione del concetto di classe," p. 455; also Luigi Sturzo, "L'organizzazione di classe e le unioni professionali," especially p. 173.

7. Toniolo, *Lettere*, 3:345–47; also my "'Germania Doceat!'" p. 43.

8. Are, "Introduzione," p. 81.

9. Quoted in Corna Pellegrini, "L'evoluzione del concetto di classe," pp. 451, 457.

10. Sturzo, "L'organizzazione di classe," p. 174. Sturzo, a priest, was one of the spokesmen for Christian Democratic activists at the turn of the century. After World War I, he became the founder and leader of the Catholic Popular Party and was a consistent opponent of fascism. Forced to live abroad after 1924, he made himself a name as a sociologist.

11. Ernesto Vercesi, *Il movimento cattolico in Italia*, pp. 243–44; Alcide De Gasperi, *I tempi e gli uomini che preparavano la "Rerum novarum,"* p. 64.

12. De Mun as quoted in Riva Sanseverino, *Il movimento sindacale cristiano*, p. 69 and Monsignor Guerry as quoted in Poulain, *L'Église et la classe ouvrière*, pp. 57ff., 75–76, 98; De Gasperi, *I tempi e gli uomini*, p. 65ff.

13. "The barbarians who ruined the country by waging a war on the church and the pope will sooner or later go to Canossa," intoned a speaker at a regional Catholic congress held in Fano in 1897 (Molinelli, *Il movimento cattolico nelle Marche*, p. 89).

14. Toniolo's methodology is outlined and Medolago's statement, dated 1885, is quoted in Brezzi, *Cristiano sociali*, p. 113ff.

15. The historian Camillo Brezzi, who noticed the absence of the resolution from the *Acts* of the congress, tracked it down among archival materials in Medolago's handwriting: he was the presiding officer of that particular session (*Cristiano sociali*, p. 282ff.)

16. Medolago, *La classi dirigenti*, pp. 6–8; Antonio Boggiano Pico, *L'importanza degli studi economici nella cultura e nell'azione del clero*, p. 16ff.; Mayeur, "Catholicisme intransigeant," p. 487; Gambasin, "L'utopia sociale," pp. 14ff., 26; René Coste, "Le développement de la pensée sociale de l'Église depuis 'Rerum novarum,' " pp. 324–25.

17. The resolution of the congress is quoted in Chiri, *Le organizzazioni operaie*, p. xv.

18. Chiri, *Le organizzazioni operaie*, p. xvi; *Voti sociali dei cattolici italiani*, p. 13ff.; also Spadolini, *L'opposizione cattolica*, p. 131ff.; Vercesi, *Il movimento cattolico in Italia*, p. 224; Brezzi, *Cristiano sociali*, p. 120ff.

19. Gambasin, "L'utopia sociale," pp. 26ff., 47–49; also Brezzi, *Cristiano sociali*, p. 120ff.

20. Quoted in Brezzi, *Cristiano sociali*, pp. 131, 182ff., 425ff.

21. Quoted in ibid., pp. 127–28, 146–47.

22. Quoted in De Gasperi, *I tempi e gli uomini*, pp. 78–80.

23. Quoted in Riva Sanseverino, *Il movimento sindacale cristiano*, p. 45ff.; also Aubert,

The Church in a Secularized Society, pp. 148–49, and Oskar Köhler, in Aubert et al., *The Church in the Industrial Age,* p. 202ff.

24. Quoted in Brezzi, *Cristiano sociali,* pp. 274–82; also *Voti sociali,* p. 39ff.; and Spadolini, *L'opposizione cattolica,* p. 243ff.

25. Toniolo's letter is quoted in Lucio Avagliano, *Alessandro Rossi e le origini dell'Italia industriale,* p. 95.

26. Cappellazzi, *Le moderne libertà,* p. 182. Similar arguments appear in Imberciadori, *L'Unione Popolare,* pp. 24–27, 74ff., and in innumerable other Catholic publications.

27. Toniolo's statement, published in 1901, is quoted in Cappellazzi, *La questione sociale,* p. 29.

28. Ketteler's famous 1864 pastoral letter, entitled the *[Industrial] Worker Question and Christianity,* as quoted in Riva Sanseverino, *Il movimento sindacale cristiano,* p. 26.

29. For Taparelli's relevant arguments, see Perego, *Forma statale,* pp. 87ff., 206ff., 280; also Talamo, *La questione sociale,* p. 35ff., and Giuseppe Toniolo, "La funzione della giustizia e della carità nell' odierna crisi sociale," p. 362.

30. Alessandro Zussini, *Luigi Caissotti di Chiusano e il movimento cattolico dal 1896 al 1915,* p. 23.

31. See the arguments voiced by the first (1874) congress of the Opera in Chiri, *Le organizzazioni operaie,* p. xv.

32. Riva Sanseverino, *Il movimento sindacale cristiano* p. 33; Hogan, *The Development of Ketteler's Interpretation,* pp. 13, 230ff.; Aubert, *The Church in a Secularized Society,* p. 146ff.; Oskar Köhler, in Aubert et al., *The Church in the Industrial Age,* p. 204ff.

33. Francesco Magri, *Dal movimento sindacale cristiano al sindacalismo democratico,* p. 6.

34. Meda's 1896 essay entitled "Parlamentarismo e sistema rappresentativo" is reprinted in Are, (ed.), *I cattolici e la questione sociale,* pp. 175–87. See also Zussini, *Luigi Caissotti di Chiusano,* p. 31ff.

35. About the program of the Partito Popolare, which advocated the transformation of the Senate into an institution based on professional-occupational representation, see Luigi Sturzo, *Riforma statale e indirizzi politici: discorsi.*

36. Toniolo, as quoted in Are, "Introduzione," pp. 19–20.

37. Hogan, *The Development of Ketteler's Interpretation,* pp. 233–34.

38. Riva Sanseverino, *Il movimento sindacale cristiano,* p. 84ff.; Zussini, *Luigi Caissotti di Chiusano,* p. 33.

39. Taparelli, "Tassa progressiva," in Perego, *Forma statale,* p. 271ff.

40. For a review of the criticism of the corporative doctrine see De Gasperi, *I tempi e gli uomini,* especially p. 83ff.; and Riva Sanseverino, *Il movimento sindacale cristiano,* p. 59ff. For a rare and early dissenting voice in Italy about the revival of the corporations, see Mario Romani, "La preparazione della 'Rerum novarum,' " p. 25. For Max Weber's charge, supported by a group of German scholars, that the promise of the resurrection of medieval group consciousness was "dishonest" and "artificial," see Fritz Nova, *Functional Representation,* p. 58ff.; for later criticism of Catholic corporativism as providing aid and comfort to fascism, see Karl Mannheim, "Christian Values and Changing Environment," in *Diagnosis of Our Time: Wartime Essays of a Sociologist,* especially p. 107.

41. Brezzi, *Cristiano sociali,* pp. 281, 285ff.; Riva Sanseverino, *Il movimento sindacale cristiano,* p. 106ff.; Rinaldo Rigola, *Storia del movimento operaio italiano,* p. 9ff.; Luigi Einaudi, *Cronache economiche e politiche di un trentennio (1893–1925),* 1:298ff.; Coste, "Le développement," p. 325.

42. Brezzi, *Cristiano sociali,* p. 284ff., and Gambasin, "L'utopia sociale," p. 50.

Chapter 5

1. Brezzi, *Cristiano sociali*, p. 287ff. The chapter title is from Leo XIII, encyclical *Rerum novarum*, p. 241.

2. Malinverni, *La Scuola Sociale*, p. 24; also Aubert, *The Church in a Secularized Society*, pp. 10, 150–61, and Oskar Köhler, in Aubert et al., *The Church in the Industrial Age*, pp. 194–95, 203, 206.

3. Leo XIII, encyclical *Rerum novarum*, especially pp. 241–42, 253–54, 256. For the background of the encyclical, see De Gasperi, *I tempi e gli uomini*, especially p. 83ff.; Romani, "La preparazione della 'Rerum novarum'," especially pp. 15, 18–19, 24–28; Lilian Parker Wallace, *Leo XIII and the Rise of Socialism*, p. 254ff.; Are, "Introduzione," p. 13ff.; Coste, "Le développement"; Aubert, *The Church in a Secularized Society*, pp. 146, 150–51.

4. For the *fasci* movement and the Catholics' reaction to it, see Francesco De Stefano and Luigi Oddo, *Storia della Sicilia dal 1860 al 1910*, pp. 271–341; Giovanna Trimarchi, *La formazione del pensiero meridionalista di Luigi Sturzo*, especially p. 16ff., 30ff.; Francesco Renda, *Socialisti e cattolici in Sicilia, 1900–1914*, p. 16ff.; Camillo Brezzi, "Capitalismo e socialismo nella cultura dei cattolici di fine '800," p. 263.

5. Camillo Brezzi, "Movimento operaio e socialismo nel giudizio dei cattolici italiani dopo il 'Rerum novarum,'" p. 223ff.

6. The text, which first appeared in January, 1894, on the pages of the *Rivista internazionale di scienze sociali*, is available in several modern reprints: Giuseppe Are, (ed.), *I cattolici e la questione sociale in Italia (1894–1904)*, pp. 143–47; Giambattista Valente, *Aspetti e momenti dell'azione sociale dei cattolici in Italia (1892–1926)*, pp. 281–87; *Voti sociali*, pp. 175–82.

7. This passage is Daniel L. Horowitz's translation. (See his *The Italian Labor Movement*, p. 99.)

8. For rather negative evaluations of the Programma, see Brezzi, "Movimento operaio," pp. 216, 232–34; and Are, who calls it a "summary list of measures considered useful to maintain the external conditions of Christian paternalism." ("Introduzione," pp. 22–23). More positive evaluations are in Vercesi, *Il movimento cattolico in Italia*, pp. 54ff., 238ff.; Spadolini, *L'opposizione cattolica*, p. 287ff.; Horowitz, *The Italian Labor Movement*, p. 98ff.

9. See the resolutions of the 1891 (Vicenza) and 1892 (Genoa) congresses of the Opera in *Voti sociali*, p. 48ff., and Chiri, *Le organizzazioni operaie*, p. xviiff.

10. Toniolo, "L'unione cattolica per gli studi sociali," p. 75. (This piece, first published in 1893, is a composite of several earlier writings, including an 1892 address to the founding congress of the Catholic Union for Social Studies.)

11. Medolago and Gusmini are quoted in De Rosa, "Introduzione," to Sturzo's *Sintesi sociali*, p. xix.

12. Chiri, *Le organizzazioni operaie*, p. xxi; also Vercesi, *Il movimento cattolico in Italia*, p. 240.

13. Chiri, *Le organizzazioni operaie*, p. xxiiff; Magri, *Dal movimento sindacale cristiano*, pp. 27–29.

14. See the "norms" suggested by Toniolo in the appendix by Sturzo's *Opera Omnia*, ser. 2, vol. 1, pp. 181–85, also *Voti sociali*, pp. 89–98, especially 94; Chiri, *Le organizzazioni operaie*, pp. xxviii–xxxi; Vercesi, *Il movimento cattolico in Italia*, p. 247ff.; Magri, *Dal movimento sindacale cristiano*, pp. 29–31; Ottavio Cavalleri, *Il movimento operaio e contadino nel Bresciano (1878–1903)*, pp. 418–19.

15. Quoted in Zussini, *Luigi Caissotti di Chiusano*, p. 84.

16. Toniolo, "L'ordinamento delle classi operaie nelle corporazioni," in part reprinted in Are (ed.), *I cattolici e la questione sociale*, pp. 499–517; Are, "Introduzione," pp. 40–48;

Riva Sanseverino, *Il movimento sindacale cristiano*, p. 37ff.; Cavalleri, *Il movimento operaio e contadino*, p. 409ff.

17. Angelo Gambasin, *Gerarchia e laicato in Italia nel secondo Ottocento*, p. 177; Francesco Vito, "L'economia al servizio dell'uomo, caposaldo della dottrina sociale cattolica," p. 3; Vincenzo Saba, "L'influsso della dottrina sociale cattolica sull'organizzazione sindacale del lavoro."

18. Giovanni D'Ascenzi, *I documenti pontifici sulla vita agraria: testo e commento*, pp. 35–39.

19. Leo XIII, encyclical *Rerum novarum;* also Wallace, *Leo XIII*, p. 271.

20. Quoted in Renda, *Socialisti e cattolici*, p. 36.

21. Renda, *Socialisti e cattolici*, pp. 34ff., 66ff.

22. Emil Ritter, *Il movimento cattolico-sociale in Germania nel XIX secolo e il Volksverein*, pp. 450–51; Angelo Gambasin, *Parroci e contadini nel Veneto alla fine dell'Ottocento*, pp. 45–72, 212.

23. Are, "Introduzione," p. 48.

24. Malinverni, *La Scuola Sociale*, p. 33.

25. Gabriele De Rosa, *Filippo Meda e l'età liberale*, pp. 122–33; Lorenzo Bedeschi, "I cappellani del lavoro a Milano nei primi anni del novecento."

26. Mario Ronchi, "Le origini del movimento contadino nel Soresinese (1901–1913)"; Mario Bardelli, "La questione operaia nell'azione e nel pensiero di Guido Miglioli," p. 59; Antonio Fappani, *Guido Miglioli e il movimento contadino*.

27. Talamo, *La questione sociale*, p. 20.

28. Zussini, *Luigi Caissotti di Chiusano*, p. 20, does not identify the writer, but the piece was from the pen of Rocca d'Adria.

29. Piergiorgio Grassi, "Neotomismo e prima Democrazia Cristiana in Romagna," p. 572.

30. Quoted in Trimarchi, *La formazione del pensiero meridionalista di Luigi Sturzo*, p. 83.

31. Sturzo, "L'organizzazione di classe," especially pp. 131–39, 162–70; also Are, "Introduzione," p. 46ff.; Renda, *Socialisti e cattolici*, pp. 41ff., 273ff.; Francesco Renda, "Luigi Sturzo e il movimento contadino in Sicilia nei primi anni del secolo," especially pp. 484–85, 491–93; Trimarchi, *La formazione del pensiero meridionalista di Luigi Sturzo*, p. 75ff.

32. Luigi Sturzo, "La lotta sociale legge di progresso," especially pp. 30–32, 48; also Maria Teresa Garutti Bellenzier, "La lotta sociale nel pensiero di Luigi Sturzo." The notion that class conflict, and, specifically, strikes are the "vehicles of social progress" came to be built into Italian historical thought (see Clough, *The Economic History of Modern Italy*, p. 153).

33. Leo XIII, encyclical *Rerum novarum*, especially p. 245ff.

34. Corna Pellegrini, "L'evoluzione del concetto di classe," p. 457.

35. As late as 1910, there were only 920,000 union members out of an estimated 7 million organizable labor force, or 13.1 percent. For Great Britain the figure was 23 percent and for Sweden 42 percent. And apparently there was no dramatic increase, at least during the next few years: in 1914 the total stood at 961,997. See Neufeld, *Italy: School for Awakening Countries*, p. 316ff., especially pp. 329, 334–35, 339, 350, 354–55; Joseph La Palombara, *Italian Labor Movement: Problems and Prospects*, pp. 6–8; Giancarlo Galli, *I cattolici e il sindacato*, pp. 120–21; Rigola, *Storia del movimento operaio italiano*, p. 306ff.

36. Alexander Gerschenkron, "Notes on the Rate of Industrial Growth in Italy, 1881–1913," p. 372; Peter N. Stearns, *European Society in Upheaval: Social History since*

1750, p. 248; Neufeld, *Italy: School for Awakening Countries*, p. 547 table 38; Renato Zangheri (ed.), *Lotte agrarie in Italia: la Federazione Nazionale dei Lavoratori della Terra (1901–1926)*, pp. xxviii–xxx; Clough, *The Economic History of Modern Italy*, p. 153ff.

37. Renda, *Socialisti e cattolici*, pp. 58ff., 276, 286.

38. Leo XIII, encyclical *Graves de communi*, especially p. 485.

39. Quoted in Are, "Introduzione," pp. 76–78; also Aubert, *The Church in a Secularized Society*, pp. 14, 161–62.

40. Chiri, *Le organizzazioni operaie*, pp. xxxi–xxxii; Magri, *Dal movimento sindacale cristiano*, pp. 240–41.

41. Fappani, "Le società operaie cattoliche nel Bresciano," p. 79; Cavalleri, *Il movimento operaio e contadino*, p. 426ff.; Riva Sanseverino, *Il movimento sindacale cristiano*, p. 240. Chiri indicates that eleven "improvement associations" were established before 1901, but he does not tell what proportion, if any, of these were mixed organizations (*Le organizzazioni operaie*, p. 21).

42. Cavalleri, *Il movimento operaio e contadino*, p. 409ff., especially pp. 424–25; Fappani, "Le società operaie cattoliche nel Bresciano," pp. 35, 76ff.; Salvadori, *Il movimento cattolico a Torino*, especially p. 134.

43. The most relevant of these articles are reprinted under the title "L'ordinamento della classe operaia nelle corporazioni," in Are, (ed.), *I cattolici e la questione sociale*, pp. 499–517. See also Are, "Introduzione," especially p. 80ff., and Cavalleri, *Il movimento operaio e contadino*, p. 425.

44. For the resolutions of the Bologna congress, see Chiri, *Le organizzazioni operaie*, pp. xxxii–xxxv; also *Voti sociali*, p. 104ff.; Magri, *Dal movimento sindacale cristiano*, p. 33–34.

45. *Voti sociali*, p. 190ff.; Vercesi is quoted in Bedeschi, "I cappellani del lavoro," pp. 306, 312–13; Sturzo is cited in Salvadori, *Il movimento cattolico a Torino*, p. 68. See also Sturzo's essay in Are (ed.), *I cattolici e la questione sociale*, pp. 420–46; Are, "Introduzione," p. 46, and Fappani, *Guido Miglioli*, p. 61ff.

46. Quoted in Gambasin, "L'utopia sociale," pp. 49–50.

47. Vercesi, *Il movimento cattolico in Italia*, p. 243ff.; Riva Sanseverino, *Il movimento sindacale cristiano*, pp. 243–244; Salvadori, *Il movimento cattolico a Torino*, pp. 67–69.

Chapter 6

1. Quoted in Are, "Introduzione," p. 73. The chapter title is from Pius X, encyclical *E supremi apostolatus*, p. 6, and was indicated as the motto for his papacy by the pontiff.

2. Malinverni, *La Scuola Sociale*, p. 52.

3. Pius X, encyclical *Il fermo proposito*, especially p. 38.

4. Papal letters in *Azione Sociale* 1, March 1907, pp. 206–8, and Sept. 1907, p. 646.

5. Arturo Jemolo, *Chiesa e Stato in Italia negli ultimi cento anni*, p. 520.

6. Sources: Chiri, *Le organizzazioni operaie*, pp. xxxi, xxxiv–xxxvii, 21–22, 144; for 1904, Vercesi, *Il movimento cattolico in Italia*, p. 250ff. The decline is usually connected with the dissolution of the Opera and the uncertainty and confusion that ensued. (For an example see Rossi, "Il movimento cattolico nelle campagne.") But this causal relationship, which points to the historical role of Pius X, is undercut somewhat by the fact that during that period the membership of non-Catholic unions declined too, as shown by the collapse of the agricultural federation, the Federterra, and the diminishing of the membership of the Socialist-led rural labor leagues. Knowing that the record-keeping of the Unione Economico Sociale was something of a disaster, one is inclined to predict that the issue of the pope's responsibility in the

decline of the Catholic organizations of labor will be open for debate even after the materials from the central archives become available. (About the damaging effects of a "paralyzing internal crisis," see Medolago's presidential address in *Azione Sociale* 4, Apr. 1910, p. 67ff.; and Rosselli's report to the congress of the Volksverein, in *Settimana Sociale* 3, (Sept. 3, 1910).

7. Neufeld, *Italy: School for Awakening Countries,* p. 547, table 38; Zangheri, *Lotte agrarie in Italia,* pp. xxviii; Clough, *The Economic History of Modern Italy,* p. 153ff. It will give an idea of the magnitude of Italian labor unrest that when an extraordinarily heavy wave of strikes peaked in France in 1906, the number of strikes registered at 1,309 and the head-count of the participants at 438,466. The peak of a similar wave in Italy in 1907 brought 2,258 strikes and 575,630 participants.

8. Murri's position is outlined in his preface to Cantono's *Le Università popolari e la democrazia.* Some of Murri's other writings were reprinted in Bedeschi (ed.), *I pioneri della D.C.* Of particular interest are two of his articles: "L'essenza della democrazia," pp. 435–48, and "La democrazia cristiana italiana," pp. 460–82. For Murri's social outlook, see Arturo Mancini, "Il pensiero sociale di Romolo Murri." As long as the papers of both Murri and Pius X remain unavailable, an exhaustive study of the conflict between the pontiff and Murri is impossible. Recent studies, however, have accumulated enough evidence to show clearly that the pope's opposition to democratic ideas was a factor. For some of the treatments of the subject, see Pietro Scoppola, "Il modernismo politico in Italia: la Lega Democratica Nazionale"; Scoppola, *Dal neoguelfismo alla Democrazia Cristiana;* Fernando Manzotti, "I 'plebei' cattolici fra integralismo e modernismo sociale (1904–1908)"; Lorenzo Bedeschi, *I cattolici disubbidienti;* Bedeschi, *Il modernismo e Romolo Murri in Emilia e Romagna;* and Sergio Zoppi, *Romolo Murri e la prima Democrazia Christiana.*

9. See Sturzo's "Per un partito nazionale dei cattolici in Italia," *Cultura Sociale* (a review edited by Murri) 9, Feb. 1, 1906, pp. 41–43. Sturzo confesses to be "an old and convinced democrat" and says that he considers it necessary to give a "democratic content" to the program of the Italian Catholic political party. In *I pioneri della D.C.,* Bedeschi reprints a selection from the writings of Christian Democrats relevant to the problems discussed here. Aside from the essays of Murri and Sturzo, those of Gennaro Avolio, Domenico Conti, Pio Molajoni, Igino Petrone, Ignazio Terragrossa, and Giovannia Battista Valente carry direct information.

10. In the diocesan archives of Faenza, Bedeschi found many letters written by parish priests who expressed their dislike of the aims and methods of the Unione Popolare and identified themselves with the goals of the Lega (Bedeschi, *Il modernismo e Romolo Murri,* p. 7).

11. This seems to be the conclusion of Federico Alessandrini, "Un pontificato," and of Scoppola, *Dal neoguelfismo alla Democrazia Cristiana,* p. 115.

12. A consideration of the story of the Sillon in connection with the response of Pius X to the challenge of Christian Democracy is advantageous also for another reason. The pope's directives about Italian Christian Democracy, and particularly about the Lega, took the form of minor documents addressed to particular situations. Thus an objective examination of the pope's motivations will not be possible while the background materials remain unavailable. The condemnation of the Sillon, on the other hand, came not through a series of occasional documents but through a papal letter, *Notre charge apostolique,* a unique document, the only one in which Pius X attempted to set forth his social and political philosophy in a systematic way. Although documents previously released by Pius X had, in terse sentences, rejected the idea of equality, its unequivocal condemnation was one of the subjects of *Notre charge apostolique.* In long, emotionally charged passages, the old pontiff declared the concept of equal-

ity "contrary to nature," and said that the Sillonists' advocacy of political, social, and economic "leveling," aimed at a future society of equals, was one of their greatest deviations from Catholic doctrine. (In my "Christian Democracy and Social Modernism," I identify the ideological elements of the controversy over the Sillon. My presentation of the pope's attitude in this study incorporates the conclusions reached in that essay. These conclusions seem to be confirmed by Aubert, *The Church in a Secularized Society,* p. 48ff., and Aubert, in Aubert et al., *The Church in the Industrial Age,* pp. 387, 420, 473ff.)

13. Molinelli, *Il movimento cattolico nelle Marche,* p. 129; Bedeschi, "I cappellani del lavoro," p. 300; De Rosa, *Il movimento cattolico,* p. 300ff.; Bedeschi, *I cattolici disubbidienti,* especially pp. 116, 125, 137ff.; Claudio Giovannini, *Politica e religione nel pensiero della Lega Democratica Nazionale (1905–1915),* pp. 122ff., 171ff.; Maurilio Guasco, *Romolo Murri e il modernismo,* p. 368ff.; Jemolo, *Chiesa e stato in Italia,* p. 515; Scoppola, *Dal neoguelfismo alla Democrazia Cristiana,* pp. 90–91. For the Vatican's position in connection with social modernism and the persecution of the Sillon and the Lega, see Pius X, encyclicals *Pascendi* and *Pieni l'animo;* Jean Rivière, *Le modernisme dans l'Église: étude d'histoire religieuse contemporaine,* p. 256ff.; Emmanuel Barbier, *Les erreurs du Sillon: histoire documentaire;* Fontaine, *Le modernisme sociologique.*

14. Pius X, encyclical *Il fermo proposito,* p. 43.

15. Bedeschi, "I cappellani del lavoro," pp. 304–5, 324; also Aubert, *The Church in a Secularized Society,* p. 197ff., and Aubert in Aubert et al., *The Church in the Industrial Age,* pp. 388, 420–23, 457ff., 468ff.

16. Bedeschi, *Il modernismo e Romolo Murri,* especially p. 143ff.

17. Ibid., pp. 139ff., 170, 315.

18. Ibid., pp. 151ff., 316ff.

19. De Rosa, *Il movimento cattolico,* p. 181ff.

20. Bedeschi, *Il modernismo e Romolo Murri,* especially pp. 109ff., 118, 142, 176ff., 302; also De Rosa, *Il movimento cattolico,* pp. 296–300. In suggesting that priests take the side of the workers in labor disputes, Ravaglia could be seen following the instructions of his bishop, who reminded his clergy that the "preference of the church always has to be for the humble, as this was the preference of Christ" (Cazzani, quoted in Fappani, *Guido Miglioli,* p. 77).

21. Grassi, "Neotomismo e la prima Democrazia Cristiana," especially pp. 559, 568ff.

22. Bedeschi, *Il modernismo e Romolo Murri,* pp. 303–4, 315–17, 325ff.; Bedeschi, *I cattolici disubbidienti,* pp. 91, 120, 147; Giampiero Cappelli, *Romolo Murri: contributo per una biografia,* p. 105; Giovannini, *Politica e religione,* pp. 39ff., 60ff., and 164ff. Guasco, *Romolo Murri,* pp. 79ff., 181–82. The issue involved a challenge to papal authority—or was it papal infallibility? Pius X perceived his authority to be virtually unlimited, certainly extending beyond religious doctrine and practice, but Murri declared that he doubted the pope enjoyed "special light from the Lord" in connection with social and political problems. My forthcoming " 'Robots Manipulated from Rome': Leadership in Italian Catholic Action during the Papacy of Pius X (1903–1914)" details the problem.

23. "Spontaneamente senza che alcuno, nemeno da lontano, possa scoprire il desiderio manifestato" (quoted in Bedeschi, *Il modernismo e Romolo Murri,* p. 325). The unrelated remark of Catholic philosopher and historian Nicholas Lash constitutes a very revealing commentary to the obsessive secrecy of Pius X: "In all societies, secrecy is a convenient weapon of power. But surely the nature of the church, as a community grounded in and existing for the sharing of living truth, is such as to make the use of this weapon even less justifiable here than in other areas of society" (Lash, *Voices of Authority,* p. 47).

24. Bedeschi, *Il modernismo e Romolo Murri,* pp. 180ff., 327.

25. Giacomo Radini Tedeschi, *La mission du prêtre dans l'action catholique*, p. 3.

26. See his statement in H. J. Leroy, *Le clergé et les oeuvres sociales*, p. 8.

27. Quoted in Lawrence Elliott, *I Will Be Called John: A Biography of Pope John XXIII*, pp. 61–64. See also Chiri, *Le organizzazioni operaie*, p. 60. The ambivalence created by the refusal to recognize strikes as legitimate means utilized by Catholic unions led to a degree of curious double-talk in Catholic publications. In his 1911 statistical study, Chiri reported that 157 of the 198 statutes of unions he examined indicated *resistenza* as one of the means they used, in the form of labor disputes and strikes to make economic gains and to assert the rights and interests of the workers against the *padroni*. In this the unions' perception of the word *resistance* coincided with the meaning that was generally accepted across the country. Yet in connection with the resolution of the 1900 Rome congress of the Opera, Chiri informed his readers in the same volume that the term *resistenza* "meant not a permanent and necessary antagonism on the part of [Catholic unions], on the contrary, a preoccupation with the fundamental solidarity of interests and common cooperation." This was like an article in *L'Osservatore Romano* in 1910 that reported the assertion of the National Association of Catholic Railroad Workers of their right to strike, which was quite dramatic, since strikes by public service employees were illegal. But because the union declared that just then it did not want to strike, the Vatican's paper headlined the item with "the Catholic railroaders against the strike," producing an intriguing item for historians as to who was trying to fool whom: was it the Catholic union *vis-à-vis* the non-Catholic one that called a strike, or the paper *vis-à-vis* the readers. (Chiri, *Le organizzazioni operaie*, pp. xxviii–xxxi, 47; *L'Osservatore Romano*, July 19, 1910.

28. Marchesan, *Papa Pio X*, p. 404.

29. For the relevant decrees, usually issued by the Concistorial Congregation, see *L'Osservatore Romano*, Aug. 11, 1910; *Azione Sociale* 4, Nov. 1910, p. 181ff.; 5, Feb.–March 1911, p. 35. For a review of these policy decisions, see D'Ascenzi, *I documenti pontifici*, pp. 60–61, and Aubert, *The Church in a Secularized Society*, pp. 132, 138, 142–43; Aubert, in Aubert et al., *The Church in the Industrial Age*, pp. 387, 472.

30. Malinverni, *La Scuola Sociale*, p. 51.

31. The advances of Catholic social theory accomplished under the direction of Leo XIII were clearly not followed through by Pius X. Even if we are not justified in talking of a regression in Catholic social thought in connection with the teachings of Pius X, a judgment implying a lack of originality and irrelevance to modern life is warranted. For instance, a collection of papal "social" encyclicals (*Le encicliche sociali dei papi*) edited by Igino Giordani, a biographer of Pius X, includes eleven encyclicals of Leo XIII and only two of Pius X. The due recognition that Leo's papacy was much longer than Pius's does not account for such a difference. Another collection of similar papal documents, edited by Francesco Vito, *Le encicliche e messaggi sociali di Leone XIII, Pio XI e Pio XII*, as the title shows, simply omits the encyclicals of Pius X, obviously considering them irrelevant to modern social problems. It might be said that the omission is due to editorial restrictions in both cases. But in *Mater et magistra*, a "social" encyclical issued in our own day, in spite of his personal admiration for Pius X, John XXIII similarly passes over the teachings of *Papa* Sarto in a review of previous papal documents that is traditionally part of papal encyclicals. For a review of the relevant issues concerning the papacy of Pius X see Aubert, *The Church in a Secularized Society*, pp. 12–19, 46–47, and Aubert, in Aubert, et al., *The Church in the Industrial Age*, p. 386.

32. Malinverni, *La Scuola Sociale*, especially pp. 18, 30, 61–68, 88ff.

33. Biederlack, *Principi dell'ordinamento*, especially pp. 44–47, 67; also Malinverni, *La Scuola Sociale*, p. 90ff; and Oskar Köhler, in Aubert et al., *The Church in the Industrial Age*, pp. 225, 231.

34. For evidence about the pope's familiarity with the courses at the Scuola Sociale, see *Azione Sociale* 4, Oct. 1910, p. 163ff. About the papal review of the curriculum and the changes in the course assignments at the end of the second academic year, see Malinverni, *La Scuola Sociale*, p. 77ff. The new program and the list of instructors is in *Azione Sociale* 8, Feb.–Mar. 1914, p. 21. The approving papal letter about Monetti's *Problemi varii*, signed by Marry del Val is in *Azione Sociale* 7, Nov. 1913, pp. 197–98.

35. Giuglio Monetti, *Errori moderni nella pratica dell'azione cattolica.*

36. Monetti, *Problemi varii*, 1:108ff.

37. Ibid., 2:18ff.

38. Ibid., 1:116ff.

39. *Azione Sociale* 2, May 1908, p. 293ff., and June 1908, p. 349ff.

40. Molteni, "Lo Sciopero," *Azione Sociale* 2, Jan.–Feb. 1908, pp. 1–27, 65–91 passim.

41. *L'Osservatore Romano*, May 10, 1906; May 11, 1906; May 16, 1906.

42. *L'Osservatore Romano*, May 13, 1906; July 15, 1906; July 18, 1906; Oct. 18, 1907; Oct. 23, 1907.

43. About the papal audience with the 1910 graduates of the Scuola Sociale see *Azione Sociale* 4, Oct. 1910, pp. 163–65; for Cazzani's suggestion, *L'Osservatore Romano*, Aug. 11, 1910.

44. Daniele Menozzi, "Orientamenti pastorali nella prima industrializzazione torinese," pp. 206–7, 223. One Catholic union with several locals in Brescia, involving both agricultural and industrial workers, reported 25 labor disputes related to wages and working hours, of which only one ended in a strike. Of the other 24, 17 resulted in completely and 2 in partially favorable resolutions for the workers, and only in 5 cases was the outcome completely negative. Of course, there is no way to tell how typical was the experience of this union, especially since the report does not mention the size of the concessions granted by the *padroni*. Incidentally, the report covers the period 1901–3, years when the labor movement was on the upswing and concessions relatively easy to gain, in part because the *padroni* were not yet well organized. (Cavalleri, *Il movimento operaio e contadino*, p. 431ff.)

45. See Molteni in *Azione Sociale* 1, Oct. 1907, pp. 688–92.

46. Giovanni Battista Scalabrini, *Il socialismo e l'azione del clero*, p. 80ff.; Bonomelli, "Proprietà," p. 53, and Bonomelli's pastoral letter written as a response to the strike wave of 1901–2, entitled *Gli scioperi: una parola amica a tutti gli operai.*

47. Chiri, *Le organizzazioni operaie*, p. 48ff., especially p. 67; also Magri, *Dal movimento sindacale cristiano*, pp. 40, 47.

48. For the description of both an opportunistic "marriage of convenience" with syndicalists, of all people, and a neutrality that positioned a numerically weak Catholic union as a "spectator" in a strike, see the description of the 1912 and 1913 strikes in the Turin automobile industry in Salvadori, *Il movimento cattolico a Torino*, pp. 174ff., 183–84.

49. Pius X, letter *Notre charge apostolique*, especially pp. 609, 621, 631; also Camp. *The Papal Ideology of Social Reform*, p. 119ff.; and my "Christian Democracy and Social Modernism."

50. See my forthcoming "'Robots Manipulated From Rome': Leadership in Italian Catholic Action During the Papacy of Pius X (1903–1914)."

51. Pius X, encyclical *Iucunda sane*, p. 24.

52. Pius X, *Visita pastorale. Lettera dell'eminentissimo sig. cardinale Giuseppe Sarto*, p. 6.

53. Speech by Cardinal Sarto, as recorded in Unione Cattolica per gli studi sociali, *Atti e documenti del secondo congresso*, p. 109; also my forthcoming "The Idea of Progress in Italian Catholic Social Thought (1846–1914)."

54. Toniolo's letter is quoted in Avagliano, *Alessandro Rossi,* p. 95; his 1901–2 articles are in Are, (ed.), *I cattolici e la questione sociale,* pp. 499–517.

55. Leone Caetani, *La crisi morale dell'ora presente: religione, modernismo e democrazia,* p. 25.

56. Even Cardinal Giovanni Battista Montini, who later became Pope Paul VI, confronted the issue in a speech he made in 1960: "We find, for sure that during previous historical periods some thought that the preservation of the established order—if we can define it as such—was the supreme good; there were some who tried to use religion in defending their own well being without taking into consideration that at the origins of well being, as a principle, lay common interests and its social and economic aim had to be to provide bread for all; we find there were some who tried to use even charity as an instrument to maintain the distance between the rich and the poor." In attempting to explain the Italian working classes' marked aversion to religion, Cardinal Montini stopped quite short of calling religion an opiate for the people. But the socialists, who argued that such was the case, were not alone in seeing that religion could be utilized to contain the dissatisfaction of the working classes and thus thwart their drive for greater equality. The conviction of Pius X that socioeconomic inequality was the handiwork of God strangely coincided with the cynical wisdom Napoleon expressed a century earlier: "There can be no society without material inequality, and there can be no material inequality without religion . . . No religion, no government." The nineteenth-century Catholic conservative credo of social immobility demanded what Cardinal Montini was to condemn later as contrary to the real spirit of Christianity. But the abuse of religion became a factor in the alienation of the working classes from religion and those who represented it, since the workers felt that "religion was an instrument used to exploit the working masses." The Church was seen taking "the side of the rich" as churchmen "defended the privileges of the rich, from whose friendship they profited while they forgot the sufferings of the humble and the precarious and insufficient conditions of entire social strata," to which they "preached that poverty was blessed and recommended resignation and nonresistance." Cardinal Montini, of course, listed these accusations only to deny them. (See Paul VI [Cardinal Montini], *Religione e lavoro: discorso tenuto a Torino il 27 marzo 1960 agli operatori del mondo del lavoro,* especially p. 27; Napoleon is quoted in A. J. P. Taylor, "The Emperor Industry" [*New York Review of Books,* Dec. 18, 1969], p. 34.)

57. Jemolo, *Chiesa e stato,* pp. 437–38, 515. The last part of Jemolo's statement quoted here was translated by Horowitz (*The Italian Labor Movement,* p. 96).

58. For examples of the debate, see Mario G. Rossi, "Movemento cattolico e capitale finanziario: appunti sulla genesi del blocco clerico-moderato"; Rossi, "Movimento cattolico nelle campagne"; Claudio Giovannini, "Come si studia il movimento cattolico"; Guido Verucci, "Storia del cattolicesimo, della Chiesa, del movimento cattolico italiano nell'età contemporanea"; Maurilio Guasco, "Proposte per una ricerca sui rapporti fra cattolici e socialisti"; Renda, *Socialisti e cattolici,* pp. 67–68.

59. *L'Osservatore Romano,* May 16, 1906.

60. Quoted in De Gasperi, *I tempi e gli uomini,* pp. 65–66.

61. Filippo Meda, *Vade mecum per il Propagandista Cattolico: istruzioni teoriche e pratiche,* p. 15.

62. Quoted in Renda, *Socialisti e cattolici,* p. 62.

63. Circular of the Unione Elettorale in *Azione Sociale* 1, July 1907, pp. 519–21.

64. Dino Secco Suardo, *Da Leone XIII a Pio X,* pp. 423, 430, 450.

65. Giordani, *Pio X,* p. 50.

66. Filippo Crispolti, a contemporary of the pope, told how Pius X was tortured by a

vision of sin engulfing virtually all mankind. And several of the other biographers seem to bear out Crispolti's assertion and tell of a fear on the mind of Pius X during the last years of his life. It was a fear of a worldwide conflagration to be followed by the betrayal of the principles of Christianity by millions, a mass desertion from the fold, a veritable *religio depopulata.* Because of this the pope felt sorry for his successor. Filippo Crispolti, *Pio IX, Leone XIII, Pio X, Benedetto XV, Pio XI: ricordi personali,* pp. 90–91, 130–31; Ernesto Vercesi, *Il pontificato di Pio X,* p. 67; Nello Vian, *Il Santo Pontefice romano Pio X,* pp. 203–4. Some expressions of an overwhelming pessimism about the future may be found even in the official pronouncements of Pius X, for instance, in his first encyclical, *E supremi apostolatus.* For a striking contrast, here is Pope John XXIII addressing the second Vatican Council: "We feel that we must disagree with those prophets of doom, who are always forecasting disaster as though the end of the world were at hand" (quoted in Elliott, *I Will Be Called John,* p. 298).

67. For the background of the lifting of the ban and the role played by socialism, particularly the 1904 general strike, see Roger Aubert, "Documents relatifs au mouvement catholique italien sous le pontificat de S. Pie X," pp. 228–29, 235–36, 358; Vercesi, *Il pontificato di Pio X,* pp. 26–27, 108; Filippo Crispolti, *Politici, querrieri, poeti: ricordi personali,* p. 99; Giovanni Semeria, *I miei quattro Papi,* p. 201; Olgiati, "La politica di S. Pio X," p. 526; Toniolo, *Lettere* 3:42–43; Giordani, *Pio X,* pp. 136ff.; Secco Suardo, *Da Leone XIII,* pp. 396ff.; Camp, *The Papal Ideology of Social Reform,* pp. 59–60.

68. Quoted in Girolamo Dal-Gal (ed.), *Insegnamenti di San Pio X,* p. 108.

69. Leo XIII, encyclical *Spesse volte,* quoted in Malinverni, *La Scuola Sociale,* p. 34ff., and Aubert, *The Church in a Secularized Society,* pp. 10–11. The proceedings of the 1899 (Ferrara) congress are reviewed in Spadolini, *L'opposizione cattolica,* pp. 504-11.

70. Marchesan, *Papa Pio X,* p. 414

71. Pius X, encyclical *E supremi apostolatus,* especially p. 7; A. William Salomone, *Italy in the Giolittian Era: Italian Democracy in the Making, 1900–1914;* my "Christian Democracy and Social Modernism"; Aubert, *The Church in a Secularized Society,* p. 48.

72. Monetti, *Problemi varii,* 2:64.

73. For examples of Toniolo's treatment of the theme, see his "La funzione della giustizia," pp. 363–64, and *Lettere,* 3:245; also Cappellazzi, *La questione sociale,* p. 27; Gambasin, *Gerarchia e laicato,* p. 220; Brezzi, *Cristiano sociali,* pp. 480-82; Danilo Veneruso, "Cattolici e socialisti in Italia tra il raggiungimento dell'unità e l'avvento del fascismo (1870–1924)," p. 75. For Toniolo's outlook on the past, present, and future of socialism, see his *Il socialismo nella storia della civiltà,* first published as a series of articles between 1899 and 1902, republished within *Opera Omnia* in a volume entitled *Capitalismo e socialismo,* and reprinted in part in Are (ed.), *I cattolici e la questione sociale,* pp. 518–30, and in Dino Del Bo (ed.), *I cattolici italiani di fronte al socialismo,* pp. 103–13. For interpretations see Are, "Introduzione," especially p. 58; Antonio Fantetti, "Giuseppe Toniolo: alcuni studi sul socialismo"; Brezzi, "Movimento operaio," especially p. 203ff.

74. Imberciadori, *L'Unione Popolare,* pp. 55, 64–65.

75. "L'Unione Popolare Italiana," p. 130.

76. *L'Osservatore Romano,* Sept. 7, 1907, p. 2; Apr. 29, 1909, pp. 1–2; *Azione Sociale* 1, Feb. 1907, p. 186; Secondo Campiglio, *L'Unione Popolare fra i cattolici d'Italia; (note illustrative e norme pratiche),* pp. 95–101; Antonio Coscetti, *Popolo all'erta!!! Ecco il nemico; opuscolo di propaganda antisocialista;* Camp, *The Papal Ideology of Social Reform,* pp. 59–60.

77. Aubert, *The Church in a Secularized Society,* p. 17; and Aubert, in Aubert et al., *The Church in the Industrial Age,* p. 381ff.

78. Sturzo, "L'organizzazione di classe," p. 157; also Renda, *Socialisti e cattolici*, p. 50.

79. Quoted in Renda, *Socialisti e cattolici*, pp. 58–59.

80. Gambasin, *Parroci e contadini*, especially pp. 48, 90, 100, 116, 141, 193–95; also Gambasin, "L'utopia sociale," p. 46.

Chapter 7

1. De Rosa, *Filippo Meda*, p. 64; Zussini, *Luigi Caissotti di Chiusano*, pp. 17, 104ff. The chapter title is from Pius X, encyclical *Pieni l'animo*, p. 60.

2. Quoted in Corna Pellegrini, "L'evoluzione del concetto di classe," p. 448. In 1898 Caissotti echoed the suggestion of a tactical cooperation between Catholic and Socialist organizations of labor (Zussini, *Luigi Caissotti di Chiusano*, p. 84).

3. Brezzi, "Movimento operaio," p. 224.

4. Scalabrini, *Il socialismo e l'azione del clero*, p. 77ff.; Are, "Introduzione," p. 60, and Danilo Veneruso, "Cattolici e socialisti in Italia tra il raggiungimento dell'unità e l'avvento del fascismo (1870–1924)," p. 80.

5. The positions taken by the Catholic papers in the Marches are reported in Molinelli, *Il movimento cattolico nelle Marche*, pp. 89–103.

6. For references to the Socialists as "barbarians" and a "deadly pestilence," see Leo's encyclical *Quod apostolici muneris*. Compare with Leo's *Graves de communi*. See also Veneruso, "Cattolici e socialisti in Italia," p. 80.

7. Renda, *Socialisti e cattolici*, especially pp. 14, 294.

8. Guasco, "Proposte per una ricerca," p. 247.

9. Avagliano, *Alessandro Rossi*, p. 340; also Molinelli, *Il movimento cattolico nelle Marche*, p. 96.

10. Guasco, "Proposte per una ricerca," p. 248.

11. Xenio Toscani, "La biblioteca del conte Stanislao Medolago Albani," p. 81.

12. See Roger Aubert's remarks about the Belgian Catholics in Rossini, (ed.), *Romolo Murri nella storia*, pp. 426–27.

13. Quoted in Brezzi, "Capitalismo e socialismo," p. 260.

14. Chiesa, *L'Unione popolare*, p. 18.

15. Giacinto Burroni, *Manipoli sparsi per l'educazione della mente e del cuore del popolo*, p. 59; Gabriele Latessa, *La società nelle teorie del Cristianesimo e della massoneria: dialogo tra socialista, massone e sacerdote*.

16. *Azione Sociale* 5, Oct. 1911, p. 177 ff. For an entertaining comparison see the report about the *Settimana Sociale* held by the Catholics, on p. 179ff.

17. Imberciadori, *L'Unione Popolare*, p. 3ff.; Campiglio, *L'Unione Popolare*, pp. 76–78, 124, 131–32; Malinverni, *La Scuola Sociale*, p. 88ff.; Valente, *Aspetti e momenti*, p.33; Jemolo, *Chiesa e stato*, p. 545; Pier Luigi Ballini, *Il movimento cattolico a Firenze (1900–1919)*, p. 204ff.; Molinelli, *Il movimento cattolico nelle Marche*, p. 53ff.; Guasco, "Proposte per una ricerca," pp. 245–62; Bell, "Worker Culture and Worker Politics," p. 14ff.

18. Valente, *Aspetti e momenti*, p. 36.

19. Renda, *Socialisti e cattolici*, p. 12ff.; also Del Bo, "Nota introduttiva," in Del Bo (ed.), *I cattolici italiani di fronte al socialismo*, p. 34ff.

20. Brezzi, "Movimento operaio," pp. 203–4.

21. Quoted in Renda, *Socialisti e cattolici*, pp. 18–19; also Molinelli, *Il movimento cattolico nelle Marche*, p. 29ff. To compare the style and substance represented by Murri with that of Toniolo, see Murri's "Socialismo e religione," a 1901 piece, reprinted in Del Bo (ed.), *I cattolici italiani di fronte al socialismo*, pp. 91–100; and Murri's "Socialismo e democrazia," first published in 1903 and reprinted in Are (ed.), *I cattolici e la questione sociale*, pp. 572–97.

22. Are, "Introduzione," pp. 60–61.
23. *Azione Sociale* 1, July 1907, p. 519ff., and 2, Dec. 1908, p. 791ff.; also Chiesa, *L'Unione popolare,* p. 20ff.; and Imberciadori, *L'Unione Popolare,* p. 90.
24. Bell, "Worker Culture and Worker Politics"; Renda, *Socialisti e cattolici,* p. 273ff.
25. Chiri, *Le organizzazioni operaie,* pp. xxxi, xxxiv–xxxvii, 21–22, 144.
26. Antonio Boggiano Pico, onetime president of the Unione Popolare, as quoted in Magri, *Dal movimento sindacale cristiano,* p. 41.
27. For an example see the situation in the automobile industry in Turin, described by Salvadori, *Il movimento cattolico a Torino.*
28. Chiri, *Le organizzazioni operaie,* pp. 23–24; De Rosa, *Il movimento cattolico,* pp. 114–15.
29. Correspondence between Caissotti and Toniolo, in Zussini, *Luigi Caissotti di Chiusano,* pp. 83–84.
30. Quoted in Are, "Introduzione," p. 81.
31.

**Percentage of Population in Towns with
20,000 or More Inhabitants**

	1850	1870	1890	1910	1930	1950	1965
Italy	(11.2)	10.6	15.0	27.5	34.5	41.2	50.0
Germany	(6.8)	12.5	21.9	34.6	43.4	......	......
GDR	......	......	......	......	......	39.1	42.9
GFR	......	......	......	......	......	41.5	49.2

SOURCE: Adapted from Peter Flora, "Historical Processes of Social Mobilization: Urbanization and Literacy, 1850–1965," in S. N. Eisenstadt and Stein Rokkan (eds.), *Building of States and Nations* (Beverly Hills, Calif.: Sage, 1973), 1:242.

32. Clough, *The Economic History of Modern Italy,* pp. 135–36.
33. Neufeld, *Italy: School for Awakening Countries,* p. 536, table 26.
34. Gerschenkron, "Notes on the Rate of Industrial Growth," p. 364; also Rosario Romeo, *Breve storia della grande industria in Italia,* pp. 63, 66.
35. Frank Coppa, *Planning, Protectionism, and Politics in Liberal Italy: Economics and Politics in the Giolittian Age,* p. 20; Romeo, *Breve storia della grande industria,* p. 111; and Neufeld, *Italy: School for Awakening Countries,* p. 536, table 25.
36. Neufeld, *Italy: School for Awakening Countries,* p. 306; Coppa, *Planning, Protectionism, and Politics,* pp. 16–17.
37. *Azione Sociale* 7, March 1913, pp. 49–50.
38. Sassoli, *La questione sociale,* pp. 26–27; also a circular signed by Medolago in *L'Osservatore Romano,* Feb. 16, 1907; and De Rosa, *Il movimento cattolico,* p. 87ff., especially 105–7, 119.
39. Gambasin, *Parroci e contadini,* especially pp. 26–49, 120, 143, 158ff.; also *Azione Sociale* 5, Oct. 1911, pp. 182ff.
40. Daniele Menozzi, "Le nuove parrocchie nella prima industrializzazione torinese (1900–1915)," p. 70.

41. For the verb *reggere*, normally applied to the reign of monarchs, used to describe the role of a village priest, see Nello Vian, "Introduzione," to Pius X, *Lettere, raccolte da Nello Vian*, p. 9.

42. Menozzi, "Le nuove parrocchie," especially pp. 85–87.

43. Briére, *Ai padroni*, p. 5.

44. Pastoral letter by Bishop Giacinto Archangeli, in *Azione Sociale* 2, Dec. 1908, p. 784.

45. Quoted in Menozzi, "Orientamenti pastorali," p. 207; also Salvadori, *Il movimento cattolico a Torino*, p. 7ff.

46. Menozzi, "Orientamenti pastorali," especially p. 206.

47. The Turin publication *La Buona Settimana*, quoted in Menozzi, "Orientamenti pastorali," pp. 211–15.

48. Imberciadori, *L'Unione Popolare*, p. 27.

Chapter 8

1. For an example see Salvadori, *Il movimento cattolico a Torino*, pp. 68–69. The chapter title is a quotation from Pius X (see Dal-Gal, *Il Papa Santo*, pp. 233–34).

2. Magri, *Dal movimento sindacale cristiano*, p. vi.

3. Chiri, *Le organizzazioni operaie*, pp. 12–13.

4. Secco Suardo, *Da Leone XIII*, pp. 530–35.

5. Toniolo, "Passato e futuro dell'azione economica fra i cattolici d' Italia."

6. *L'Osservatore Romano*, April 6, 1910.

7. Ibid., June 5, 1910; July 10, 1910; Sept. 25, 1910; Oct. 29, 1910.

8. *Azione Sociale* 4, Sept. 1910, p. 151–54.

9. The entire text of Medolago's presidential address is in *Azione Sociale* 4, April 1910, pp. 67–77.

10. Toniolo's letter, dated Aug. 31, 1910, is in Zussini, *Luigi Caissotti di Chiusano*, p. 145.

11. *Azione Sociale* 4, Oct. 1910, pp. 168–72; *L'Osservatore Romano*, Oct. 30, 1910.

12. For an example see Lorenzo Bedeschi, "L'autonomia politica dei cattolici italiani."

13. Secco Suardo, *Da Leone XIII*, especially pp. 367, 426, 405ff.; his evidence is based on the archives of the *Civiltà Cattolica*.

14. Giuseppe Toniolo, "Atteggiamenti e doveri dei cattolici nell'ora presente," p. 440: "Ed è con tale convinzione e previsione, che noi dell'ordinamento di tutte le classi, lavoratrici e proprietarie, in distinti ma cordiali enti corporativi professionali, facciamo il fulcro di codesta ristorazione; perchè entro questi organismi autonomi, fra loro ravvicinati nel quotidiano e parallelo esercizio dei rispettivi doveri e dirritti e nella comunanza finale degli interessi di tutti, rinasca e si cementi il sentimento della solidarietà sociale."

15. In the pope's wishes, Toniolo perceived the "safe indication of the will of the Lord." He felt that "even in areas where the pope's authority is not infallible . . . even if the pope is mistaken we have to obey him. God rewards those who are good and obedient" (see his *Lettere*, 3:236, 253–54, 331–32; also quoted in A. Fantetti, "Eco di dibattiti: Murri, Toniolo, Meda," pp. 63–64.)

16. Secco Suardo, *Da Leone XIII*, pp. 483, 560ff.

17. The concluding part of Rezzara's report and the resolutions as accepted are in *Azione Sociale* 4, Nov. 1910, p. 183ff.; the latter are also cited in Riva Sanseverino, *Il movimento sindacale cristiano*, p. 250ff., and in *Voti sociali*, p. 107ff.

18. For the coverage of the congress in *L'Osservatore Romano*, see editions of Nov. 11–14, 1910.

19. Rezzara, Cecconelli, and Crispolti are cited in De Rosa, *Il movimento cattolico,* pp. 319–22. For additional information about the debate, see Galli, *I cattolici e il sindacato,* p. 128ff.; Caetani, *La crisi morale dell'ora presente,* p. 33; Fappani, *Guido Miglioli,* p. 174ff.; Magri, *Dal movimento sindacale cristiano,* p. 36ff.; Scoppola, *Dal neoguelfismo alla Democrazia Cristiana,* p. 110ff.; Gaetano Di Mariano, "Il movimento cattolico e le masse contadine," p. 265.

20. Pius X is quoted in Emile Poulat, "La dernière bataille du pontificat de Pie X," p. 105. For Toniolo's statement see his *Lettere,* 3:93.

21. *L'Osservatore Romano,* Nov. 18, 1910.

22. Ibid., April 4, 1912; also Biederlack, *Principi dell'ordinamento,* p. 25ff.

23. *Azione Sociale* 6, Nov. 1912, p. xxixff.; also 7, July 1913, p. 118, and Nov. 1913, p. 211ff.

24. Rigola, *Storia del movimento operaio italiano,* p. 317ff.; Neufeld, *Italy: School for Awakening Countries,* pp. 318, 341; Coppa, *Planning, Protectionism, and Politics,* pp. 186ff., 222–25, 237ff.

Chapter 9

1. Vercesi, *Il movimento cattolico in Italia,* p. 252; Neufeld, *Italy: School for Awakening Countries,* p. 358. The chapter title is from Pius X, letter to G. M. Cazares Y Martinez, bishop of Zamora (Mexico), Oct. 7, 1906, in D'Ascenzi (ed.), *I documenti pontifici,* p. 63.

2. For rather rare extant evidence suggesting that the Catholics' reorientation of their organizational efforts toward the peasantry was indeed conscious and considered, see a report about the meeting of the presidents of the Diocesan Directorates of the Venetian region in *Azione Sociale* 3, Aug. 1909, p. 206ff., and a speech by Boggiano, reported in *L'Osservatore Romano,* Feb. 4, 1910. An article published in *Civiltà Cattolica* in 1907 suggests that the Catholics' refocussing of their organizational efforts toward the peasantry might have been something that originated with Pius X, who maintained a direct contact with the writers of the *Civiltà.* The article was written at the time when the reorganization of Italian Catholic Action, which the Pope ordered, was being finalized. The writer of the unsigned article, who was in fact the Jesuit Antonio Pavissich, set out in an authoritative manner the goals for the Unione Popolare, the propaganda organization of Catholic Action. The Popular Union, Pavissich suggested, should concentrate on organizing and propagandizing the rural population, not only because peasants constituted the majority of the country's population, but also because "for the most part they remained faithful to religion" ("L'Unione Popolare Italiana," p. 141).

3. For a review of a clerical "vanguard" that advanced class consciousness in the countryside and its ultimate fate in the hands of Pius X, see Lorenzo Bedeschi, "Precedenti storici delle avanguardie contadine miglioline"; Molinelli, *Il movimento cattolico nelle Marche,* pp. 15, 20–21, 179–89; Antonio Fappani, *Il movimento contadino in Italia: cento anni di storia,* p. 96ff.; Gambasin, *Parroci e contadini,* pp. 216–19.

4. Mario Bandini, *Cento anni di storia agraria italiana,* p. 73ff. Cf. Neufeld, *Italy: School for Awakening Countries,* p. 528, table 13.

5. Clough, *The Economic History of Modern Italy,* p. 142; Renato Zangheri, "Introduzione," in Zangheri (ed.), *Lotte agrarie in Italia,* pp. ix–xix.

6. Bonomelli, "Proprietà e socialismo," pp. 36–37; also Fappani, *Guido Miglioli,* p. 12ff.

7. Zangheri, "Introduzione," pp. xxiff., and xxxviiiff.; Alberto Caracciolo, "Le origini della lotta di classe nell'agro romano (1870–1915)," p. 632ff.

8. Robert Michels, for one, is referred to in Alberto Caracciolo, "Per una storia del movimento contadino in Italia," pp. 472–73.

9. I will give away my own philosophical disposition by quoting the great pragmatist Prime Minister Giovanni Giolitti, who declared with biting sarcasm in the Italian Parliament in 1908 that the conflict between socialism and Catholicism was "one church against another. The Socialist party has its ecumenical councils that declare the dogma and its conclaves that nominate those in high office, has its missionaries and its grand inquisitors and it excommunicates. The Honorable Bissolati [who was eventually read out of the Socialist party] knows that there is excommunication" (Giovanni Giolitti, *Discorsi parlamentari, pubblicati per deliberazione della Camera dei Deputati,* 3:108).

10. See the minutes of the founding congress of the socialist-led Federterra, a national federation of rural labor, held in 1901 (Zangheri [ed.], *Lotte agrarie in Italia,* especially pp. 10–15, 19, 39, 59–61; also Zangheri's "Introduzione," especially p. lxxivff.).

11. Alessandro Cantono, *Storia del socialismo italiano,* p. 47; Zangheri, "Introduzione," p. lxxix; Caracciolo, "Per una storia," pp. 474–77; Bardelli, "La questione operaia," p. 59; di Mariano, "Il movimento cattolico"; Rossi, "Il movimento cattolico nelle campagne"; remarks by A. Stella in Tramontin (ed.), *Il movimento cattolico,* pp. 71–72.

12. Zangheri, "Introduzione," pp. xxxivff., lviii; Renda's remarks in Tramontin (ed.), *Il movimento cattolico,* pp. 54–61, Neufeld, *Italy: School for Awakening Countries,* p. 331; Caracciolo, "Le origini della lotta di classe," especially p. 634.

13. Fappani, *Il movimento contadino in Italia,* p. 129; Amos Zanibelli, *Le "leghe bianche" nel Cremonese dal 1900 al "Lodo Bianchi,"* p. 12.

14. Ronchi, "Le origini del movimento contadino nel Soresinese"; also Bardelli, "La questione operaia," p. 59. For Miglioli's long career, see Fappani, *Guido Miglioli.*

15. Fontaine, *Le modernisme sociologique,* p. 163. For the papal letter praising Fontaine, signed by Merry del Val, see *Acta Apostolicae Sedis,* 1 (1909): 719. For others expressing an attitude similar to Fontaine's, see a circular of the Unione Economico Sociale in *L'Osservatore Romano,* Oct. 22, 1907; Talamo, *La questione sociale,* p. 38; Biederlack, *Principi dell'ordinamento,* p. 17; Gambasin, *Parroci e contadini,* pp. 170–73, 198–200; Avagliano, *Alessandro Rossi,* p. 132.

16. For early instances of this in Italy, see Gambasin, "L'utopia sociale," pp. 41–43; also De Rosa, *Il movimento cattolico,* p. 106.

17. Spadolini, *L'opposizione cattolica,* pp. 267–68.

18. See Franco Rizzo, *Luigi Sturzo e la questione meridionale nella crisi del primo dopoguerra, 1919–1924,* especially p. 78ff.; Trimarchi, *La formazione del pensiero meridionalista di Luigi Sturzo,* particularly p. 18. Salvemini's arguments coincided with Sturzo's in many important aspects. Salvemini was especially emphatic about the political consequences of the system of *latifondi;* he pointed to the overbearance in southern politics of the *latifondista* and the consequences of this—political corruption and a stultifying conservatism that served the economic interests of the upper classes (see Salvemini's "La questione meridionale e il federalismo"; also Rosario Villari, "Il meridionalista," Villari et al., *Gaetano Salvemini,* p. 108).

19. For Sturzo's arguments in favor of land reform, see Rizzo, *Luigi Sturzo,* pp. 78–79, 84; also Trimarchi, *La formazione del pensiero meridionalista di Luigi Sturzo,* pp. 74–75; Renda, "Luigi Sturzo e il movimento contadino," especially pp. 468–76, 492ff.; Renda, *Socialisti e cattolici,* pp. 27ff., 60ff. Salvemini's suggestion of land reform and his insistence upon the importance of *piccola proprietà democratica* ran against the convictions of many of the theoreticians in the Socialist party who considered it one of the basic aims of socialism to do away with private property, the source of social ills for them. This issue appears to have been involved in Salvemini's eventual break with the Socialist party. (See his, "La questione meri-

dionale"; also Villari, "Il meridionalista," pp. 99ff., 106ff., 111–15.) Eventually Sturzo became convinced that there existed a "Southern Question," which went beyond the problems of southern society to involve the semicolonial status of the south in united Italy. Thus by 1910 he sought to orient the discussion of the *questione meridionale* toward the ways and means of winning for the southern working classes a genuine social autonomy as well as a voice in the political affairs of the country. At Sturzo's insistence the 1910 (Modena) congress adopted a resolution that urged the study of the Southern Question and special organizational efforts in the south. (See *L'Osservatore Romano,* Nov. 14, 1910; also Rizzo, *Luigi Sturzo,* particularly p. 80ff.; De Stefano and Oddo, *Storia della Sicilia,* pp. 428–49.) Salvemini, like Sturzo, a southerner, accomplished for the Socialist movement what Sturzo did for Catholic Action: with an authentic voice, he aroused in Italian Socialists an interest in the south and urged the study of the *questione meridionale* in realistic terms. (See Giampiero Carocci, *Giolitti e l'età giolittiana,* p. 81; and Villari, "Il meridionalista," pp. 126–27.) Prime Minister Giolitti apparently thought that he would be presiding over the dissolution of the unitary state if he granted a genuine political autonomy to the south, the demand for which soon emerged as the theme in the discussions of the Southern Question. Nevertheless, Giolitti became aware of the increasing aggravation of the situation in the south. Speaking of the problems connected with the *latifondi* in 1913, he went so far as to say that he "did not exclude" the possibility of the "expropriation" of these (*Discorsi parlamentari,* 3:1671). How ironic it was that Sturzo, a proponent of regional autonomy at the turn of the century, after World War II became concerned, as Giolitti once was, about the threat to unity represented by regionalism.

20. An 1895 statement by Avolio is quoted in Rizzo, *Luigi Sturzo,* p. 41.

21. D'Ascenzi, *I documenti pontifici,* pp. 19–22.

22. Jemolo, *Chiesa e stato in Italia,* p. 519.

23. Caracciolo, "Le origini della lotta di classe," especially p. 642.

24. See the resolutions of the 1894 congress of the Opera in Chiri, *Le organizzazioni operaie,* p. xxiii. About the debate at the 1896 (Padua) congress of the Catholic Union for Social Studies, see Unione Cattolica per gli Studi Sociali, *Atti e documenti,* especially pp. 119ff., 149–69, 192–94, 241–77. For the years of the papacy of Pius X, see *L'Osservatore Romano,* Jan. 6, 1910; May 29, 1911; *Settimana Sociale,* Nov. 23, 1912; Dec. 28, 1912; Jan. 25, 1913; Feb. 8, 1913; July 4, 1914. Biederlack's was a dissenting opinion among Catholics as he argued against smallholdings because these, he said, were inefficient and tended to break up into ever smaller units that could not support a family, thus leading to the proletarianization of the peasantry (*Principi dell'ordinamento,* p. 18ff.). The 1896 Padua congress anticipated this argument (which, by the way, coincides with the perception of a large number of historians, especially those of Neo-Marxist orientation), by suggesting that the breakup of smallholdings should be prevented by legal means, through laws that would require the inheritance of smallholdings by a single offspring, somewhat like the case used to be with the *latifundia.* (For the historiographical appearance of the problems of the *piccola proprietà,* and Catholics' attitude toward it, see Zussini, *Luigi Caissotti di Chiusano,* pp. 54, 112ff.; Nino Mazzoni, *Lotte agrarie nella vecchia Italia,* pp. 49–52; Zanibelli, *Le "leghe bianche" nel Cremonese,* p. 13; Fappani, *Il movimento contadino in Italia,* p. 101ff.; Ronchi, "Le origini del movimento contadino nel Soresinese," especially p. 433ff.; Di Mariano, "Il movimento cattolico e le masse contadine"; Caracciolo, "Per una storia del movimento contadino in Italia," especially p. 488; Caracciolo, "Le origini della lotta di classe," especially p. 642ff.; Caracciolo, *Il movimento contadino nel Lazio: 1870–1922,* particularly pp. 124–25, 137ff.; Giuseppe Are, *Economia e politica nell'Italia liberale (1890–1915),* particularly pp. 167–81.

25. The presence of smallholdings, like that of the *latifondi,* was very uneven in Italy.

The *piccola proprietà* was widespread in Piedmont, for instance. As to the area around Rome, see Caracciolo, "Le origini della lotta di classe," p. 642, and *Il movimento contadino nel Lazio*, p. 125.

26. One is at a loss in trying to translate terms like *mezzadria* and words denoting similar contractual arrangements, the equivalents of which did not exist in North America. For *mezzadria* I used the word *sharecropping* with a good deal of hesitation, since I realize that in American English it can be somewhat misleading. (For a historiographical treatment of the *mezzadria*, and similar arrangements, see the resolutions of the 1875 congress of the Opera in *Voti sociali*, p. 23ff.; D'Ascenzi, *I documenti pontifici*, p. 26ff.; Pier Luigi Ballini, "La lotta politica e movimento sindacale in Toscana agli inizi dell'età giolittiana. Lo sciopero generale di Firenze," p. 246. Ballini, *Il movimento cattolico a Firenze (1900–1919)*, p. 198, quotes a Catholic paper characteristically declaring the *mezzadria* "an institution of justice and of social peace." (See also Zanibelli, *Le "leghe bianche" nel Cremonese*, p. 14ff.; Bedeschi, "I cappellani del lavoro," pp. 307–9; and Giorgio Mori, "I cattolici e il problema della mezzadria.")

27. The *inurbamento*, the urban settlement of the landholding aristocracy, was not new. Given the traditions of urbanism as manifest even in the writings of Aquinas and the concomitant perception of urban life as the good life, residence in urban *palazzi* became the life-style of the Italian aristocracy already during the Middle Ages, as shown by the efforts late medieval and Renaissance towns had to exert in taming the still rampaging feudal but already urban nobles. For several centuries only those Italian nobles who could not afford to maintain an urban residence lived in the countryside. The facts of history and custom made a mockery of the conservative Catholic argument about the tutelage and personalized care given to their peasants in times past by the landlords. "Kings" they may have been in behavior, but they were absentee kings whom their loyal "subjects" rarely saw.

Sassoli's 1879 speech was emphatic about the necessity for the landlord to reside on his property in order to have his beneficial influence felt among his "subjects" and "obtain" through a benevolent "tutelage" their observance of "religious and civic duties" (Sassoli, *La questione sociale nelle campagne*, p. 21ff.). It was the absenteeism and the obvious failure of the aristocratic landowners in performing the paternalistic obligations imposed by the law of charity that alarmed doctrinaire Catholic conservatives as they railed against the aristocrats' turn to capitalistic enterprises that made the landowners' absence something final and permanent, thus precluding a moral regeneration. That absenteeism was a problem before the large-scale turn of the aristocracy to capitalism was obvious already at the congress of the Opera held in 1875. It passed a resolution reminding the landowners that it was their "charitable obligation to reside on their holdings" and lashed out at those who were inclined to see with the Angelic Doctor heaps of dirt and misery to be avoided, if possible, in life in the countryside. But lounging in their urban *palazzi*, they could not "extend to their dependents the benevolent and paternal tutelage in the cordial and charitable exercise of which rested the secret of the closure of the split between the ruling and working classes [*le classi dirigenti e la diretta*] that is growing wider every day in our countryside." Thus the resolution insisted somewhat pathetically that landowners should reside on their lands "at least during the major part of the year" so that their "subjects" would only be partially deprived of the "moral and economic" benefits accrued to them from the presence of the landlords. ("V Congresso Cattolico Italiano. (Modena, 21-24, 10. 1875), "Deliberazioni," reprinted in *Voti sociali dei cattolici italiani*, pp. 23–33; also Bandini, *Cento anni di storia*, p. 55ff.)

With its warning of the growing separation of classes and the implied threat of class struggle, this resolution set the tone of the Catholics' discussion of the social issues of the countryside for decades to come. Because of the large-scale presence of the *latifondi*, at least in some regions, this discussion inevitably included the absenteeism of the aristocratic landlords, some of whom must have squirmed uncomfortably on their seats as speaker after speaker told them that they were sinners who increased the misery of their faithful "subjects" by leaving them without moral guidance. An exasperated village priest, seeing his flock diminishing by the emigration of the parishioners who imitated the landlords by leaving the land, called the aristocrats the "assassins of the family"(Gambasin, *Parroci e contadini,* especially p. 116). Yet the assassins were but sinners deviating somewhat from God's commandments, and the campaign of "repent or burn" continued. Perhaps because absenteeism was becoming more marked as time went by, so did the shrillness of the warning about class struggle and the wipeout to be inflicted on the rural landowning class for their sins.

Count Eduardo Soderini apparently could not take it anymore, when he was reminded of all this once again at the second congress of Catholic social scientists, held in Padua in 1896. Concluding a presentation about the "rural crisis," the young activist Angelo Mauri suggested a resolution to remind the landowners once more of the sins and omissions involved in their habitual absenteeism. He did this after Toniolo, in the opening remarks he delivered as the president of the Catholic Union for Social Studies, pondered the same issue. Soderini's hand must have gone up very fast since Medolago, the presiding officer, recognized him as the first speaker when the discussion on the proposed resolution began. Count Soderini then showed his skill as an objective social scientist by remarking, that "if it was right to remind the landlords (*padroni*) of the need to do their duties, it is equally right to do the same to the peasants, since they too inculpate themselves of absenteeism as they succumb to the desire to emigrate to nearby urban centers and even to far away countries."

What followed was akin to a shouting match between the aged count and young Mauri, supported by Toniolo. Mauri was quick to respond that "if the peasants abandon the fields and emigrate, this happens very frequently because they are forced to do so by misery. Thus if the absenteeism of the *padroni* is voluntary and sinful, the same cannot be imputed to the peasants whose [absenteeism] is in fact a necessary consequence of the absenteeism of the landlords." Despite Toniolo's efforts on the rostrum to defend Mauri's position several times and to remind the audience that the rural upper classes placed their very existence in jeopardy by failing to carry out their charitable obligations "for the sake of impartial Christian equity," as the minutes recorded it, Mauri's proposition did not carry in the end. In fact, the resolution accepted "by a great majority" according to the minutes began by reminding first the peasants and then the landlords of their obligations. This represented solid good social scientific sense, since more peasants than landlords absented themselves from the countryside. Unfortunately, many of the peasants could not read and thus were unable to take to heart the ringing declaration of the illustrious assembly of objective social scientists, recognize their sins, repent and mend their sinful ways by staying on the farm:

The second Catholic congress for the social studies;

Preoccupied by the increasing aggravation of the rural crisis in Italy,

While it reminds the land workers of their obligations of justice toward the landowners, and at the same time invites them to revive their affection toward the land and proper peasant attitudes (*abitudini campagnuole*), and affirms the need to restore the notion of the moral and civic duties of landed property, only the reinvigorated awareness of which can arrest the class separation between the workers and their employers. [This separation] was initiated by the absenteeism from the countryside of the superior social stratum which showed itself ignorant or forgetful of its providential mission among the rural laboring folks, [has to be reminded of these] in order to reunite the disordered threads of the social order, by leading the landowners back to the fruitful exercise of their natural functions involving both individual and collective patronage [. . . etc.]

(Unione cattolica per gli studi sociali, *Atti e documenti*, pp. 119ff., 149ff., especially 173–74, 192–93.)

28. Catholic economic institutions tabulated by Chiri:

Nomenclature	Number of institutions	Membership
Cooperative	57	3,652
Affitanze collettive	64	9,612
Cooperative di consumo	105	26,488
Cooperative agricole	487	50,410
Società di mutuo soccorso	799	88,508
Società di assicurazione contro la mortalità del bestiame	261	23,852
Società di assicurazione contro danni degli incendi	62	2,187
Casse rurali	942	94,188
Casse operaie di dipositi e prestiti	83	10,022
Banche	31	....
Totals	**2,891**	**308,919**

SOURCE: Chiri, *Le organizzazione operaie*, pp. 173, 179, 199, 230, 276, 290, 295, 349, 356, 360. A report by Medolago mentions that the total number of the organizations attached to the Unione Economico Sociale in 1910 was about 6,000 (see *Azione Sociale* 4, Aug. 1910, p. 65ff.).

29. Gambasin, *Gerarchia e laicato*, p. 129.

30. *Voti sociali*, p. 75ff.; D'Ascenzi, *I documenti pontifici*, p. 35ff.; Unione Cattolica per gli Studi Sociali, *Atti e documenti*, especially pp. 169, 193; Riva Sanseverino, *Il movimento sindacale cristiano*, pp. 85–86, 217, 222–23; Zussini, *Luigi Caissotti di Chiusano*, p. 64ff.; Molinelli, *Il movimento cattolico nelle Marche*, p. 46ff.

31. Giuseppe Toniolo, "Passato e futuro dell'azione economica fra i cattolici d'Italia"; also Chiri, *Le organizzazioni operaie*, p. li.

32. *Azione Sociale* 1, Feb. 1907, p. 187; Vercesi, *Il movimento cattolico in Italia*, pp. 227, 236–37; Neufeld, *Italy: School for Awakening Countries*, pp. 334–35; Horowitz, *The Italian Labor Movement*, p. 100ff.; Bell, "Worker Culture and Worker Politics". For Medolago's mention of the figure 2,000 in connection with mutual aid societies, see *Azione Sociale* 4, Apr. 1910, p. 72.

Chapter 10

1. The chapter title is a statement ("*Il Papa tacera*") by Pius X on the occasion of the partial lifting of the Non Expedit, quoted in Richard Webster, *The Cross and the Fasces*, p. 14.

2. Zussini, *Luigi Caissotti di Chiusano*, p. 251.

3. Murri, as quoted in Cappelli, *Romolo Murri*, pp. 6 and 105.

4. Pius X, as quoted in Dal-Gal, *Il Papa santo,* pp. 233–34.

5. Casoli, *Un campione,* p. 33.

6. Aubert, *The Church in a Secularized Society,* p. 19; Aubert, in Aubert et al., *The Church in the Industrial Age,* p. 387; and Ritter, *Il movimento cattolico-sociale in Germania,* especially p. 258ff. Admiration for things German was a European-wide phenomenon in the aftermath of the Franco-Prussian war. In following this trend, Pius X was somewhat selective in emphasizing the example of the *Volksverein,* which, unlike the Center, the German Catholic political party, was under the direct control of the church hierarchy.

7. James O'Gara, "Introduction," to O'Gara (ed.), *The Layman in the Church,* p. 12. For the post-Vatican II reoccurrence of the problem, see report, complete with a photo of pickets carrying signs "Autonomy to laymen in temporal matters" in the Rome daily *Il Messagero,* Feb. 24, 1968.

8. Pius X, encyclical *Vehementer nos,* pp. 47–48.

9. Aubert, *The Church in a secularized Society,* p. 194ff.; also Pietro Scoppola, "L'autonomia nell'azione politica dei cattolici"; Scoppola, "Per una valutazione del popolarismo"; and De Rosa, *Filippo Meda,* p. 52ff.

10. Toniolo, "Lettera aperta al conte Grosoli," p. 395.

11. For examples see *L'Osservatore Romano,* Sept. 28, 1907; Imberciadori, *L'Unione Popolare,* p. 64ff.

12. The cry of Bishop Bonomelli is a chilling comment about the style of leadership established by Pius X: in a climate of "adulation" and fear, he says, some of the bishops are afraid to speak their minds and "see themselves reduced to simple executors and transmitters" of orders coming from Rome. (Bedeschi, *La curia romana,* especially pp. 3, 8, 121ff., 198ff. My forthcoming " 'Robots Manipulated from Rome': Leadership in Italian Catholic Action during the Papacy of Pius X (1903–1914)" details the centralization and clericalization of Catholic Action during the period.)

13. Chiri, *Le organizzazioni operaie,* p. xxiiff.; also Pius X, *motu proprio* "Fin dalla prima," and Dal-Gal, *Il Papa Santo,* p. 278.

14. The letter of Pius X to Medolago is cited in Casoli, *Un campione della causa cattolica,* pp. 30–31.

15. For a series of very forceful and highly orthodox arguments in favor of the church control and religious orientation of Catholic Action, see Toniolo's 1901–2 series of articles in *Are* (ed.), *I cattolici e la questione sociale,* p. 515ff.; also a letter written by Toniolo to Pius X (was the pope's letter to Medolago leaked and is this in self-defense?) in *Lettere,* 3:177–78. Murri is quoted in Cappelli, *Romolo Murri,* p. 72.

16. *Azione Sociale* 1, Nov.–Dec. 1907, pp. 751–58, 661–65; 4, Jan.–Feb. 1910, pp. 1–6; May 1910, pp. 81–83; also D'Ascenzi, *I documenti pontifici,* pp. 67–73; also Aubert, *The Church in a Secularized Society,* pp. 132–33, and Aubert, in Aubert et al., *The Church in the Industrial Age,* p. 505.

17. The text of the papal letter is in *Azione Sociale* 1, March 1907, pp. 207–8; see also Medolago's circular reflecting it in *L'Osservatore Romano,* Oct. 22, 1907, p. 2; Magri, *Dal movimento sindacale cristiano,* p. 35; Aubert, *The Church in a Secularized Society,* pp. 133, 142–43, 574; also Aubert, in Aubert et al., *The Church in the Industrial Age,* pp. 418–19.

18. See the papal letter, dated Nov. 22, 1909, in *Azione Sociale* 3, Nov.–Dec., 1909, pp. 257–58; another letter, dated March 15, 1910, signed by Merry del Val in *Acta Apostolicae Sedis,* 2:223–24; Pius X, letter *Notre charge apostolique,* p. 624ff.; also *Azione Sociale* 3, Nov.–Dec., 1909, p. 259; *L'Osservatore Romano,* July 21, 1910; Jemolo, *Chiesa e stato in Italia,* p. 520ff., and Malinverni, *La Scuola Sociale,* p. 59ff.

19. Chiri, *Le organizzazioni operaie,* pp. iv, xxxvff., 16–20.

20. Salvadori, *Il movimento cattolico a Torino,* pp. 71–72; Magri, *Dal movimento sindacale cristiano,* p. 36.

21. Casoli, *Un campione,* p. 33.

22. Text in *Azione Sociale* 5, April 1911, pp. 59–63; the new *statuto* is in ibid., Feb.–March 1911, pp. 24–32; related arguments in ibid., 6, March 1912, p. 43ff. and 7, Nov. 1913, p. 211ff.

23. Pius X, encyclical *Singulari quadam,* especially pp. 136–37. For background see Riva Sanseverino, *Movimento sindacale cristiano,* p. 31ff.; Hogan, *The Development of Ketteler's Interpretation,* especially pp. 246–47; Dal-Gal, *Il Papa Santo,* p. 278ff.; Emile Poulat, "La dernière bataille du pontificat de Pie X"; Aubert, *The Church in a Secularized Society,* p. 92ff., 203; and Aubert, in Aubert et al., *The Church in the Industrial Age,* pp. 476ff., 498ff., 503, 523.

24. See my " 'Germania Doceat!' "

25. Ballini, *Il movimento cattolico a Firenze,* p. 292ff.

26. Zussini's presentation of the affair (*Luigi Caissotti di Chiusano,* pp. 145–96) is based on the correspondence between Toniolo and Caissotti. His documentation appears to be impeccable and is accepted as such by Poulat, whose "La dernière bataille" adds to the tale mostly in the way of interpretation. For Secco Suardo's remark about Monetti, see his *Da Leone XIII,* p. 562.

27. In attacking that "socialistic prejudice," the concept of the social functions of property, Monetti was not breaking new ground. Some of the earlier Italian Neo-Thomists gave a very un-Thomistic twist to social theory and betrayed the influence of liberal economic doctrine by stressing the owners' rights in connection with property and neglecting its social function. (see Köhler, in Aubert et al., *The Church in the Industrial Age,* pp. 196–99.)

28. Quoted in Zussini, *Luigi Caissotti di Chiusano,* pp. 154–57.

29. Quoted in De Rosa, *Il movimento cattolico,* pp. 325–26.

30. *Azione Sociale* 8, May 1914, pp. 93–94. For the echoes of the "last battle of the papacy of Pius X," see also ibid., 6, Nov. 1912, p. xxvff., 8, July 1914, pp. 131–32, and Aug.–Sept. 1914, pp. 163–65; and Riva Sanseverino, *Il movimento sindacale cristiano,* pp. 258–59.

31. Zussini, *Caissotti di Chiusano,* p. 169ff.

32. Luigi Caissotti di Chiusano, *Il sindacalismo cristiano in un articolo della "Civiltà Cattolica."*

33. See a papal statement made on May 27, 1914, that seems to be favorable toward the activities of the organizations of labor, quoted extensively in Poulat, "La dernière bataille," p. 104ff.; also in Dal-Gal, *Il Papa santo,* p. 285ff. This statement might have represented a change in the pope's attitude as manifest in his earlier approval of Monetti's articles. On May 27, 1914, Pius X clearly stated that he "approved" of organizations that worked toward improving the spiritual as well as material conditions of workers and peasants. Although he called these organizations "Catholic associations," he seems to have referred to labor unions, and simple ones at that. The word *mixed* appeared in the papal address, but it referred to the religious affiliation of members. Pius X declared that although he preferred an exclusively Catholic membership, "in certain determined conditions" "mixed associations, alliances with non-Catholics" were also "permissible." It is possible that the pope was not reaffirming the position taken by *Singulari quadam,* for he did not mention in his May 27, 1914 statement that those "determined conditions" applied only to religiously "mixed" societies, such as Germany. If indeed Pius X changed his mind about the principle of *confessionalità,* this pointed in the direction of the decision of his successor, who soon after taking office eased the strict religious

requirements for the membership of Italian Catholic unions. The instructions sent by Cardinal Pietro Gasparri, the secretary of state of Benedict XV, to the leaders of Catholic Action stated that the religious character of Catholic organizations of labor "should not be imposed through explicit articles in the statutes, but guided by the criteria of prudence and charitable largess" (quoted in Zussini, *Luigi Caissotti di Chiusano,* p. 202). The strict enforcement of the religious nature of labor unions, which Pius X insisted upon, was self-defeating, for it closed the door on Italian workers who were nominal but not practicing Catholics. With its exclusiveness *confessionalità* created a climate of "us" against "them," led to divisiveness in the Italian labor movement, hindered working-class solidarity, and prevented the workers from making economic gains. Whether Pius X realized this during the last months of his life and changed his position remains, at least for the time being, an open question.

Conclusions

1. Sturzo, "La lotta sociale legge di progresso," p. 52.

2. Matteo Liberatore, *Il progresso: dialogo filosofico;* also my forthcoming "The Idea of Progress in Italian Catholic Social Thought (1846–1914)."

3. Etienne Gilson, *The Spirit of Thomism,* pp. 84–102; Ralph M. McInerny, *Thomism in the Age of Renewal,* especially p. 172ff.

4. Masnovo, "Il neotomismo in Italia," p. 101.

5. *Prima lettera pastorale dell'illustrissimo e reverendissimo Mons. Giuseppe Sarto, vescovo di Mantova al clero e al popolo della sua diocesi,* p. 27: "The spring from which the healthy waters to extinguish the insatiable thirst of knowledge flow, is open, all you that thirst, come to the waters, to which the most wise pontiff invited us with his encyclical *Aeterni Patris,* and I refer to the doctrine of St. Thomas Aquinas, which is useful not only for the religious defense of revealed truths and for resisting those who attempt to refute them, but also for offering arguments in the defense of the Catholic faith, the well-being of society and the enrichment of all the sciences." For the last year of the papacy of Pius X, see *Acta Apostolicae Sedis,* 6 (1914): 336–41, 383–86. The *Acta* print several other papal documents that stress the importance of Thomism: *motu proprio* "Sacrum antistitum," 2 (1910): 655–80; papal letters to Mgr. Dubois, 4 (1912): 45; to Joseph Gredt, 4 (1912): 564–65; to P. E. Hugon, 5 (1913): 487; and *motu proprio* "Preclara inter," 6 (1914): 333–35, which stated, "Quo in studio magistrum semper secuti sunt ipsum S. Thomam, cuius aurea doctrina mentes splendore suo illuminat; cuius via et ratio usque ad profundissimam divinarum rerum cognitionem sine ullo erroris periculo perducit."

6. Quoted in McInerny, *Thomism in the Age of Renewal,* pp. 179–80.

7. *Rivista di filosofia neo-scolastica* 3 (1911): 2–3.

8. Quoted in Cappelli, *Romolo Murri,* p. 105.

9. Pius X, encyclical *Pascendi,* especially pp. 88–89; also Giuseppe Prezzolini, *Cos'è il modernismo?,* especially pp. 7ff., 19; Giordani, *Pio X,* p. 191.

10. Papal letter signed by Merry del Val, in *Acta Apostolicae Sedis,* 2 (1910): 176.

11. *Rivista di filosofia neo-scolastica* 6 (1914): 331–33.

12. In spite of its apparent waning on the eve of the Great War, Thomism did not completely disappear as a social and political philosophy. There was a revival of the revival during fascism, when some Catholic conservatives used Thomistic ideas, *volere nolere,* in support of the fascist corporative doctrine. One would have expected that this was enough to discredit Thomistic social and political notions, especially since some of the fascistoid Thomistic arguments, such as the attacks on the concept of democracy, upon examination turned out to be against the spirit and the words of the Angelic Doctor. But Thomism apparently has a way of

surviving use and abuse, and it is still around as a social philosophy advocated by conservative Catholics. Spiazzi et al., *Teologia e storia della carità,* written in the 1960s, still insists on the validity of Thomistic ideas for society (see pp. 178, 419–21). The volume still seems to assume that the "poor" are a permanent element in the social structure. The solution for the social problems involving the "poor" is framed in terms of *assistenza.* The most important form of assistance, the writers maintain, is private charity. Public assistance, one of them says, is only to supplement private and church charity. Disregarding, at least to some extent, the Thomistic tradition of the social responsibility of the state, this writer, Carlo Messori, argues that the social activity of the state should be limited to those problems that private and church charity cannot solve. Like social and political conservatives in other countries, these Italian Catholic authors seem to fear that the welfare state would sooner or later turn into a totalitarian state. And this leads them into arguments that characterized the laissez-faire arguments of yester-year used against Socialists by conservative liberals. Considering that it was born as a counter-ideology to liberalism, Neo-Thomism seems to have run full circle. But during the 1980s, Pope John Paul II might have set in motion an initiative aimed at reinstating the thought of Aqui-nas as more than just a source of theological precepts—indeed, as a social philosophy. (See Bortolaso, "Il centenario.") Whether this revival, if it materializes, will lead to a renewed hostility toward the labor movement, is an intriguing question. With conservativism on the upswing in most parts of the world and labor on the decline, the prognosis appears to be positive for both Neo-Thomism and a Thomistic new corporativism, which could become a threat to the autonomy of the labor movement by sapping its strength. By suggesting that Aquinas become once more what Pius X used to call him, "leader and teacher" in social thought and social action, is not John Paul II contradicting himself? For the pope is on the record not only arguing forcefully that labor unions are "indispensable and irreplaceable" but also defending the workers' right to strike. (The statements by John Paul II referred to in these "Conclusions" were reported in the *London* [Ontario] *Free Press,* May 23, June 21, 1983, and Dec. 22, 1984.)

13. For Gentiloni's statement see the interview in the *Giornale d'Italia,* 13, No. 310, Nov. 8, 1913. For the recriminations against Giolitti and his reaction, see *Atti del Parlamento Italiano, Camera dei Deputati, Sessione 1913–1914, Discussioni,* 1:94–478.

14. In spite of obvious contrasts, there were points of convergence between the Catho-lics' and Giolitti's outlook and political practice. In my "Giolitti's Reform Program," I detail the intellectual and practical considerations that led the prime minister to conclude the Genti-loni Pact.

References

Azione Sociale. Monthly published by the Unione Economico Sociale.
Civiltà Cattolica. Periodical published by the Jesuit Fathers of Rome.
L'Osservatore Romano. Daily published in the Vatican.
La Settimana Sociale. Weekly published by the Unione Popolare.
Agócs, Sándor. "Giolitti's Reform Program: An Exercise in Equilibrium Politics." *Political Science Quarterly* 86 (1971): 637–53.
———. "The Road of Charity Leads to the Picket Lines: The Neo-Thomistic Revival and the Italian Catholic Labor Movement." *International Review of Social History* 18 (1973): 28–50.
———. "Christian Democracy and Social Modernism in Italy during the Papacy of Pius X." *Church History* 42 (1973): 73–88.
———. " 'Germania Doceat!' The Volksverein, the Model for Italian Catholic Action, 1905–1914." *Catholic Historical Review* 61 (1975): 31–47.
Alessandrini, Federico. "Un pontificato." *Studium* 50 (1954): 373–80.
Antonelli, Ferdinando. "La santità di Pio X." *Studium* 50 (1954): 381–85.
Aquinas, Thomas. *Summa Theologica.* 22 vols. London: Burns, Oates & Washbourne, 1920.
———. *De Regimine Principum.* Turin: Paravia, 1928.
Arcari, Paolo. *Il concetto cristiano del progresso.* Parma: Buffetti, 1900.
Are, Giuseppe (ed.). *I cattolici e la questione sociale in Italia (1894–1904).* Milan: Feltrinelli, 1963.
———. "Introduzione." *I cattolici e la questione sociale in Italia.*
———. *Economia e politica nell'Italia liberale (1890–1915).* Bologna: Il Mulino, 1974.
Arena, Antonio. *Il lavoro manuale e la chiesa cattolica.* Rome: Tipografia dell'Unione Editrice, 1912.
Aubert, Roger. "Documents relatifs au mouvement catholique italien sous le pontificat de S. Pie X." *Rivista di storia della Chiesa in Italia* 12 (1958): 202–43, 334–70.
———. "Aspects divers du néo-thomisme sous le pontificat de Léon XIII." In Rossini (ed.). *Aspetti della cultura cattolica nell'età di Leone XIII.* pp. 133–227.
———. *The Church in a Secularized Society.* New York: Paulist Press, 1978.
———. et al. *The Church in the Industrial Age.* New York: Crossroad, 1981.
Avagliano, Lucio. *Alessandro Rossi e le origini dell'Italia industriale.* Naples: Libreria Scientifica, 1970.
Avolio, Gennaro. *I cattolici di fronte a'mali sociali.* Naples: Bicchierai, 1895.

Bacchion, Eugenio. *Pio X, Giuseppe Sarto, Arciprete di Salzano (1867–1878) nella tradizione e negli atti di Archivio Parrochiale e Communale.* Padua: Tipografia del Seminario, 1925.

Ballini, Pier Luigi. *Il movimento cattolico a Firenze (1900–1919).* Rome: Cinque lune, 1969.

————. "La lotta politica e movimento sindacale in Toscana agli inizi dell'età giolittiana. Lo sciopero generale di Firenze." *Rassegna storica toscana* 21 (1975): 243–95.

Bandini, Mario. *Cento anni di storia agraria italiana.* Rome: Cinque lune, 1957.

Barbier, Emmanuel. *Les erreurs du Sillon: histoire documentaire.* Poitiers: Blais et Roy, n.d.

Bardelli, Mario. "La questione operaia nell'azione e nel pensiero di Guido Miglioli." In Pierantozzi et al., *Leghe bianche e leghe rosse,* pp. 57–69.

Basevi, Paolo. "Lo sciopero agrario a Parma nel 1908." *Emilia,* April, 1951, pp. 144–47.

Bazin, René. *Pie X.* Paris: Flammarion, 1928.

Bedeschi, Lorenzo. *I cattolici disubbidienti.* Rome: Bianco, 1959.

————. "L'autonomia politica dei cattolici italiani." *Humanitas,* n.s. 17 (1962): 409–28.

————. (ed.). *I pioneri della D.C.: modernismo cattolico, 1896–1906.* Milan: Il Saggiatore, 1966.

————. *Il modernismo e Romolo Murri in Emilia e Romagna.* Parma: Guanda, 1967.

————. *La curia romana durante la crisi modernista; episodi e metodi di governo.* Parma: Guanda, 1968.

————. "I cappellani del lavoro a Milano nei primi anni del novecento." *Ricerche di storia sociale e religiosa* 3 (1974): 295–327.

————. "Precedenti storici delle avanguardie contadine miglioline." In Pierantozzi et al., *Leghe bianche e leghe rosse,* pp. 47–56.

Bell, Donald H. "Worker Culture and Worker Politics: The Experience of an Italian Town, 1880–1915" *Social History* 3 (1978): 1–21.

Bendix, Reinhard. *Work and Authority in Industry.* New York: Harper Torch, 1963.

Bettazzi, R. "Il compito sociale delle Società di S. Vincenzo de'Paoli." *Settimana Sociale* 4 (1911): 218–19.

Biederlack, Giuseppe. *Principi dell'ordinamento economico-sociale cristiano.* Bergamo: Tipografia S. Alessandro, 1911.

Boggiano Pico, Antonio. *L'importanza degli studi economici nella cultura e nell'azione del clero.* Rome: Società Italiana Cattolica di Cultura Editrice, 1901.

————. "L'attualità del pensiero di Giuseppe Toniolo." In Boggiano Pico et al., *Per una coscienza sociale.* Rome, 1943. Pp. 55–72.

Bonomelli, Geremia. "Il clero e la società moderna." In *Questioni religiose, morali e sociali del giorno,* Rome: Desclée, 1903. Pp. 262–311.

————. "La questione sociale è questione morale." 1892; reprinted in *Questioni religiose,* pp. 121–72.

————. "Proprietà e socialismo." In *Questioni religiose,* pp. 1–65.

————. *La Chiesa e i tempi nuovi.* Cremona: Tipografia Unione Diocesana, 1906.

————. *Gli scioperi: una parola amica a tutti gli operai.* Rome: Desclée, 1910.

Bortolaso, Giovanni. "Il centenario dell'enciclica 'Aeterni Patris'." *Civiltà Cattolica* 131 (1980), vol. 1, pp. 43–50.

Brezzi, Camillo. *Cristiano sociali e intransigenti. L'opera di Medolago Albani fino alla 'Rerum novarum.'* Rome: Cinque lune, 1971.

————. "Movimento operaio e socialismo nel giudizio dei cattolici dopo il 'Rerum novarum.' " *Storia e politica* 12 (1973): 198–234.

————. "Capitalismo e socialismo nella cultura dei cattolici di fine '800." *Bollettino dell'Archivio per la storia del movimento sociale cattolico in Italia* 9 (1974): 251–66.

Briére, Eduardo P. *Ai padroni: loro missione e doveri*. Vicenza: Galla, 1911.
Brucculeri, Angelo. *La funzione sociale della proprietà*. Rome: Civiltà Cattolica, 1944.
Burri, Antonio. *Le teorie politiche di San Tommaso e il moderno diritto pubblico*. Rome: Tipografia della Società Cattolica Istruttiva, 1884.
Burroni, Giacinto. *Manipoli sparsi per l'educazione della mente e del cuore del popolo*. Turin: Tipografia Emilio Bono, 1910.
Bury, J. B. *The Idea of Progress*. New York: Dover, 1955.

Caetani, Leone. *La crisi morale dell'ora presente: religione, modernismo e democrazia*. Rome: Casa Editrice Italiana, 1911.
Caissotti di Chiusano, Luigi. *Il sindacalismo cristiano in un articolo della "Civiltà Cattolica."* Turin: Libreria Ecclesiastica Clemente Tappi, 1914.
Camp, Richard L. *The Papal Ideology of Social Reform: A Study in Historical Development, 1878–1967*. Leyden: Brill, 1968.
Campiglio, Secondo. *L'Unione Popolare fra i cattolici d'Italia; (note illustrative e norme pratiche)*. Tortona: Tipografia S. Giuseppe, 1910.
Cantono, Alessandro. *Le Università popolari e la democrazia*. Rome: Società Italiana di cultura, 1902.
———. *Storia del socialismo italiano*. Turin: L.E.I., 1912.
Capecelatro, Alfonso. *La quistione sociale e il Cristianesimo*. Rome: Desclée, 1907.
———. *La povertà, l'industria e il sapere in relazione al Cristianesimo*. Rome: Desclée, 1908.
———. *Amiamo il popolo*. Rome: Desclée, 1912.
Cappellazzi, Andrea. *Le moderne libertà esaminate secondo i principii della filosofia scolastica*. Crema: Cazzamalli, 1890.
———. *La questione sociale*. Rome: Unione Cooperativa Editrice, 1902.
Cappelli, Giampiero. *Romolo Murri: contributo per una biografia*. Rome: Cinque lune, 1965.
Caracciolo, Alberto. "Le origini della lotta di classe nell'agro romano (1870–1915)." *Società* (1949): 602–45.
———. "Per una storia del movimento contadino in Italia." *Società* (1952): 469–96.
———. *Il movimento contadino nel Lazio: 1870–1922*. Rome: Rinascita, 1952.
Carlen, Claudia. *The Papal Encyclicals*. 5 vols. Wilmington, N.C.: McGrath, 1981.
Carocci, Giampiero. *Giolitti e l'età giolittiana*. Turin: Einaudi, 1961.
Casella, Graziosa. *S. Pio X. I più significativi episodi sulla vita di Giuseppe Sarto, 1835–1914*. Venice: I.T.E., 1959.
Casoli, Alfonso. *Un campione della causa cattolica: il Conte Stanislao Medolago Albani. Commemorazione*. Acquapendente: Lemurio, 1922.
Cavalleri, Ottavio. *Il movimento operaio e contadino nel Bresciano (1878–1903)*. Rome: Cinque lune, 1972.
Chiesa, F.F. *L'Unione popolare spiegata ai contadini*. Alba: Tipografia Albese, 1908.
Chiri, Mario. *Le organizzazioni operaie cattoliche in Italia*. Series B, No. 35. Ministero di Agricoltura, Industria e Commercio, Ufficio del Lavoro. Rome: Officina Poligrafica Italiana, 1911.
Clough, Shepard. *The Economic History of Modern Italy*. New York: Columbia University Press, 1964.
Colish, Marcia L. "St. Thomas Aquinas in Historical Perspective: The Modern Period." *Church History* 44 (1975): 433–49.
Coplestone, F. C. *Aquinas*. Baltimore: Viking, Penguin, 1967.

Coppa, Frank. *Planning, Protectionism, and Politics in Liberal Italy: Economics and Politics in the Giolittian Age.* Washington (D.C.): Catholic University Press, 1971.

Corna Pellegrini, Giacomo. "L'evoluzione del concetto di classe: dal pensiero del Toniolo al pensiero cattolico contemporaneo." In Rossini (ed.), *Aspetti della cultura cattolica nell'età di Leone XIII,* pp. 445–64.

Coscetti, Antonio. *Popolo all'erta!!! Ecco il nemico; opuscolo di propaganda antisocialista.* S. Miniato: Tipografia Vescovile Taviani, 1911.

Coste, René. "Le développement de la pensée sociale de l'Église depuis 'Rerum novarum.' " *Nouvelle Revue Théologique* 114 (1982): 321–45.

Crispolti, Crispolto. *Pio X e un episodio nella storia del partito cattolico in Italia.* Rome: Bontempelli e Invernizzi, 1913.

Crispolti, Filippo. *Politici, querrieri, poeti: ricordi personali.* Milan: Treves, 1938.

————. *Pio IX, Leone XIII, Pio X, Benedetto XV, Pio XI; ricordi personali.* Milan: Garzanti, 1939.

Croce, Benedetto. "I 'neo' in filosofia." *La Critica* 39 (1941): 289–95.

Dal-Gal, Girolamo. *Il Papa santo Pio X. Vita ufficiale della Postulazione per la causa di canonizzazione.* Padua: Il Messagiero di S. Antonio, 1954.

———— (ed.). *Insegnamenti di San Pio X.* Bari: Edizioni Paoline, 1957.

Dalla Torre, Giuseppe. *I cattolici e la vita pubblica italiana: articoli, saggi, discorsi.* Edited by Gabriele De Rosa. 2 vols. Rome: Cinque lune, 1962.

————. *Memorie.* Milan: Mondadori, 1965.

D'Ascenzi, Giovanni (ed.). *I documenti pontifici sulla vita agraria: testo e commento.* Rome: Università Gregoriana, 1961.

De Concilio, Januarius. *The Doctrine of St. Thomas on the Right of Property and Its Use.* New York: Pustet, 1887.

De Gasperi, Alcide. *I tempi e gli uomini che preparavano la "Rerum novarum."* Milan: Vita e pensiero, 1945.

Del Bo, Nino (ed.). *I cattolici italiani di fronte al socialismo.* Rome: Cinque lune, 1956.

De Mattei, Rodolfo. "Le prime discussioni in Italia sull'esistenza e sull'essenza d'una 'Questione Sociale.' " *Storia e Politica* 6 (1967): 377–94.

Deploige, Simon. "La théorie thomiste de la propriété." *Revue néo-scolastique* (1895): 61–82, 163–75, 286–301.

De Rosa, Gabriele. "La crisi del sistema giolittiano." *Rassegna di politica e storia* 1 (1955): No. 8, pp. 4–11; No. 10, pp. 6–11.

————. *Filippo Meda e l'età liberale.* Florence: Le Monnier, 1959.

————. *Il movimento cattolico in Italia dalla Restaurazione all'età giolittiana.* Bari: Laterza, 1970.

————. "Introduzione" to Sturzo's *Sintesi sociali.*

————. "Gramsci et la question catholique." *Archives des sciences sociales des religions* 23 (1978): 5–26.

De Stefano, Francesco, and Luigi Oddo. *Storia della Sicilia dal 1860 al 1910.* Bari: Laterza, 1963.

Di Carlo, Eugenio. *La filosofia giuridica e politica di San Tommaso d'Aquino.* Palermo: Palumbo, 1945.

Di Mariano, Gaetano. "Il movimento cattolico e le masse contadine." *Critica Marxista* (1970): 263–85.

Einaudi, Luigi. *Cronache economiche e politiche di un trentennio (1893–1925)*. 6 vols. Turin: Einaudi, 1959.

Elliott, Lawrence. *I Will Be Called John: A Biography of Pope John XXIII*. New York: Dutton, 1973.

Falcucci, Franca. "Lo Stato nel pensiero di Giuseppe Toniolo." *Civitas*, n.s. 10 (1959): 22–30.

Fantetti, Antonio. "Eco di dibattiti: Murri, Toniolo, Meda." *Civitas*, n.s. 5 (1954): 54–64.

———. "Giuseppe Toniolo: alcuni studi sul socialismo." *Civitas*, n.s. 6 (1955): 3–19.

Fappani, Antonio. *Il movimento contadino in Italia: cento anni di storia*. Rome: A.C.L.I., 1956.

———. *Guido Miglioli e il movimento contadino*. Rome: Cinque lune, 1964.

———. "Le società operaie cattoliche nel Bresciano." *Bollettino dell'Archivio per la storia del movimento sociale cattolico in Italia* 4–5 (1969–70): 29–80.

Farrell, Walter. "The Fate of Representative Government." In Robert Brennan (ed.), *Essays in Thomism*. New York: Steed & Ward, 1942. Pp. 287–309.

Finley, M. I. *The Ancient Economy*. London: Chatto & Windus, 1973.

Flora, Peter. "Historical Processes of Social Mobilization: Urbanization and Literacy, 1850–1965. In S. N. Eisenstadt and Stein Rokkan (eds.), *Building of States and Nations*. Beverly Hills, Calif.: Sage, 1973. Vol. 1.

Flori, Ezio. *Il trattato "De Regimine Principum" e le dottrine politiche di S. Tommaso*. Bologna: Zanichelli, 1928.

Fontaine, Julien. *Le modernisme sociologique: décadence ou régénération?* Paris: Lethielleux, 1909.

Fonzi, Fausto. *I cattolici e la società italiana dopo l'unità*. Rome: Studium, 1953.

Franzina, Emilio. "Intransigenti e clerico-moderati nella società veneta di fine '800." In Franzina. et al., *Movimento cattolico e sviluppo capitalistico*.

——— et all. *Movimento cattolico e sviluppo capitalistico. Atti del Convegno sul movimento cattolico e sviluppo capitalistico nel Veneto*. Padua: Marsilio, 1974.

Galli, Giancarlo. *I cattolici e il sindacato*. Milan: Palazzi, 1969.

Gambasin, Angelo. *Gerarchia e laicato in Italia nel secondo Ottocento*. Padua: Antenore, 1969.

———. *Parroci e contadini nel Veneto alla fine dell'Ottocento*. Rome: Edizioni di storia e letteratura, 1973.

———. "L'utopia sociale dei congressi cattolici in Italia prima della 'Rerum novarum.'" *Bollettino dell'Archivio per la storia del movimento sociale cattolico in Italia* 9 (1974): 7–51.

Garutti Bellenzier, Maria Teresa. "La lotta sociale nel pensiero di Luigi Sturzo." *Humanitas* n.s. 17 (1962): 119–29.

Gentile, Giovanni. "Neotomisti." In Giovanni Gentile, *Le origini della filosofia contemporanea in Italia*. Rpt. *Opera Omnia*, vol. 33. Florence: Sansoni, 1957. Pp. 139–53.

Gerschenkron, Alexander. "Notes on the Rate of Industrial Growth in Italy, 1881–1913." *Journal of Economic History* 15 (1955): 360–75.

Gilson, Etienne. *The Spirit of Thomism*. Rpt. New York: Harper and Row, Torch Books, 1966.

Giolitti, Giovanni. *Discorsi extraparlamentari*. Turin: Einaudi, 1952.

————. *Discorsi parlamentari, pubblicati per deliberazione della Camera dei Deputati.* 4 vols. Rome: Tipografia della Camera dei Deputati, 1953–56.

————. *Dalle carte di Giovanni Giolitti. Quarant' anni di politica italiana.* 3 vols. Milan: Feltrinelli, 1962.

————. *Memorie della mia vita.* 2 vols. Milan (?): Treves, 1922.

Giordani, Igino. *Pio X, un prete di campagna.* Turin: S.E.I., 1951.

———— (ed.). *Le encicliche sociali dei papi da Pio IX a Pio XII, 1864–1956.* Rome: Studium, 1956.

Giovannini, Claudio. *Politica e religione nel pensiero della Lega Democratica Nazionale (1905–1915).* Rome: Cinque lune, 1968.

————. "Come si studia il movimento cattolico." *Studi storici* 14 (1973): 140–46.

Grassi, Piergiorgio. "Neotomismo e prima Democrazia Cristiana in Romagna." In Rossini (ed.), *Romolo Murri nella storia,* pp. 557–75.

Guasco, Maurilio. *Romolo Murri e il modernismo.* Rome: Cinque lune, 1968.

————. "Proposte per una ricerca sui rapporti fra cattolici e socialisti." In Passerin d'Entreves (ed.), *Il cattolicesimo politico e sociale,* pp. 245–62.

Hogan, William Edward. *The Development of Bishop Wilhelm Emmanuel von Ketteler's Interpretation of the Social Problem.* Washington, D.C.: Catholic University Press, 1946.

Horowitz, Daniel L. *The Italian Labor Movement.* Cambridge, Mass.: Harvard University Press, 1963.

Imberciadori, I. *L'Unione Popolare fra i cattolici d'Italia. Manuale teoretico-pratico.* Rome: Pustet, 1909.

Ionescu, Ghitta, and Ernest Gellner. *Populism.* New York: Macmillan, 1969.

Jemolo, Arturo. *Chiesa e Stato in Italia negli ultimi cento anni.* Turin: Einaudi, 1955.

John XXIII. Encyclical *Mater et magistra.* Milan: Vita e pensiero, 1963.

————. *Journal of a Soul.* Rpt. New York: New American Library, Signet Books, 1966.

Josephson, Eric and Mary (eds.). *Man Alone: Alienation in Modern Society.* New York: Dell, 1977.

Lanaro, Silvio. "Movimento cattolico e sviluppo capitalistico nel Veneto fra '800 e '900. Linee interpretative." In Franzina et al., *Movimento cattolico e sviluppo capitalistico.* Pp. 11–51.

La Palombara, Joseph. *Italian Labor Movement: Problems and Prospects.* Ithaca, N.Y.: Cornell University Press, 1957.

Lash, Nicholas. *Voices of Authority.* London: Sheed & Ward, 1976.

Latessa, Gabriele. *La società nelle teorie del Cristianesimo e della massoneria: dialogo tra socialista, massone e sacerdote.* S. Maria C.V.: Di Stefano, 1905.

Legitimo, Gianfranco. *Sociologi cattolici italiani.* Rome: Il Quadrato, 1963.

Leo XIII. Encyclical *Inscrutabili Dei consilio* (1878). In Carlen, *The Papal Encyclicals, 1878–1903,* pp. 5–10.

————. Encyclical *Quod apostolici muneris* (1878). In Carlen, *The Papal Encyclicals, 1878–1903,* pp. 11–16.

_____. Encyclical *Aeterni Patris* (1879). In Carlen, *The Papal Encyclicals, 1878–1903,* pp. 17–27.

_____. Encyclical *Rerum novarum* (1891). In Carlen, *The Papal Encyclicals, 1878–1903,* pp. 241–61.

_____. Encyclical *Graves de communi* (1901). In Carlen, *The Papal Encyclicals, 1878*–1903, pp. 479–85.

Leone, Enrico. *Il sindacalismo.* Milan: Sandron, 1907.

Leroy, H. J. *Le clergé et les oeuvres sociales.* Paris: Lecoffre, n.d.

Liberatore, Matteo. *Il progresso: dialogo filosofico.* Naples: Torchi del Tramater, 1846.

McInerny, Ralph M. *Thomism in the Age of Renewal.* Garden City, N.Y.: Doubleday, 1966.

McLaughlin, J. B. "S. Thomas and Property." *Studies, an Irish Quarterly* 9 (1920): 571–78.

Magnani, Giovanni Franceso. *Il progresso materiale ed il clero.* Recanati: Badaloni, 1858.

Magri, Franceso. *Dal movimento sindacale cristiano al sindacalismo democratico.* Milan: La Fiaccola, 1956.

Malagola, Achille. *Le teorie politiche di San Tommaso d'Aquino.* Bologna: Berti, 1912.

Malgeri, Francesco (ed.). *Luigi Sturzo nella Storia d'Italia.* 2 vols. Rome: Edizioni di storia e letteratura, 1973.

Malinverni, Bruno. *La Scuola Sociale Cattolica di Bergamo (1910–1932).* Rome: Cinque lune, 1960.

Mancini, Arturo. "Il pensiero sociale di Romolo Murri." *Idea* 8 (1952): 652–54.

Mandonnet, P., and J. Destrez. *Bibliographie Thomiste.* Paris: Vrin, 1960. (Reprint of an indispensible bibliographical volume originally published in 1920.)

Mannheim, Karl. *Diagnosis of Our Time: Wartime Essays of a Sociologist.* London: Kegan Paul, 1943.

_____. "Conservative Thought." In *Essays on Sociology and Social Psychology.* New York: Oxford University Press, 1953. Pp. 74–164.

Manzotti, Fernando. "I 'plebei' cattolici fra integralismo e modernismo sociale (1904–1908)." *Convivium* 26 (1958): 423–45.

Marchesan, Angelo. *Papa Pio X nella sua vita e nella sua parola.* Rome: Istituto Pontificio di Arte Cristiana, 1905.

Masnovo, Amato. "Il prof. G. Gentile e il Tomismo italiano dal 1850 al 1900." *Rivista di filosofia neo-scolastica* 4 (1912): 115–25, 260–69, 646–49.

_____. "Il neotomismo in Italia dopo il 1870." *Rivista di filosofia neo-scolastica* 16 (1924): 97–108.

_____. "Il significato storico del neotomismo." *Rivista di filosofia neo-scolastica* 32 (1940): 17–30.

Mathis. "Introduzione" to Aquinas's *De Regimine.*

Mazzoni, Nino. *Lotte agrarie nella vecchia Italia.* Milan: Domus, 1946.

Mayeur, Jean-Marie. "Catholicisme intransigeant, catholicisme social, démocratie chrétienne." *Annales: Économies, Sociétés, Civilisations* 27 (1972): 483–99.

Meda, Filippo. *Vade Mecum per il Propagandista Cattolico: istruzioni teoriche e pratiche.* Milan: Ghezzi, 1898.

Medolago Albani, Stanislao. *Le classi dirigenti nella società: conferenza tenuta il giorno 4 Marzo 1883 in Bergamo.* Bergamo: Tipografia S. Alessandro, 1883.

_____. *Due campioni dell'azione cattolica bergamasca: Prof. Comm. Nicolo Rezzara, Prof. Cav. Giambattista Caironi.* Bergamo: S. Alessandro, 1916.

Menna, Antonio. *Expedit o non expedit? Considerazioni storico-giuridico-morali.* Naples: Pierro, 1904.

Menozzi, Daniele. "Orientamenti pastorali nella prima industrializzazione torinese." *Annali della fondazione Luigi Einaudi* 5 (1971): 191–235.

──────. "Le nuove parrocchie nella prima industrializzazione torinese (1900–1915)." *Rivista di storia e letteratura religiosa* 9 (1973): 69–87.

Merry Del Val, Raffaele. *Pio X, impressioni e ricordi.* Padua: Il Messagiero di S. Antonio, 1949.

Mitchell, Hary. *Pie X et la France.* Paris: Les Editions du Cèdre, 1954.

Molinelli, Raffaele. *Il movimento cattolico nelle Marche.* Florence: La Nuova Italia, 1959.

Molteni, G. "Lo sciopero." *Azione Sociale* 2 (1908): 1–27, 65–91.

Monetti, Giulio. *Problemi varii di sociologia generale.* 2 vols. Bergamo: Tipografia S. Alessandro, 1913.

──────. *Errori moderni nella pratica dell'azione cattolica.* Bergamo: Tipografia S. Alessandro, 1914.

Mori, Giorgio. "I cattolici e il problema della mezzadria." *Studi storici* 3 (1962): 543–58.

Natale, G. *Giolitti e gli Italiani.* Milan: Garzanti, 1949.

Neufeld, Maurice. *Italy: School for Awakening Countries; The Italian Labor Movement in Its Political, Social, and Economic Setting from 1800 to 1960.* Ithaca, N.Y.: Cornell University Press, 1961.

Nova, Fritz. *Functional Representation.* Dubuque, Iowa: Brown, 1950.

O'Connor, Daniel. *Catholic Social Doctrine.* Westminster, Md.: Newman Press, 1956.

O'Gara, James (ed.). *The Layman in the Church.* New York: Herder, 1962.

Olgiati, Francesco. "La politica di S. Pio X e il conservatorismo." *Vita e Pensiero* 37 (1954): 525–40.

Olivetti, A. O. *Problemi del socialismo contemporaneo.* Lugano: Avanguardia, 1906.

O'Rahilly, Alfred. "S. Thomas's Theory of Property." *Studies: an Irish Quarterly* 9 (1920): 337–54.

Orlando, Pasquale. *Il tomismo a Napoli nel secolo XIX. La scuola del Sanseverino. Fonti e documenti.* Rome: Università Lateranense, 1968.

Passerin d'Entreves, Alessandro. *La filosofia politica medioevale.* Turin: Giappichelli, 1934.

Passerin d'Entreves, Ettore, and Konrad Repgen (eds.). *Il cattolicesimo politico e sociale in Italia e Germania dal 1870 al 1914.* Bologna: Il Mulino, 1977.

Paul VI (Cardinal Montini). *Religione e lavoro: discorso tenuto a Torino il 27 marzo 1960 agli operatori del mondo del lavoro.* Milan: Scuola Tipografica S. Benedetto, 1960.

──────. Encyclical *Populorum progressio.* Naples: Edizioni Domenicane, 1967.

Perego, Angelo. *Forma statale e politica finanziaria nel pensiero di Luigi Taparelli d'Azeglio.* Milan: Giuffrè, 1956.

Pernot, Maurice. *Le Saint Siège, L'Église catholique et la politique mondiale.* Paris: A. Colin, 1924.

Pierantozzi, Libero, et al. *Leghe bianche e leghe rosse. L'esperienza unitaria di Guido Miglioli.* Rome: Editori riuniti, 1972.

Pius X. *Prima lettera pastorale dell'illustrissimo e reverendissimo Mons. Giuseppe Sarto, vescovo di Mantova al clero e al popolo della sua diocesi.* Treviso: Tipografia della Scuola apostolica, 1885.

————. *Visita pastorale. Lettera dell'eminentissimo sig. cardinale Giuseppe Sarto.* Venice: Tipografia Patriarcale, 1895.

————. *Il Santo Padre Leone XIII. Lettera pastorale di S. Em. il cardinale Giuseppe Sarto, Patriarca di Venezia per la Quaresima 1898.* Venice: Tipografia Patriarcale, 1898.

————. *L'indifferenza religiosa. Lettera pastorale dell'eminentissimo cardinale Giuseppe Sarto.* Venice: Tipografia Patriarchale, 1903.

————. Encyclical *E supremi apostolatus* (1903). In Carlen, *The Papal Encyclicals, 1903–1939,* pp. 5–10.

————. *Motu proprio,* "Fin dalla prima" (1904). *Civiltà Cattolica* 55 (1904), vol. 1, pp. 3–8.

————. Encyclical *Iucunda sane* (1904). In Carlen, *The Papal Encyclicals, 1903–1939,* pp. 19–28.

————. Encyclical *Il fermo proposito* (1905). In Carlen, *The Papal Encyclicals, 1903–1939,* pp. 37–44.

————. Encyclical *Vehementer nos* (1906). In Carlen, *The Papal Encyclicals, 1903–1939,* pp. 45–51.

————. Encyclical *Pieni l'animo* (1906). In Carlen, *The Papal Encyclicals, 1903–1939,* pp. 57–61.

————. Encyclical *Pascendi Dominici gregis* (1907). In Carlen, *The Papal Encyclicals, 1903–1939,* pp. 71–98.

————. Encyclical *Communium rerum* (1909). In Carlen, *The Papal Encyclicals, 1903–1939,* pp. 99–113.

————. Letter *Notre charge apostolique* (1910). *Acta Apostolicae Sedis* 2 (1910): 607–33.

————. Encyclical *Iamdudum* (1911). In Carlen, *The Papal Encyclicals, 1903–1939,* pp. 127–30.

————. Encyclical *Lacrimabili statu* (1912). In Carlen, *The Papal Encyclicals, 1903–1939,* pp. 131–33.

————. Encyclical *Singulari quadam* (1912). In Carlen, *The Papal Encyclicals, 1903–1939,* pp. 135–38.

————. *Motu proprio* "Praeclara inter" (1914), *Acta Apostolicae Sedis* 6 (1914): 333–35.

————. *Lettere, raccolte da Nello Vian.* Rome: Belardetti, 1954.

————. *Insegnamenti di San Pio X.* Ed. Girolamo Dal-Gal. Bari: Edizioni Paoline, 1957.

Pius XI. Encyclical *Quadragesimo anno* (1931). In Giordani (ed.), *Le encicliche sociali dei papi,* pp. 431–88.

Poulain, Jean-Claude. *L'Église et la classe ouvrière.* Paris: Editions sociales, 1961.

Poulat, Emile. "La dernière bataille du pontificat de Pie X." *Rivista di storia della Chiesa in Italia* 25 (1971): 83–107.

Pratesi, Piero. "Luci e ombra nella sociologia di Toniolo." *Rassegna di politica e di storia* 1 (1955): 11–18.

Prezzolini, Giuseppe. *Cos'è il modernismo.* Milan: Treves, 1908.

————. *La teoria sindacalista.* Naples: Perella, 1909.

Quadrotta, Guglielmo. *Il colloquio di un secolo fra cattolici e socialisti 1864–1963.* Rome: Libreria Editrice Romana, 1964.

Radini Tedeschi, Giacomo. *Discorso tenuto nell'adunanza generale della Società di S. Vincenzo di Paoli in Piacenza addi 3 Giugno 1890.* Piacenza: Bertola, 1890.

————. *San Giorgio M. e la questione operaia*. Genoa: Tipografia delle Letture Cattoliche, 1890.

————. *La mission du prètre dans l'action catholique*. Paris: Maison de la Bonne Presse, 1897.

Renda, Francesco. *Socialisti e cattolici in Sicilia, 1900–1914*. Caltanisetta: Sciascia, 1972.

————. "Luigi Sturzo e il movimento contadino in Sicilia nei primi anni del secolo." In Malgeri (ed.), *Luigi Sturzo nella storia*, 2:455–97.

Rigola, Rinaldo. *Storia del movimento operaio italiano*. Milan: Domus, 1947.

Ritter, Emil. *Die Katholisch-Soziale Bewegung Deutschlands im Neunzehnten Jahrhundert und der Volksverein*. (In Italian: *Il movimento cattolico-sociale in Germania nel XIX secolo e il Volksverein*), translated by Anna Maria Pozzan. Rome: Cinque lune, 1967.

Riva Sanseverino, Luisa. *Il movimento sindacale cristiano dal 1850 al 1939*. Rome: Zuffi, 1950.

Rivière, Jean. *Le modernisme dans l'Église: étude d'histoire religieuse contemporaine*. Paris: Letouzey et Ané, 1929.

Rizzo, Franco. *Luigi Sturzo e la questione meridionale nella crisi del primo dopoguerra, 1919–1924*. Rome: Centro Democratico di cultura e di documentazione, 1957.

Robert, Mathieu. "Hiérachie nécessaire des fonctions économique d'après Saint Thomas d'Aquin." *Revue Thomiste* 21 (1913): 419–31.

Roland-Gosselin, Bernard. *La doctrine politique de Saint Thomas d'Aquin*. Paris: Rivière, 1928.

Romani, Mario. "La preparazione della 'Rerum novarum.' " In Vito et al., *Nel LXX anniversario della "Rerum novarum,"* pp. 11–28.

Romeo, Rosario. *Breve storia della grande industria in Italia*. Rocca San Casciano: Cappelli, 1963.

Ronchi, Mario. "Le origini del movimento contadino nel Soresinese (1901–1913). *Movimento operaio*, (1955), pp. 423–38.

Rossi, Mario G. "Il movimento cattolico nelle campagne fino al primo dopo querra." *Critica Marxista* (1970): 286–304.

————. "Movimento cattolico e capitale finanziario: appunti sulla genesi del blocco clerico-moderato." *Studi storici* 13 (1972): 249–88.

Rossini, Giuseppe (ed.). *Aspetti della cultura cattolica nell'età di Leone XIII*. Rome: Cinque lune, 1961.

————, (ed.). *Romolo Murri nella storia politica e religiosa del suo tempo. Atti del convegno di studio. Fermo 9-11 ottobre, 1970*. Rome: Cinque lune, 1972.

Ryan, John A. "The Economic Philosophy of St. Thomas." In Robert E. Brennan (ed.), *Essays in Thomism*. New York: Sheed & Ward, 1942. Pp. 237–60.

Saba, Vincenzo. "L'influsso della dottrina sociale cattolica sull'organizzazione sindacale del lavoro." In Vito et al., *Nel LXX anniversario della "Rerum novarum,"* pp. 63–77.

Salomone, A. William. *Italy in the Giolittian Era: Italian Democracy in the Making, 1900–1914*. Philadelphia: University of Pennsylvania Press, 1960.

Salvadori, Massimo. *Il movimento cattolico a Torino 1911–1915*. Turin: Giappichelli, 1969.

Salvemini, Gaetano. "La questione meridionale e il federalismo." First published in 1900; reprinted in *Opere di Gaetano Salvemini*, ser. 4, vol. 2. Milan: Feltrinelli, 1963. Pp. 157–91.

Sassoli de' Bianchi, Achille. *La questione sociale nelle campagne*. Speech made in 1879; reprinted, Acquapendente: Lemurio, 1922.

Scalabrini, Giovanni Battista. *Il socialismo e l'azione del clero.* Turin: Libreria Salesiana Editrice, 1899.

Schenk, H. G. *The Mind of European Romantics.* Garden City, N.Y.: Doubleday, Anchor Books, 1969.

Schorske, Carl. "The Idea of the City in European Thought." In Carl Schorske et al., *The Historian and the City.* Cambridge, Mass.: MIT Press, 1963. Pp. 95–114.

Scoppola, Pietro. "L'autonomia nell'azione politica dei cattolici." *Comunità* 6 (1952): 6–8.

———. "Per una valutazione del popolarismo." *Quaderni di cultura e storia sociale* 2 (1953): 185–97.

———. "Il modernismo politico in Italia: la Lega Democratica Nazionale." *Rivista Storica Italiana* 69 (1957): 61–109.

———. *Dal neoguelfismo alla Democrazia Cristiana.* Rome: Studium, 1957.

Secco Suardo, Dino. *Da Leone XIII a Pio X.* Rome: Cinque lune, 1967.

Semeria, Giovanni. *I miei quattro Papi.* Milan: Ambrosiana Editoriale, 1930.

Sinistri, Giovanni. *La Chiesa e il progresso.* Rome: Tipografia Vaticana, 1888.

Spadolini, Giovanni. *L'opposizione cattolica da Porta Pia al 98.* Florence: Vallecchi, 1961.

Spiazzi, Raimondo, et al., *Teologia e storia della carità.* Rome: Caritas, 1965.

Stearns, Peter N. *European Society in Upheaval: Social History since 1750.* New York: Macmillan, 1975.

Sturzo, Luigi. "L'organizzazione di classe e le unioni professionali." First published in 1901; reprinted in *Opera Omnia,* ser. 2, vol. 1. Bologna: Zanichelli, 1961. Pp. 131–77.

———. "La lotta sociale legge di progresso." Lecture first delivered in 1902; reprinted in *Sintesi sociali,* pp. 24–56.

———. *Riforma statale e indirizzi politici: discorsi.* Florence: Vallechi, 1923.

———. *Sintesi sociali.* Bologna: Zanichelli, 1961.

Talamo, Salvatore. *L'odierna scuola tomistica e i suoi avversari.* Siena: S. Bernardino, 1880.

———. *Il cristianesimo e il lavoro manuale.* Rome: Tipografia degli Artigianelli di S. Giuseppe, n.d.

———. *La questione sociale e i cattolici.* Rome: Unione Cooperativa Editrice, 1896.

Talmon, J. L. *Romanticism and Revolt.* New York: Harcourt, 1968.

Taviani, Paolo Emilio. "Il concetto di democrazia cristiana in Giuseppe Toniolo." *Civitas* n.s. 6 (1955): 3–22.

Toniolo, Giuseppe. "La funzione della giustizia e della carità nell'odierna crisi sociale." First published in 1893; reprinted in *Opera Omnia,* ser. 4, vol. 3. Vatican City: Comitato Opera Omnia di G. Toniolo, 1951. Pp. 359–67.

———. "L'Unione cattolica per gli studi sociali in Italia." First published in 1893; reprinted in *Opera Omnia,* ser. 4, vol. 3, pp. 75–133.

———. "Lettera aperta al conte Grosoli." First published in 1902; reprinted in *Opera Omnia,* ser. 4, vol. 3, pp. 385–98.

———. *L'Unione cattolica popolare italiana, ragioni, scopi, incitamenti.* First published in 1905; reprinted in *Opera Omnia,* ser. 4, vol. 3, pp. 1–72.

———. "Atteggiamenti e doveri dei cattolici nell'ora presente." Speech delivered in 1910; reprinted in *Opera Omnia,* ser. 4, vol. 3, pp. 435–42.

———. "Passato e futuro dell'azione economica fra i cattolici d'Italia." *Azione Sociale* 1, Dec. 1906, pp. 1–10.

———. "La genesi storica dell'odierna crisi sociale." First published in 1893; reprinted in Are (ed.), *I cattolici e la questione sociale,* pp. 123–42.

————. "L'ordinamento della classe operaia nelle corporazioni." First published as a series of articles in 1901–2; in part reprinted in Are (ed.), *I cattolici e la questione sociale,* pp. 499–517.

————. *Lettere.* 3 vols. Vatican City: Comitato Opera Omnia di G. Toniolo, 1953.

Toscani, Xenio. "La biblioteca del conte Stanislao Medolago Albani." *Rassegna di politica e storia* 12 (1966): 76–82.

Tozzi, Glauco. *I fondamenti dell'economia in Tommaso d'Aquino.* Milan: Mursia, 1970.

Tramontin, Silvio. "A cento anni dal primo congresso dei cattolici italiani." In Tramontin (ed.), *Il movimento cattolico e la società italiana,* pp. 22–26.

————(ed.). *Il movimento cattolico e la società italiana in cento anni di storia.* Rome: Edizioni di storia e letteratura, 1976.

Trimarchi, Giovanna. *La formazione del pensiero meridionalista di Luigi Sturzo.* Brescia: Morcelliana, 1965.

Troeltsch, Ernst. *The Social Doctrine of Churches and Christian Groups.* Translated by Olive Wyon. New York: Harper, Torch Books, 1960.

Unione cattolica per gli studi sociali in Italia. *Atti e documenti del secondo congresso cattolico italiano degli studiosi di scienze sociali tenutosi in Padova nei giorni 26, 27, 28 Agosto 1896.* Padua: Tipografia del Seminario, 1897.

Unione Elettorale Cattolica Italiana. *Statuto, Regolamento, Programma, Norme.* Rome: Officina Poligrafica Laziale, 1912.

"L'Unione Popolare Italiana: avertenze." *Civiltà Cattolica* 58 (1907), vol. 1, pp. 129–43.

Valente, Giambattista. *Aspetti e momenti dell'azione sociale dei cattolici in Italia (1892–1926).* Rome: Cinque lune, 1968.

Valeri, Nino. "Introduzione" to Giolitti's *Discorsi extraparlamentari.*

Veneruso, Danilo. "Cattolici e socialisti in Italia tra il raggiungimento dell'unità e l'avvento del fascismo (1870–1924)." *Studium* 62 (1966): 73–86.

Vercesi, Ernesto. *Il movimento cattolico in Italia.* Florence: La Voce, 1923.

————. *Il pontificato di Pio X.* Milan: Libreria Pontificia ed Arcivescovile, 1935.

Verucci, Guido. "Storia del cattolicesimo, della Chiesa, del movimento cattolico italiano nell'età contemporanea," *Quaderni storici* (1974), pp. 559–68.

Vian, Nello. *Il Santo Pontefice romano Pio X.* Genoa: Stringa, 1954.

————. "Umanità e umorismo di Pio X." *Studium* 50 (1954): 386–92.

————. "Introduzione" to Pius X, *Lettere raccolte da Nello Vian.*

Villari, Rosario. "Il meridionalista." In Villari et al., *Gaetano Salvemini.* Bari: Laterza, 1959. Pp. 95–148.

Vistalli, Francesco. *Giuseppe Toniolo.* Vatican City: Comitato Opera Omnia di G. Toniolo, 1954.

Vito, Francesco. "L'economia a servizio dell'uomo, caposaldo della dottrina sociale cattolica." In Francesco Vito et al., *Nel LXX anniversario della "Rerum novarum."* Milan: Vita e pensiero, 1962.

————. "Trasformazioni economiche e dottrina cattolica." In Francesco Vito (ed.), *I nuovi termini della questione sociale e l'enciclica "Mater et magistra."* Milan: Vita e pensiero, 1962.

Voti sociali dei cattolici italiani. Rome: Cinque lune, 1956.

Vykopal, Adolfo. *La dottrina del superfluo in San Tommaso.* Brescia: Morcelliana, 1961.

Wallace, Lilian Parker. *Leo XIII and the Rise of Socialism*. Durham, N.C.: Duke University Press, 1966.

Walzel, Oskar. *German Romanticism*. Translated by Elise Lussky. New York: Capricorn, 1966.

Wandruszka, Adam. "Il cattolicesimo politico e sociale nell'Austria-Ungheria degli anni 1870–1914." In Passerin d'Entreves and Repgen (eds.), *Il cattolicesimo politico e sociale*, pp. 151–77.

Webster, Richard. *The Cross and the Fasces*. Stanford, Calif.: Stanford University Press, 1960.

Zangheri, Renato (ed.). *Lotte agrarie in Italia: la Federazione Nazionale dei Lavoratori della Terra (1901–1926)*. Milan: Feltrinelli, 1960.

————. "Introduzione" to Zangheri (ed.), *Lotte agrarie in Italia*, pp. ix–xcii.

Zanibelli, Amos. *Le "leghe bianche" nel Cremonese dal 1900 al "Lodo Bianchi."* Rome: Cinque lune, 1961.

Zocchi, Gaetano. *La questione sociale ossia onde il popolo possa sperare pane, lavoro e pace*. S. Pier d'Arena: Tipografia Saleziana, 1892.

Zoppi, Sergio. *Romolo Murri e la prima Democrazia Cristiana*. Florence: Vallecchi, 1968.

Zussini, Alessandro. *Luigi Caissotti di Chiusano e il movimento cattolico dal 1896 al 1915*. Turin: Giappichelli, 1965.

Index

246

Sándor Agócs teaches in the University Studies, Weekend College Program of the College of Lifelong Learning of Wayne State University. He earned his M.A. at Eötvös University in Budapest and pursued graduate studies at Italian and American universities, receiving a Ph.D. degree from the University of Rochester. His published works include a series of articles about modern Italian history.

The manuscript was edited by Bob Demorest. The book was designed by Joanne Kinney. The typeface for the text is Times Roman. The display face is Times Roman and Italic. The book is printed on 55-lb. Glatfelter text paper and is bound in Holliston Mills' Roxite Linen.

Manufactured in the United States of America.